**PERGAMON INTERNATIONAL LIBRARY**
of Science, Technology, Engineering and Social Studies

*The 1000-volume original paperback library in aid of education, industrial training and the enjoyment of leisure*

Publisher: Robert Maxwell, M.C.

# PRACTICAL SPANISH
# FOR
# SCHOOL PERSONNEL, FIREMEN, POLICEMEN
# AND
# COMMUNITY AGENCIES
## (Second Edition)

### THE PERGAMON TEXTBOOK
### INSPECTION COPY SERVICE

An inspection copy of any book published in the Pergamon International Library will gladly be sent to academic staff without obligation for their consideration for course adoption or recommendation. Copies may be retained for a period of 60 days from receipt and returned if not suitable. When a particular title is adopted or recommended for adoption for class use and the recommendation results in a sale of 12 or more copies, the inspection copy may be retained with our compliments. The Publishers will be pleased to receive suggestions for revised editions and new titles to be published in this important International Library.

**OTHER PERGAMON TITLES**

Bomse — *Practical Spanish Grammar*

Bomse & Alfaro — *Practical Spanish for Medical and Hospital Personnel* — Second Edition

Seymann — *Basic Spanish for Elementary Teachers*

# PRACTICAL SPANISH FOR SCHOOL PERSONNEL, FIREMEN, POLICEMEN AND COMMUNITY AGENCIES

(Second Edition)

by

Marguerite D. Bomse

and

Julian H. Alfaro

*Staten Island Community College*

PERGAMON PRESS
NEW YORK/OXFORD/TORONTO/SYDNEY/FRANKFURT/PARIS

*Pergamon Press Offices:*

| | |
|---|---|
| U.S.A. | Pergamon Press Inc., Maxwell House, Fairview Park, Elmsford, New York 10523, U.S.A. |
| U.K. | Pergamon Press Ltd., Headington Hill Hall, Oxford OX3, OBW, England |
| CANADA | Pergamon of Canada, Ltd., 75 The East Mall, Toronto, Ontario M8Z 5W3, Canada |
| AUSTRALIA | Pergamon Press (Aust) Pty. Ltd., 19a Boundary Street, Rushcutters Bay, N.S.W. 2011, Australia |
| FRANCE | Pergamon Press SARL, 24 rue des Ecoles, 75240 Paris, Cedex 05, France |
| WEST GERMANY | Pergamon Press GmbH, 6242 Kronberg/Taunus, Pferdstrasse 1, West Germany |

Copyright © 1978 Pergamon Press Inc.

**Library of Congress Cataloging in Publication Data**

Bomse, Marguerite D.
   Practical Spanish for school personnel, firemen, policemen, and community agencies.

   1.   Spanish language -- Conversation and phrase books.   I.   Alfaro, Julian, joint author.
II.   Title.
PC4121.B58     1978     468'.3'421     78-1414
ISBN 0-08-023002-4

*All Rights Reserved. No part of this publication may be reproduced, stored in a retrieval system or transmitted in any form or by any means: electronic, electrostatic, magnetic tape, mechanical, photocopying, recording or otherwise, without permission in writing from the publishers.*

TABLE OF CONTENTS

1. School (familiar forms)................ 1
2. School I
   Teacher in Class..................... 2
3. School II
   School Secretary.................... 12
4. School III
   Illness............................. 28
5. School IV
   School Doctor....................... 31
6. Fire Department....................... 36
7. Police I
   Burglary............................ 40
8. Police II
   Accident............................ 48
9. Police III
   Drug Arrest......................... 55
10. Police IV
    Family Dispute..................... 59
11. Police V
    Family Dispute (Alcoholic)......... 74
12. Police VI
    Holdup............................. 78
13. Police VII
    Narcotics Arrest................... 88
14. Police VIII
    Intoxicated Driver................. 91

15. Police IX
    Traffic Accident..................... 96
16. Police X
    Traffic Ticket....................... 100
17. Police XI
    Missing Person....................... 102
18. Social Service I
    Family............................... 107
19. Social Service II
    Abandoned Wife....................... 115
20. Housing I
    Looking for an apartment............. 127
21. Housing II
    Complaints........................... 137
22. Food Stamps............................. 145
23. Unemployment............................ 153
24. Workmen's Compensation.................. 163
25. Banking................................. 170
26. Travel Agency........................... 180
27. Airlines................................ 190

## VOCABULARY

Vocabulary............................. 195
Español-Inglés......................... 197
English-Spanish........................ 221

## FOREWORD

Language should be the bridge between different cultures but all too often language becomes a barrier which prevents understanding. Such a lack of understanding is unfortunate in any context, but in police work it can have tragic consequences. A police officer, no matter how motivated or well-intentioned, can not serve a public with whom he can not communicate. Today, most of our urban centers and many of our suburbans are becoming increasingly bilingual; for a significant number of our citizens Spanish is their native and primary language. We can not sit back and "wait for them to learn English;" the police mandate is service-now. The burden is ours; we must view and accept language instruction as another in the technological advances which make us more proficient in our mission.

Language instruction, as any other aspect of technical progress, must be geared to meet the needs of the police officer on the street -- the man or woman who must work with the Hispanic community.

This manual is an outstanding contribution to the bi-lingual education of the law enforcement and criminal justice community. The attention to detail and realism make the text one with which the police officer can quickly relate.

The end result of this learning effort can only be a more effective relationship between the police and the Hispanic community.

Lt. John P. Oliver,<br>
Emergency Medical Service<br>
Long Island City, N. Y.

## FOREWORD

Anyone employed by a social agency who does not have a knowledge of Spanish soon experiences the frustration of trying to communicate across a language barrier. This problem is especially acute in the large urban areas and in the South and Southwestern part of the country where there are large concentrations of Spanish-speaking people. To properly fulfill our obligation, we in the field of social work must be able to communicate with our clients, to understand them and to make ourselves understood.

I have found that this book deals in a very practical manner with a variety of fields, utilizing authentic situations and well-researched realistic conversations. With a little time and effort one can rapidly acquire from this book the fundamentals to carry on a conversation with a Spanish-speaking client. I found the grammatical explanations and the appended vocabulary especially helpful.

Gerda L. Schulman,
Ph.D., M.S., A.C.S.W.,
Adjunct Associate Professor,
School of Social Work,
Adelphi University and Hunter College.

## PREFACE TO THE 1978 EDITION

This manual is meant to help break the language barrier that exists between the ever growing Spanish-speaking community in the United States and those who serve it in various capacities. In answer to the demand for greater relevance in language studies, many schools and colleges have introduced courses in Practical Spanish. Many social agencies have also found it necessary to offer Spanish courses in order to give their personnel a basic knowledge that will enable them to communicate with their Spanish-speaking clients.

We present authentic spoken Spanish recorded from conversations of people working in various social agencies at their work. The Spanish dialogue appears on the right of the page and the English translation on the left. Wherever possible, Spanish constructions similar to the English are given rather than the idiomatic Spanish. Additional words needed in English or Spanish are placed between diagonal lines. Every dialogue is followed by grammar notes and a few English sentences to be translated into Spanish.

Since the appearance of the preliminary edition of this text, which has received a very favorable response, we have made a number of revisions and additions, including many suggested by teachers who have used the text. We have added some new dialogues, notably 10 more dialogues for police, one on food stamps and one on unemployment insurance.

The grammar notes that follow each dialogue now contain cross references to the <u>Practical Spanish Grammar</u> (by Marguerite D. Bomse), also published by Pergamon Press. The examples that illustrate grammatical points in the grammar text are taken from the dialogues in this manual or from everyday situations in hospitals, doctors' offices, police stations, schools and social agencies, in contrast with the literary examples that appear in most grammar texts. By employing the grammar together with this manual the teacher can cover specific interests in depth without having to resort to vocabulary unnecessary to anyone studying Spanish in order to communicate with Spanish speaking clients.

The present manual now contains a Spanish/English and English/Spanish end vocabulary, covering all expressions used in the dialogues. Feminine and masculine forms of nouns and adjectives, as well as changes in the stems and orthography in verbs are indicated in parentheses in the vocabulary. Irregular verbs are printed in capitals.

A <u>Spanish Dictionary & Phrase Book</u> (Bomse, Pergamon, 1978) of important idiomatic expressions used in conversations between people working in social agencies and their clients, together with word lists organized by subject matter such as welfare, police, traffic, house, travel, etc., is being published later this year. The book will make it possible for the student to learn the most important vocabulary for his or her particular field.

We have been able, with the support of the Research Foundation of the City University of New York, to produce several video tapes based on the revised dialogues in this book. A list of the tapes can be found at the end of this Preface. They are being distributed by Campus Films, Scarsdale, N. Y. In these tapes, the dialogues are presented at normal speed and then repeated with pauses at important questions asked by the police officer or the interviewer in a social agency and at difficult constructions, which then appear in writing on the screen, with time for the student to repeat the construction. This new tool will make both the teacher's and the students' task much easier and more enjoyable.

Use of the present text in conjunction with the <u>Practical Spanish Grammar</u> and the <u>Practical Spanish Dictionary & Phrase Book</u> with the video tapes will enable the student to enlarge basic skills as well as the vocabulary needed in his or her occupation.

We wish to express our thanks for their assistance in preparing this new edition, and for their help with preparing the video tapes, to the City University

Research Foundation for its financial support; to Professor Jerry Melmed, his staff and to the College of Staten Island for the use of audio-visual production facilities; to the Nuestro Teatro group which performed the scenes on the video tapes, and to Professors Carl Erickson, Marion Holt and Amado Ricon for their advice and assistance.

We thank once more the Staten Island Community College Alumni Association for the Faculty Fellowship awarded to us in support of the original work on this manual.

Our thanks also go to Emanuel M. Bomse, M.D. for his suggestions which enabled us to present credible conversations between doctor, nurse or paraprofessional and the Spanish-speaking patient, and for his help in contacting various medical professionals, to Lt. John Oliver of the Emergency Medical Service, Long Island City, and to the many people in various social agencies whom we interviewed. Finally, we thank Mrs. Frances Armada Adamo for her help in typing the photoready copy of this text.

                        Marguerite D. Bomse
                        Julián H. Alfaro
                        Staten Island Community College

VIDEO TAPES AVAILABLE FROM
STEVE CAMPUS PRODUCTIONS, INC.
2 Overhill Road
Scarsdale, N. Y. 10583

- Banking
- First Day of School
- Food Stamps
- Housing
- Police (Robbery)
- Social Service I
- Social Service II (Abandoned Wife)
- Travel Agent
- Unemployment Insurance

SCHOOL I             ESCUELA 1

When an adult addresses children he or she uses the familiar (<u>tú</u>) form. In Spain, <u>vosotro(a)s</u> is used for the plural. However, in most Spanish-American countries, <u>vosotro(a)s</u> is replaced by <u>ustedes</u>. We will be using the <u>ustedes</u> (<u>Vds</u>.) form for the plural.

Children speaking to adults, address him (or her) with <u>usted</u> (<u>Vd</u>.).

Where a phrase may be addressed to one child or to a whole group, the plural verb form is indicated in parenthesis.

## SCHOOL I
### TEACHER IN CLASS

## ESCUELA I
### EL MAESTRO (LA MAESTRA) EN CLASE

|  |  | |
|---|---|---|
| What is your name? | ¿Cómo te llamas? | 1 |
| Do you have /any/ brothers or sisters? | ¿Tienes hermanos o hermanas? | 2 |
| Close the door, please. | Cierra la puerta, por favor. | 3 |
| Take off your hat(s). | Quítate (Quítense) el sombrero. | 4 |
| Hang /up/ your coat(s). | Cuelga (Cuelguen) el abrigo. | 5 |
| I am going to help you. | Voy a ayudarte (ayudarles). | |
| Why are you (arriving) late? | ¿Por qué llegas (llegan) tarde? | |
| Can you hear me? | ¿Puedes (pueden) oírme? | 6 |
| Do you understand me? | ¿Me comprendes (comprenden)? | |
| Open your book(s). | Abre el libro (abran los libros). | |
| Close your (the) book(s). | Cierra el libro (cierren los libros). | |
| Listen. | Oye (oigan). | 7 |
| Look /at/ this. | Mira (miren) esto. | 8 |
| Read what it says here. | Lee (lean) /lo/ que dice aquí. | 9 |
| Speak slowly and clearly. | Habla (hablen) despacio y claramente. | 10 |
| Write your name /over/ here. | Escribe (escriban) tu (su) nombre aquí. | |

| | | |
|---|---|---|
| Write today's date. | Escribe (escriban) la fecha /de/ hoy. | 11 |
| Are (have) you finished? | ¿Has (han) terminado? | 12 |
| Take this paper home. | Lleva (lleven) este papel a casa. | |
| Your parents should sign it. | Tus (sus) padres deben firmarlo. | |
| Bring your milk money tomorrow. | Trae (traigan) el dinero para la leche mañana. | 13 |
| Come to the blackboard, please. | Ven (vengan) a la pizarra, por favor. | 14 |
| Write this on the board. | Escribe (escriban) esto en la pizarra. | |
| Erase the board, please. | Borra (borren) la pizarra, por favor. | |
| Pay attention. | Pon (pongan) atención. | 15 |
| Don't do that. | No hagas (hagan) eso. | 16 |
| Bring your mother to school tomorrow. | Trae a tu madre a /la/ escuela mañana. | 17 |
| Speak louder, please. | Habla (hablen) más alto, por favor. | |
| What do you want? | ¿Qué quieres (quieren)? | 18 |
| Tomorrow there is no school. /It/ is /a/ holiday. | Mañana no hay escuela. Es fiesta. | 19 |
| Stand up. | Levántate (levántense). | 20 |
| Wash your hands. | Lávate (lávense) las manos. | 21 |

| | | |
|---|---|---|
| Get on line. | Ponte (pónganse) en fila. | 22 |
| Walk quickly and quietly (in silence). | Camina (caminen) rápidamente y en silencio. | |
| Wait /for/ me. | Espérame (espérenme). | 23 |
| Watch your step. | Ten (tengan) cuidado al caminar. | 24 |
| Eat your lunch. | Come (coman) tu (su) almuerzo. | |
| Drink the milk. | Bebe (beban) la leche. | |
| Don't fight. | No pelees (peleen). | |
| Don't push. | No empujes (empujen). | |
| Don't yell. | No grites (griten). | |
| What's the matter? | ¿Qué pasa? | 25 |
| Aren't you feeling well? | ¿No te sientes (se sienten) bien? | |
| Use your handkerchief. | Usa tu pañuelo. | |
| If you cough, cover your (the) mouth with your (the) hand. | Si toses (tosen) tápate (tápense) la boca con la mano. | 26 |
| What hurts you? | ¿Qué te duele? | |
| Does your (the) head hurt you? | ¿Te duele la cabeza? | 27 |
| Go to the nurse with this note. | Ve a la enfermera con esta nota. | |
| Bring a note telling why you were absent. | Trae una nota diciendo porqué estuviste ausente. | 28 |
| Your mother is going to come for you. | Tu madre va a venir por ti. | 29 |

| INSTRUCTIONS TO PARENTS | INSTRUCCIONES PARA /LOS/ PADRES | |
|---|---|---|
| Send your children to school every day except on holidays. | Manden /a/ sus hijos a /la/ escuela todos los días excepto /los/ días de fiesta. | 30 |
| Teach him (or her) that he (or she) must come to school clean. | Enséñenle que debe venir a la escuela limpio(a). | 31 |
| Give him (or her) a good breakfast. | Denle un buen desayuno. | 32 |
| Put him (or her) to bed early. | Acuéstenlo(la) temprano. | 33 |
| Mark all clothing with his (or her) name. | Marquen toda /la/ ropa con su nombre. | 34 |
| Keep (attend to) all appointments with the teacher | Asistan a todas /las/ citas con el maestro (la maestra) | 35 |
| the doctor the nurse the dentist | el doctor la enfermera el dentista. | |
| If you move, give your new address to the school. | Si /se/ mudan, den su nueva dirección a la escuela. | |

### NOTES

1. ¿Cómo te llamas?: What is your name?
   Literally: How do you call yourself?
   Use of familiar (tú) form. Reflexive verb.
                            IIIB1a(Present Tense)
             VIIB and E(Reflexive
                          Constructions)

2. ¿Tienes hermanos (o hermanas)?: Do you have /any/ brothers or sisters?
Tienes: tú form, Present Tense of tener
IIIB1b (Present Tense)
Hermanos means brothers or brothers and sisters. Here, in order not to be misunderstood, both hermanos and hermanas is used.

3. Cierra la puerta: Close the door.
Familiar command (tú) form of cerrar.
Cerrar is a stem changing verb.
VIB (Familiar Commands)

4. Quítate (quítense) el sombrero: Take off your hat(s).
When referring to parts of the body or articles of clothing, Spanish uses a reflexive construction (quítate) and the definite article (el sombrero), while English uses the possessive adjective (your hat/s/). Whether speaking to one person or to a whole group, el sombrero remains in the singular because each person takes off only one hat.
VIB (Familiar Commands)
VIID2 (Reflexive Construction)
IIA2e (Use of Definite Article)

5. Cuelga (cuelguen) el abrigo: Hang /up/ your coat(s).
Colgar (to hang, to hang up) is a stem changing verb. In addition, before an ending that begins with e, a u is added to the g, in order to preserve the original sound of g.
XVIC (Verbs and Prepositions)
VIA and B (Command Forms)
Here again, each one hangs up one coat (el abrigo).

6. ¿Puedes (pueden) oírme?: Can you hear me?
Poder is stem changing in the Present Tense.
IIIB1b (Stem Changing Verbs)

7. Oye (oigan): Listen.
Oír is an irregular verb.
VIA and B (Command Forms)

8. <u>Mira (miren) esto</u>: Look /at/ this.
   <u>Mirar</u>: to look <u>at</u>
                   XVIC(Verbs and Prepositions)
   cf. buscar: to look <u>for</u>

9. <u>Lee (lean) /lo/ que dice aquí</u>: Read what it says here.
   The relative pronoun <u>what</u> has no antecedent. Therefore, the compound relative pronoun <u>lo</u> <u>que</u> is required in Spanish.
                   XXIIIB(Relative Pronouns)

10. <u>Habla (hablen) despacio y claramente</u>: Speak slowly and clearly.
    <u>Despacio</u> is both adjective and adverb.

11. <u>Escribe (escriban) la fecha /de/ hoy</u>: Write today's date (the date of today). Use of <u>de</u> in lieu of the English '<u>s</u>.
                    IXD(de)

12. <u>¿Has (han) terminado?</u>: Have you finished?
    <u>Has (han)</u>: Present Tense of <u>haber</u>.
                    XXIB(Present Perfect)

13. <u>Trae (traigan) el dinero /para/ la leche</u>: Bring the milk money.
    <u>Trae (traigan)</u>: Command forms of <u>traer</u>.
                VIA1 & VIB1(Command Forms)
    el dinero /para/ la leche: the milk money (the money for milk)
    para: meant for
                    IA16(Compound Nouns)
                    XVIA6b(para)

14. <u>Ven (vengan) a la pizarra</u>: Come to the blackboard.
    <u>Ven (vengan)</u>: Command forms of <u>venir</u>.
                    VIA3(Irregular Command Forms)

15. <u>Pon (pongan) atención</u>: Pay attention.
    <u>Poner</u> atención: to pay attention. Dict(Idioms)
    <u>Poner</u> is an irregular verb.
                    VIA1(Command Forms)

16. No hagas (hagan) eso: Don't do that.
    Hacer is an irregular verb.
    In the negative command, both formal and familiar forms have the same stem.
                            VIB3(Negative Familiar Commands)

17. Trae /a/ tu madre a /la/ escuela: Bring your mother to school.
    Use of personal a before a direct object referring to a person.
                            XVIA1m(Personal a)
    a /la/ escuela: to (the) school.
                            IA2s(Use of Definite Article)
    cf. a /la/ iglesia: to church.

18. ¿Qué quieres (quieren)?: What do you want?
    Querer is stem changing in the Present Tense.
                            IIIB1b(Stem Changing Verbs)

19. No hay escuela: There is no (there isn't any) school.
    Hay: there is, there are.
                            XD(hay)

20. Levántate (levántense): Get up.
    Levantarse: to get up. For many actions which a person carries out on himself, Spanish uses a reflexive verb.
    cf. levantar algo: to lift something.
                            VIID4(Reflexive Constructions)
    In the command form, the reflexive pronoun is attached. An accent mark is needed on the originally stressed syllable.
                            VIIC(Pos. of Reflexive Pronoun)

21. Lávate (lávense) las manos: Wash your hands.
    Use of reflexive construction (lávate, lávense) and definite article (las) in Spanish, possessive adjective (your) in English.
    Mano (fem.).    VIID1(Reflexive Construction)
           IA2(note), VIB1 and VIB4(Familiar Commands)

22. Ponte (pónganse) en fila: Get in line.
    Ponerse en fila: to get on line.
                            Dict(Idioms)
    Poner is an irregular verb.
                            VIA1(Command Forms)

23. **Espérame (espérenme)**: Wait for me.
    Esperar: to wait for.
            XVIC(Verbs and Prepositions)
    When an object pronoun is attached to the command form, a written accent mark must be placed on the originally stressed syllable.
            XIF(Position of Object Pronouns)

24. **Ten (tengan) cuidado al caminar**: Watch your step.
    Literally: be careful walking.
            Dict(Idioms)
    Tener is an irregular verb.
            VIA1(Command Forms)

25. **¿Qué pasa?** What is the matter? What is happening?  Dict(Idioms)

26. **Si toses (tosen), tápate (tápense) la boca con la mano**: If you cough, cover your (the) mouth with your (the) hand.
    Use of reflexive construction in Spanish, possessive adjective in English.
            VIID2(Use of Reflexive Const.)

27. **¿Te duele la cabeza?**: Does your (the) head hurt you?
    The person whom something hurts, is the indirect object of doler.
            XIK(doler)
    Doler is a stem changing verb.
            IIIB1b(Stem Changing Verbs)
    Use of definite article (la cabeza) in Spanish, possessive adjective (my head) in English.
            VIID2(Use of Reflexive Const.)

28. **Trae una nota diciendo porqué estuviste ausente**: Bring a note telling why you were absent.
    diciendo: Present Participle of decir (to say, to tell)
            XVIIA(Present Participle)
    estuviste: Preterite Tense of estar
            XIIB3(Irregular Preterite)
    Use of estar for temporary condition.
            XB(estar)

29. <u>Tu madre va a venir por ti</u>: Your mother is going to come for you.
venir por alguien (algo): to come for someone (something)      XVIB7o(por)
por ti: for you. Use of stressed pronoun after a preposition.
XID1(Object of Preposition)

30. <u>Manden /a/ sus hijos a /la/ escuela todos los días</u>: Send your children to school every day.
a sus hijos: Use of personal <u>a</u> before a direct object referring to persons.
XVIA1m(Personal <u>a</u>)
a /la/ escuela: to school
IIA2s(Use of Definite Article)
todos los días: every day
cf. todo el día: all day (long)

31. <u>Enséñenle</u>: Teach him (or her).
Enseñar algo a alguien: to teach something to someone. The direct object of <u>enseñar</u> is what one teaches. The person <u>to whom</u> one teaches something, becomes the indirect object.
XIC(Indirect Object Pronouns)

32. <u>Denle un buen desayuno</u>: Give (to) him (or her) a good breakfast.
<u>Le</u> is the indirect object pronoun. <u>Un buen desayuno</u> is the direct object.
XIC1(Indirect Object Pronouns)

33. <u>Acuéstenlo(la)</u>: Put him (her) to bed.
<u>Acostar a alguien</u>: (to put someone to sleep) is a stem changing verb.
cf. Acostarse: to go to bed.
VIA4(Command Forms)

34. <u>Marquen toda /la/ ropa</u>: Mark all the clothing.
The <u>c</u> in marcar changes to <u>qu</u> before <u>e</u>.
VIA5(Spelling Changes)
<u>La ropa</u> (the clothes) is always used in the singular.      IB9(Singular Nouns)

35. <u>Asistan /a/ todas las citas</u>: Keep all appointments.
Asistir a: to be present at.
Dict(Idioms)

## TRANSLATE

1. What is your name?
2. Take off your hats, and hang up your coats.
3. Read what it says.        (singular and plural)
4. Pay attention.            (singular and plural)
5. Bring your mother to school.
6. Get up. Sit down.         (singular and plural)
7. Wash your hands.          (singular and plural)
8. Get on line.              (singular and plural)
9. Watch your step.          (singular and plural)
10. What is the matter?
11. Put your child to bed early.
12. My head (foot, hand, throat) hurts.
13. My ears hurt.
14. If you cough, cover your mouth with your hand.
15. Look at the blackboard (plural).
16. Speak slowly and clearly.
17. There is no school tomorrow.

## SCHOOL II

### SCHOOL SECRETARY

MOTHER: Is this where I come to register my child?

SECRETARY: Yes. I am the school secretary.

What can I do for you?

MOTHER: I want to register my son in school.

SECRETARY: Fine. Sit down, please, Mrs.....

MOTHER: Ayala. Mrs. Ayala.

SECRETARY: Here we have the form which we have to fill /out/.

Is this the first day of school for the child?

MOTHER: Yes, /it/ is (it).

SECRETARY: What is the child's name?

MOTHER: His name is Miguel Ayala.

SECRETARY: Does he have a nickname?

MOTHER: No. We always call him Miguel.

## ESCUELA II

### SECRETARIA DE LA ESCUELA

MADRE: ¿Es aquí donde vengo a matricular a mi niño?  1

SECRETARIA: Sí. Soy la secretaria de la escuela. ¿En qué puedo servirla?  2

MADRE: Quiero inscribir a mi hijo en la escuela.  see 1

SECRETARIA: Bien. Siéntese, por favor, señora....  3

MADRE: Ayala. Señora Ayala.

SECRETARIA: Aquí tenemos el formulario que debemos llenar. ¿Es este el primer día de escuela para el niño?  4

MADRE: Sí, /lo/ es.  5

SECRETARIA: ¿Cómo  6
se llama el niño?

MADRE: Se llama  6
Miguel Ayala.

SECRETARIA: ¿Tiene un apodo?

MADRE: No, siempre le llamamos Miguel.

| | |
|---|---|
| SECRETARY: Are you his mother? | SECRETARIA: ¿Es Vd. su madre? |
| MOTHER: Yes, I am. | MADRE: Sí, /lo/ soy. |
| SECRETARY: How old is Miguel? | SECRETARIA: ¿Cuántos años tiene Miguel?    7 |
| MOTHER: He was 5 years old on March 9th. | MADRE: Cumplió cinco años el nueve de marzo.    8 |
| SECRETARY: Where was he born? | SECRETARIA: ¿Dónde nació?    9 |
| MOTHER: In Ponce, Puerto Rico. | MADRE: En Ponce, Puerto Rico. |
| SECRETARY: He was born in Puerto Rico. Does he have /a/ birth certificate? | SECRETARIA: Nació en Puerto Rico. ¿Tiene certificado de nacimiento?    10 |
| MOTHER: Yes. Here it is. | MADRE: Sí. Aquí lo tiene.    11 |
| SECRETARY: Thank you. Where do you live? | SECRETARIA: Gracias. ¿Dónde vive Vd? |
| MOTHER: At 230 East 120th Street. | MADRE: En /el/ doscientos treinta este /de la/ calle ciento veinte. |
| SECRETARY: What is your name? | SECRETARIA: ¿Cómo se llama Vd? |
| MOTHER: Carmen Ayala. | MADRE: Carmen Ayala. |
| SECRETARY: And what is the father's name? | SECRETARIA: ¿Y cómo se llama el padre? |
| MOTHER: Julián Ayala. | MADRE: Julián Ayala. |
| SECRETARY: Do you have /a/ telephone in your house? | SECRETARIA: ¿Tiene teléfono en su casa?    12 |

MOTHER: Yes, the number is 872-3478.

MADRE: Sí, el número es: ocho, setenta y dos, treinta y cuatro, setenta y ocho.

SECRETARY: Are there /any/ other children of your family in this school?

SECRETARIA: ¿Hay otros niños de su familia en esta escuela?  13

MOTHER: Yes, Pedro is in the second grade and María in the fourth.

MADRE: Sí, Pedro está en el segundo grado y María en el cuarto.

SECRETARY: How many rooms are there in your house?

SECRETARIA: ¿Cuántos cuartos hay en su casa?  see 13

MOTHER: Five.

MADRE: Cinco.

SECRETARY: Does Miguel have a room for himself?

SECRETARIA: ¿Tiene Miguel un cuarto para él?

MOTHER: No, he shares it with his two brothers.

MADRE: No, lo comparte con sus dos hermanos.

SECRETARY: What kind of work does your husband do?

SECRETARIA: ¿Qué clase de trabajo hace su marido?  14

MOTHER: He works in a plastics factory.

MADRE: Trabaja en una fábrica /de/ plásticos.

SECRETARY: Do you work also?

SECRETARIA: ¿Trabaja Vd. también?

MOTHER: Yes. I work in a dress factory.

MADRE: Sí, trabajo en una fábrica /de/ vestidos.

SECRETARY: Who cares for the child when you are away?

SECRETARIA: ¿Quién cuida al niño cuando Vd. está fuera?  15

| | |
|---|---|
| MOTHER: My sister. She lives in the same building. | MADRE: Mi hermana. Ella vive en el mismo edificio. |
| SECRETARY: What is your sister's name? | SECRETARIA: ¿Cómo se llama su hermana? |
| MOTHER: Juana Rodríguez. | MADRE: Juana Rodríguez. |
| SECRETARY: Please tell me the address of your employer and that of your husband's. | SECRETARIA: Por favor, dígame las señas de su patrono y las del patrono de su marido. |
| MOTHER: I work for Brown Dresses, 24 East 39th Street and my husband works for Plastics, Inc., 444-4th Ave., Long Island City. | MADRE: <u>Trabajo para Brown Dresses, /en el/ veinticuatro este /de la/ calle treinta y nueve</u> y mi marido trabaja para Plastics, Inc., /en el/ cuatrocientos cuarenta y cuatro de la cuarta avenida, Long Island City. |
| SECRETARY: Has anyone in your family had tuberculosis? | SECRETARIA: <u>¿Hay alguien en su familia que haya padecido de tuberculosis</u>? |
| MOTHER: No. | MADRE: No. |
| SECRETARY: Heart disease? | SECRETARIA: ¿Enfermedad del corazón? |
| MOTHER: No. | MADRE: No. |
| SECRETARY: Cancer or rheumatism? | SECRETARIA: ¿Cáncer o reumatismo? |
| MOTHER: My husband had rheumatism when he was a child. | MADRE: Mi marido tuvo reumatismo cuando era niño. |

| | |
|---|---|
| SECRETARY: Was Miguel immunized against smallpox? | SECRETARIA: ¿Fue Miguel inmunizado contra la viruela? |
| MOTHER: Yes. | MADRE: Sí. |
| SECRETARY: Against diphtheria, chicken pox and scarlet fever? | SECRETARIA: ¿Contra la difteria, la varicela y la fiebre escarlatina? |
| MOTHER: Yes, he had all the injections and vaccinations. | MADRE: Sí, recibió todas las inyecciónes y vacunas. |
| SECRETARY: Has he had mumps or measles? | SECRETARIA: ¿Ha tenido paperas o sarampión? |
| MOTHER: He had measles two years ago. | MADRE: <u>Tuvo sarampión hace dos años.</u>    18 |
| SECRETARY: Has he ever been hospitalized? | SECRETARIA: ¿Ha estado él hospitalizado <u>alguna vez</u>?    19 |
| MOTHER: They took out his (the) tonsils two years ago. He had to spend a night in the hospital. | MADRE: <u>Le quitaron las amígdalas hace dos años.</u> see 18<br><u>Tuvo que pasar una</u>   20<br><u>noche en el hospital.</u> |
| SECRETARY: Does he often get (suffer from) sore throats? | SECRETARIA: ¿<u>Sufre</u>   21 <u>de dolores de garganta a menudo</u>? |
| MOTHER: Sometimes. | MADRE: A veces. |
| SECRETARY: Does he have (suffer from) any allergy? | SECRETARIA: ¿Padece él de alguna alergia? |
| MOTHER: I don't think so. | MADRE: <u>Creo que no.</u>   22 |
| SECRETARY: How is his appetite? | SECRETARIA: ¿<u>Cómo está él de apetito</u>?   23 |

| | |
|---|---|
| MOTHER: Fair. | MADRE: Regular. |
| SECRETARY: What did he eat for breakfast this morning? | SECRETARIA: ¿Qué comió de desayuno esta mañana? |
| MOTHER: Hot cereal and milk. | MADRE: Cereal caliente y leche. |
| SECRETARY: Does he hear and see well? | SECRETARIA: ¿Oye y ve bien? |
| MOTHER: Oh, yes. | MADRE: Oh, sí. |
| SECRETARY: At what time does Miguel usually go to bed? | SECRETARIA: ¿A qué hora se acuesta Miguel por lo común?  24 |
| MOTHER: That depends. Most of the time he is in bed before seven. | MADRE: Eso depende. La mayoría de las veces está acostado antes /de/ las siete.  25 |
| SECRETARY: At what time does he wake up? | SECRETARIA: ¿A qué hora se despierta?  26 |
| MOTHER: He generally wakes up before seven. | MADRE: Generalmente se despierta antes /de las/ siete. |
| SECRETARY: Does he sleep well? | SECRETARIA: ¿Duerme bien? |
| MOTHER: Yes, he sleeps well. | MADRE: Sí, duerme bien. |
| SECRETARY: Does he have any nervous habit? | SECRETARIA: ¿Tiene algún hábito nervioso? |
| MOTHER: No. | MADRE: No. |
| SECRETARY: Does he have any kind of fear(s)? | SECRETARIA: ¿Tiene él cualquier clase de temor? |
| MOTHER: He is afraid of doctors. | MADRE: Tiene miedo de /los/ médicos.  27 |

| | |
|---|---|
| SECRETARY: Does he bite his nails or suck his thumb? | SECRETARIA: ¿<u>Se muerde las uñas o se chupa el dedo</u>?   28 |
| MOTHER: Sometimes he bites his nails. | MADRE: Algunas veces se muerde las uñas. |
| SECRETARY: Does he wet his bed? | SECRETARIA: ¿<u>Se orina en la cama</u>?   29 |
| MOTHER: Sometimes. | MADRE: A veces. |
| SECRETARY: Which hand does he use? | SECRETARIA: ¿Qué mano usa él? |
| MOTHER: The right /one/. | MADRE: La derecha. |
| SECRETARY: Does he have any speech problem? | SECRETARIA: ¿<u>Tiene alguna dificultad en hablar</u>?   30 |
| MOTHER: I don't think so, but he doesn't speak English. | MADRE: No creo, pero no habla inglés. |
| SECRETARY: Does he dress himself? | SECRETARIA: ¿<u>Se viste solo</u>?   31 |
| MOTHER: Yes. Moreover, he helps me dress the baby. | MADRE: Sí. Además, <u>me ayuda /a/ vestir al bebé</u>.   32 |
| SECRETARY: Does he have any other responsibilities? | SECRETARIA: ¿Tiene él alguna otra responsibilidad? |
| MOTHER: Sometimes he goes shopping for me, and he takes care of the baby. | MADRE: Algunas veces <u>va de compras por mí</u> y cuida al bebé.   33 |
| SECRETARY: Does he watch much television? | SECRETARIA: ¿<u>Ve él mucho la televisión</u>?   34 |
| MOTHER: He likes television very much. | MADRE: <u>Le gusta mucho la televisión</u>.   35 |

| | | |
|---|---|---|
| If I don't stop him, he sits (is) all day in front of the television set. | Si no le paro, está <u>todo el día</u> <u>frente al televisor</u>. | 36<br>37 |
| SECRETARY: Does he have any books? | SECRETARIA: ¿Tiene él algunos libros? | |
| MOTHER: No. | MADRE: No. | |
| SECRETARY: Does he get along well with other children? | SECRETARIA: ¿<u>Se</u> <u>lleva bien con</u> <u>otros niños</u>? | 38 |
| MOTHER: Yes, he always plays with other children. | MADRE: Sí, siempre juega con otros niños. | |
| SECRETARY: Has Miguel been to the dentist? | SECRETARIA: ¿<u>Ha</u> <u>estado Miguel en</u> <u>el dentista</u>? | 39 |
| MOTHER: Yes, he had some cavities filled. | MADRE: Sí, <u>le</u> <u>curaron algunas</u> <u>caries</u>. | 40 |
| SECRETARY: Would you like to have an appointment (interview) with the (guidance) counsellor? | SECRETARIA: ¿Le gustaría a Vd. tener una entrevista con la consejera? | |
| MOTHER: Not now, because I have to go to work. But if you give me her name, my husband or I could see (visit) her another time. | MADRE: No ahora, porque <u>tengo que</u> <u>ir al trabajo</u>. Pero si Vd. me da su nombre, mi marido o yo podríamos visitarla <u>en otra</u> <u>ocasión</u>. | 41<br><br>42 |
| SECRETARY: Fine. Her name is Miss Salerno. You can visit her any morning, between 10 and 12. | SECRETARIA: Bien. Su nombre es señorita Salerno. Puede visitarla cualquier mañana, entre /las/ diez y /las/ doce. | |

Good-bye, Mrs. Ayala.          Adiós, señora Ayala.
MOTHER: Good-bye,              MADRE: Adiós,
Miss.                          señorita.

## NOTES

1. ¿Es aquí donde vengo a matricular /a/ mi niño?:
   Is this (here) where I come to register my child?
   Use of personal a for a person who is the direct object.         XVIAlm(Personal a)

2. ¿En qué puedo servirla?: What can I do for you?
   Literally: In (with) what can I serve you?
                                      Dict(Idioms)
   The direct object (la) is attached to the infinitive.         XIF(Pos. of Object Pronouns)

3. Siénte/se: Sit /down/.
   Sentarse: to sit down. Use of Reflexive Construction in Spanish.
   Sentarse is a stem changing verb.
                          VIIE(Reflexive Construction)
                          IIIBlb(Present Tense)

4. Para el niño: For the child.
   Para: meant for.
   cf. por mí: for me (instead of myself)
                          XVIA6b(Para)

5. Sí, lo es: Yes, /it/ is (it).
   Accent mark on sí (meaning yes) to distinguish it from si meaning if. Introduction G
   The subject pronoun it is not expressed.
   The object pronoun lo refers to el primer día.
                          XIA3(Omission of it)

6. ¿Cómo se llama el niño?: What is the child's name?         VIIE(Reflexive Construction)
   Llamarse: to be called.

7. ¿Cuántos años tiene Miguel?: How old is Michael?
   tener...años: to be ...years old.
   XE1(tener)

8. Cumplió cinco años /el/ nueve /de/ marzo: He was 5 years old (reached 5 years) /on/ March 9th.
   cumplir...años: to reach a certain age (to finish...years)  Dict(Idioms)
   El nueve de marzo: On March 9th.
   Use of cardinal number (nueve) for dates where English uses ordinal numbers (ninth).
   XVC(Dates)

9. ¿Dónde nació?: Where was he born?
   nacer: to be born.  XF & Dict(Idioms)

10. ¿Tiene certificado /de/ nacimiento?: Does he have /a/ birth certificate?
    Omission of a (any) in questions and negative statements.        IIB2e(Indefinite Article)
    un certificado /de/ nacimiento: a birth certificate.    IA16 (Compound Nouns)
    Dict(Compound Nouns)

11. Aquí lo tiene: Here it is. Here you have it.

12. ¿Tiene teléfono?: Do you have /a/ telephone?
    Omission of indefinite article (a), see No. 10.

13. ¿Hay otros niños...en esta escuela?: Are there /any/ other children in this school?
    Hay: there is, there are, are there?, etc.
    XC(hay)
    Omission of any in questions.
    XXA1

14. ¿Qué clase de trabajo?: What kind of work?
    Dict(Idioms)

15. ¿Quién cuida al niño?: Who takes care of the child?
    cuidar: to take care of
    Use of personal a before a person that is the direct object of the verb.
          XVIA1m(Personal a)

16. Trabajo para Brown Dresses, /en el/ veinticuatro este /de la/ calle treinta y nueve: I work for Brown Dresses, 24 East 39th Street.
    trabajar para: to work for
          XVIA6(para)
    Use of definite article in addresses.
          IIA2p(Definite Article)

17. ¿Hay alguien en su familia que haya padecido de tuberculosis?: Has anyone in your family had tuberculosis?
    Literally: Is there anyone in your family who has (may have) suffered from tuberculosis?
    Hay: is there?, are there?, etc.
          XD(hay)
    alguien: anyone, someone.
          XX(Indefinites)
    haya: Subjunctive of haber.
    The subjunctive is needed here because of the indefinite antecedent (alguien) and because it is not known what the answer will be.
          XXVA1h(Irregular
            Subjunctive)
          XXVB1D(Use of Subjunctive)

18. Tuvo sarampión hace dos años: He had measles two years ago.
    Tuvo: Preterite tense of tener.
          XIIB3a(Preterite of tener)
    Hace, used with the Preterite Tense, is the equivalent of the English ago.
          XVG2(Hace and Preterite)

19. Alguna vez: ever, at any time, sometime.
          XVE3(vez)

20. Tuvo /que/ pasar una noche en el hospital:
He had to spend a night in the hospital.
Tener que: to have to
pasar: to spend (time)
cf. gastar: to spend money.
                Dict(Idioms)

21. ¿Sufre de dolores /de/ garganta a menudo?:
Does he often get sore throats?
Literally: Does he often suffer from pains in the throat?
dolor /de/ garganta: sore throat.
                Dict(Idioms)

22. Creo que no: I don't think /so/.
                Dict(Idioms)

23. ¿Cómo está él de apetito?: How is his appetite?    Dict(Idioms)

24. ¿A qué hora /se/ acuesta Miguel por lo común?:
At what time does Miguel usually go to bed?
¿A qué hora?: at what time?
                XVF(Time)
acostarse is a stem changing verb.
                IIIB1b(Present Tense)
cf. Le acuesto: I put him to sleep.
                VIIE(Reflexive Construction)
Por lo común: generally, usually.
                XVIA7n(Por)

25. Antes /de/ las siete: Before seven.
Antes de: before.
las siete: seven o'clock.
cf. la una: one o'clock.
                XVF(Time of day)

26. ¿A qué hora /se/ despierta?: At what time does he wake /up/?
despertarse: (to wake up) is a stem changing verb which is used reflexively.
cf. Le despierto: I wake him.
                IIIB1b(Present Tense)
                VIIE(Reflexive Construction)

27. Tiene miedo de /los/ médicos:  He is afraid
    (has fear)of  doctors.
    tener miedo de:  to be afraid of.
                          XE(tener) & Dict(Idioms)
    The definite article is required in Spanish, if
    one refers to the noun in general (he is afraid
    of doctors, in general).
                          IIa2b(Use of Def. Article)

28. ¿/Se/ muerde las uñas o /se/ chupa el dedo?:
    Does he bite his nails or suck his thumb
    (finger)?
    morderse(ue) las uñas:  to bite one's nails.
    Chuparse el dedo:  to suck one's thumb (finger).
                          Dict(Idioms)
    Use of reflexive construction in Spanish and
    definite article and possessive adjective in
    English when speaking about an action referring
    to one's body.    VIID1(Reflexive Construction)
                      IIIB1b(Present Tense)
    morder is a stem changing verb.

29. ¿Se orina en la cama?:  Does he wet his
    (urinate in the) bed?
    orinarse:  to urinate.  Reflexive Construction.
                      VII(Reflexive Constructions)

30. ¿Tiene alguna dificultad en hablar?:  Does he
    have any speech problem (difficulty in
    speaking)?        Dict(Idioms)

31. ¿Se viste solo?:  Does he dress himself
    (alone)?

32. Me ayuda /a/ vestir al bebé:  He helps me
    dress the baby.
    ayudar:  to help (to do something)
                          XVID(Verbs & Prepositions)
    al bebé:  Use of Personal a
                          XVIA1m(Personal a)

33. Va /de/ compras por mí:  He goes shopping for me.
    Ir /de/ compras:  To go shopping.
           Dict(Idioms)
    va:  Present Tense of ir  IVA3(Present Tense)
    por mí:  for me.  Use of por (instead of me)
           XVIA7f(por)
    Use of stressed pronoun (mí) after a
    preposition.   XID1(Object of Preposition)
    Mí has an accent mark to distinguish it from the
    possessive adjective (mi).
          Intr. G

34. ¿Ve él mucho la televisión?:  Does he watch television a lot?
    Ver (mirar) la televisión:  to watch TV.
    Mirar:  to look at.  XVIC(Verbs and Prep.)
    Use of definite article (la televisión).
          IIA2(Use of Definite Art.)

35. Le gusta mucho la televisión:  He likes television very much.
    Literally:  Television is pleasing to him.
    gustar:  to like.  The subject of gustar
    is la televisión.  The person who likes it is
    the indirect object. XIJ(gustar)

36. Todo /el/ día:  All day. Dict(Idioms)

37. Frente al televisor:  In front of the television set.
    Frente a:  in front of.  XVIB(Compound Prep.)
    la televisión:  TV (programs, etc.)
    el televisor:  the TV set.

38. ¿/Se/ lleva bien con otros niños?:  Does he get along well with other children?
    LLevarse bien con:  to get along well with.
          Dict(Idioms)

39. ¿Ha estado Miguel en el dentista?:  Has Miguel been to the dentist?
    Use of estar for location.
          XB(estar)

40. <u>Le curaron algunas caries</u>: He had some cavities filled.
Use of Active voice in Spanish, Passive voice in English.
Literally, what is said in Spanish is: They cured some cavities for him.
Spanish uses the passive voice much less frequently than English.
      XXIVA1(Active Voice for
        Passive)

41. <u>¿Le gustaría a Vd. tener una entrevista</u>?:
Would you like to have an appointment?
gustar: see No. 35.
<u>gustaría</u> is the Conditional of <u>gustar</u>. Just like in English, the Conditional of <u>gustar</u>, <u>poder</u>, etc. is often used for politeness (would you like to, could you, etc.).
      XIVB2b(Conditional Use)
      XIVB1(Forms of Conditional)

42. <u>Tengo /que/ ir al trabajo</u>: I have to go to work.

43. <u>Podríamos visitarla en otra ocasión</u>: We could visit her another time (on some other occasion). <u>Podríamos</u> is the conditional of <u>poder</u> ( to be able to).  XIVB2b(Use of Conditional)
      XIVB1b.(Irregular
        Conditional)


      TRANSLATE


1. What is the child's name?
2. How old is he?
3. When was he born?
4. What kind of work does your husband do?
5. He had chicken pox three years ago.

6. They took out his tonsils.
7. At what time does he get up (go to sleep)?
8. He is afraid of doctors.
9. Does he bite his nails or suck his thumb?
10. Does he wet his bed?
11. He does not get along well with other children.
12. She goes shopping for us.
13. He takes care of the other children.
14. He likes the television programs.
15. He had some cavities filled.

## SCHOOL III
### SCHOOL SECRETARY
### ILLNESS

| | |
|---|---|
| SCHOOL III | ESCUELA III |
| SCHOOL SECRETARY | SECRETARIA DE LA ESCUELA |
| ILLNESS | ENFERMEDAD |

SECRETARY: Hello. Are you Pedro López' mother?

SECRETARIA: Hola. ¿<u>Es Vd. la madre /de/ Pedro López</u>?   1

MRS. LÓPEZ: Yes.

SRA. LÓPEZ: Sí.

SECRETARY: Pedro does not feel well. He vomited several times and the teacher thinks that he should go home. He may have a virus.

SECRETARIA: <u>Pedro no /se/ siente bien</u>. Vomitó varias veces y la maestra cree que <u>debe ir a casa</u>. Puede tener un virus.   2, 4, 5

Can you come for him?

¿<u>Puede Ud. venir por él</u>?   6

MRS. LÓPEZ: I can't leave right now because the baby is sick too.

SRA. LÓPEZ: No puedo salir <u>ahora mismo</u> porque el bebé <u>está enfermo</u> también.   7, 8

I have to wait for my neighbor.

<u>Tengo que esperar /a/ mi vecina</u>.   9

SECRETARY: All right.

SECRETARIA: <u>Está bien</u>.   10

In the meantime, Pedro will be with the nurse.

<u>Mientras tanto Pedro estará con la enfermera</u>.   11

## NOTES

1. ¿Es Vd. la madre /de/ Pedro López?: Are you Pedro López' mother?
   (the mother of Pedro López): Spanish always expresses the possessive by the preposition <u>de</u>.
   IXD(Possessives)
   XVIA3a(de)

2. Pedro no /se/ siente bien: Pedro does not feel well.
Sentirse bien (mal): to feel good (bad).
Reflexive construction.
Sentirse is a stem changing verb.
VIIE(Reflexive Construction)
IIIB1b(Present - stem changing)

3. Varias veces: Several times.
veces is the plural of vez.
IB4(Noun Plurals)
XVE3(vez)

4. Debe ir /a/ casa: He should go home.
Deber: to be supposed to, should
ir a casa: to go home.
cf. Estar en casa: to be at home.
XVIA1a(a)

5. Puede tener un virus: He may have a virus.
Poder: to be able to, can, may (permission and conjecture).
Poder is a stem changing verb.
IIIB1b(Present Tense)

6. ¿Puede Vd. venir por él?: Can you come for him?
Venir por alguien (algo): to come for someone (something). XVIA7n(por)

7. Ahora mismo: Right now.
Dict(Idioms)

8. El bebé está enfermo: The baby is sick.
Use of estar for health.
XB1(estar)

9. <u>Tengo /que/ esperar /a/ mi vecina</u>: I have to wait for my neighbor.
   Tener que: to have to
   　　　　　　　　　　Dict(Idioms)
   esperar: to wait <u>for</u>
   　　　　　　　　XVIC(Verbs and Prep.)
   <u>A</u> mi vecina: Use of personal <u>a</u> before a direct object referring to a person.
   　　　　　　　　　　XVIAlm(Personal <u>a</u>)
   cf. Espero el tren.

10. <u>Está bien</u>: All right.
    　　　　　　　　Dict(Idioms)

11. <u>Mientras tanto Pedro estará con la enfermera</u>: In the meantime, Pedro will be with the nurse.
    Mientras tanto: In the meantime.
    　　　　　　　　　Dict(Idioms)
    Use of <u>estar</u> for location.
    estará: future tense of <u>estar</u>.
    　　　　　　　　XB2(estar)

## TRANSLATE

1. Are you Pedro's father?
2. He is going to be with the nurse.
3. Pedro does not feel well.
4. I have to wait for my husband.
5. He should go home.
6. He may have a virus.
7. I can't come for him right now.

## SCHOOL IV

### SCHOOL DOCTOR

DR. SMITH: What is your name?
MIGUEL: Miguel Hernández.
DR. SMITH: How old are you?
MIGUEL: Seven and /a/ half.
DR. SMITH: Where do you live?
MIGUEL: 320 East 110th Street.

DR. SMITH: What is your father's and mother's name?
MIGUEL: María Hernández and Juan Hernández.
DR. SMITH: Do your father and mother work?
MIGUEL: Yes, they both work.
DR. SMITH: What is the trouble?
MIGUEL: I vomited and I have /a/ stomach ache.
DR. SMITH: What did you eat for breakfast this morning?

## ESCUELA IV

### MÉDICO DE LA ESCUELA

DR. SMITH: ¿Cómo te llamas?  1
MIGUEL: Miguel Hernández.
DR. SMITH: ¿Cuántos años tienes?  2
MIGUEL: Siete /años/ y medio.  3
DR. SMITH: ¿Dónde vives?
MIGUEL: /En la/ calle ciento diez, /número/ trescientos veinte, Este.  4

DR. SMITH: ¿Cómo se llaman tu padre y /tu/ madre?
MIGUEL: María Hernández y Juan Hernández.
DR. SMITH: ¿Trabajan tu padre y /tu/ madre?
MIGUEL: Sí, trabajan los dos.  5
DR. SMITH: ¿Qué tienes?  6
MIGUEL: Vomité y tengo dolor /de/ estómago.  7
DR. SMITH: ¿Qué comiste de desayuno esta mañana?  8

MIGUEL: Cereal, milk and orange juice.

MIGUEL: Cereal, leche y jugo /de/ naranja.

DR. SMITH: What did you eat for supper last night?

DR. SMITH: ¿Qué comiste de cena anoche? 9

MIGUEL: Chicken and rice and ice cream.

MIGUEL: Pollo y arroz y helado.

DR. SMITH: Take off your clothing.

DR. SMITH: <u>Quítate la ropa</u>. 10

Sit /down/.

<u>Siéntate</u>. 11

Bend /over/.

<u>Dóblate</u>. 12

Stick your tongue out.

<u>Saca la lengua</u>. 13

Stand /up/.

<u>Levántate</u>. 14

Is anyone at your house now?

¿<u>Hay alguien</u> en tu casa ahora? 15

MIGUEL: No, there is no one but my aunt lives in the same building.

MIGUEL: No, <u>no hay nadie</u> pero mi tía vive en el mismo edificio. 16

DR. SMITH: Does she have /a/ telephone?

DR. SMITH: ¿<u>Tiene teléfono</u>? 17

MIGUEL: Yes, it is 756-8960.

MIGUEL: Sí, es /el/ siete-cincuenta y seis - ochenta y nueve - sesenta.

DR. SMITH: Wait here.

DR. SMITH: Espera aquí.

The nurse is going to call your aunt.

<u>La enfermera va a llamar /a/ tu tía</u>. 18

She is going to pick you /up/. Give her this note.

Ella va a recogerte. <u>Dale esta nota</u>. 19

## NOTES

1. ¿Cómo te llamas?: What is your name?
   llamarse: to be called, to call oneself.
   >VIIE(Reflexive
   > Constructions)
   >Dict(Idioms)

2. ¿Cuántos años tienes?: How old are you?
   >XE1(Tener)
   >Dict(Idioms)

3. Siete /años/ y medio: Seven and /a/ half.

4. /En la/ calle ciento diez, /número/ trescientos veinte, Este: 320 East 110th Street.

5. Los dos: both (the two).

6. ¿Qué tienes?: What is the trouble? What is the matter with you?
   >XE1(Tener)
   >Dict(Idioms)

7. Tengo dolor /de/ estómago: I have /a/ stomach ache.
   >IA16(Compound Nouns)

8. ¿Qué comiste de desayuno?: What did you eat for breakfast?

9. Anoche: last night.
   >Dict(Idioms)

10. Quítate la ropa: Take off your clothes.
    Use of reflexive construction in Spanish, possessive adjective in English.
    >VIID2(Reflexives)
    
    In the affirmative command form, the reflexive pronoun, like all object pronouns is attached to the command form. A written accent mark is required to maintain the original stress.
    >VIIC(Pos. of Reflexive
    > Pronouns)

11. <u>Siéntate</u>: Sit /down/.
    sentarse: to sit down.
    cf. sentar a alguien: to seat someone.
    >Dict(Idioms)
    >VIIC(Pos. of Reflexive Pronouns)

12. <u>Dóblate</u>: Bend /over/.
    doblarse: to bend over.
    cf. doblar: to fold, bend (something)
    >VIID1(Reflexives)

13. <u>Saca la lengua</u>: Stick /out/ your (the) tongue.
    Sacar: to take out, to stick out.
    Use of definite article (la lengua) in Spanish, possessive adjective (your tongue) in English (when referring to parts of the body).
    >IIA2e(Definite Article)

14. <u>Levántate</u>: Get up
    Levantarse: to get up.
    cf. levantar algo: to lift something
    >VIID4(Reflexives)

15. ¿<u>Hay alguien en tu casa</u>?: Is anyone at (in) your house now?
    Hay: there is, there are, is there? are there?
    alguien: somebody, anybody, anyone.
    >XD(hay)
    >XX(Indefinites)

16. <u>No hay nadie</u>: There is no-one, there isn't anyone.
    Use of Double Negative.
    >XXB1(Double Negative)

17. ¿<u>Tiene teléfono</u>?: Does she have /a/ telephone?
    In questions and negative constructions, the English <u>any</u> is generally not translated.
    >IIB2e

18. La enfermera va a llamar /a/ tu tía:
    The nurse is going to call your aunt.
    va a llamar: she is going to call. Use of
    the verb <u>ir a</u> in lieu of the future (English:
    <u>going to</u>).           XVIAlh(ir a)

    /a/ tu tía:           XVIAlm(Personal <u>a</u>)

19. <u>Dale esta nota</u>: Give her this note.
    Give this note to her.
    The person to whom something is given becomes
    the indirect object (le). Object pronouns
    are attached to the command form.
                    XIF(Position of Object
                          Pronouns).


                    TRANSLATE


1.  What is the trouble?

2.  My head (throat, arm, leg) hurts.

3.  What did you have for breakfast (supper, lunch)?

4.  Is anyone in your house?

5.  Sit up; bend over; get up.

6.  Take off your clothes.

7.  I am going to call your mother.

8.  Stick your tongue out.

9.  There isn't anyone in my house.

| FIRE DEPARTMENT | DEPARTAMENTO DE INCENDIOS (CUERPO /DE/ BOMBEROS) | |
|---|---|---|
| A. <u>Fire</u> | A. <u>Un fuego</u> | |
| MRS. CARDONA: There is a fire in my apartment.<br>Please, come right away. | SRA. CARDONA: <u>Hay un fuego en mi apartamento.</u><br>Por favor, vengan <u>enseguida.</u> | 1<br><br>2 |
| FIREMAN: What is your address? | BOMBERO: <u>¿Cuál es su dirección?</u> | 3 |
| MRS. CARDONA: 350 East 10th Street, Apartment 8H. | SRA. CARDONA: <u>Trescientos cincuenta Este, calle diez.</u> Apartamento ocho H (hache). | 4 |
| FIREMAN: What is the telephone number from which you are calling? | BOMBERO: <u>¿Cuál es el número /de/ teléfono</u> de donde llama usted? | see 3 |
| MRS. CARDONA: 475-6097. | SRA. CARDONA: Cuatro-siete-cinco-seis-cero-nueve-siete. | |
| FIREMAN: Make everybody leave the apartment.<br>We will be there in a few minutes. | BOMBERO: <u>Haga salir /a/ todo el mundo del apartamento.</u><br><u>Estaremos allí en unos minutos.</u> | 5<br><br>6 |
| B. <u>At the fire</u> | B. <u>En el incendio</u> | |
| Where is the fire? | ¿Dónde está el fuego? | |
| Is /there/ anyone in the house? | <u>¿Hay alguien en la casa?</u> | see 1 |
| Are all the children out? | ¿Están fuera todos los niños? | 7 |
| Don't go near there, please. | <u>No se acerque(n)</u> ahí, por favor. | 8 |
| Don't go /in/to the apartment. | No vaya(n) al apartamento. | |

| | | |
|---|---|---|
| Where are your parents? | ¿Dónde están tus padres? | 9 |
| Who is your landlord? | ¿Quién es su casero? | 10 |

| C. Inspection | C. Inspección | |
|---|---|---|
| The hallway is obstructed by furniture. | El pasillo está obstruído de muebles. | 11 |
| There is rubbish in the hall. | Hay basura en el vestíbulo. | see 1 |
| The door to the roof is locked. | La puerta de la azotea está cerrada con llave. | 12 |
| There are inflammable liquids in the basement. | Hay líquidos inflamables en el sótano. | |
| The hallway is dark. | El corredor está obscuro. | 13 |
| The electric wires are exposed (in the air). | Los cables de la luz eléctrica están al aire. | |

## NOTES

1. Hay un fuego en mi apartamento: There is a fire in my apartment.
   Hay: there is, there are, are there? is there?
                 XD(hay)
2. En seguida: Right away  Dict(Idioms)
3. ¿Cuál es su dirección?: What is your address?
   What? is translated by ¿cuál? before the verb to be.
                 VC3b(Interrogatives)

4. **Trescientos cincuenta Este, calle diez:** 350 East 10th Street.
   Use of cardinal number (diez) in Spanish - ordinal number (tenth) in English.
         XVA(numbers)

5. **Haga salir /a/ todo el mundo del apartamento:** Make everybody leave the apartment.
   Haga: Command form of <u>hacer</u>.  VIA2(Commands)
   Todo el mundo: everybody (literally: the whole world).     Dict(Idioms)
   salir de: to leave (from).
         XVIA3g(Verbs & Prepos.)

6. **Estaremos allí en unos minutos:** We will be there in a few minutes.
   Use of <u>estar</u> for location.  XB2(estar)
   ahí: there (near the speaker)
   cf. allí: there (away from the speaker).

7. **¿Están fuera todos los niños?:** Are all the children out(side)?
   Use of <u>estar</u> for location.  XB2(estar)

8. **No se acerquen:** Don't go near (there).
   Acercarse: to go near, to come close to.
   Use of reflexive construction in Spanish.
         VII(Reflexive Verbs)
   When the ending begins with an <u>e</u>, the <u>c</u> of the infinitive changes to <u>qu</u>, in order to maintain the original hard sound of <u>c</u>.
         IIIB1c(Spelling Changes)

9. **¿Dónde están tus padres?:** Where are your parents?
   Use of <u>estar</u> for location.  XB2(estar)
   Los padres: the fathers or the parents.
         IB8(Plural Nouns)
   cf. los hijos: the sons or sons and daughters.

10. **¿Quién es su casero?:** Who is your landlord?
    Use of <u>ser</u> for occupation.
          XA1(ser)

11. **El pasillo está obstruído de muebles**: The hallway is obstructed by furniture.
    Use of <u>estar</u> for a condition which is the result of an action (obstruir).
    $\qquad$ XB3(estar)
    Los muebles (plural): the furniture (singular)
    $\qquad$ IB8(Plural Nouns)

12. **La puerta de la azotea está cerrada con llave**: The door to (of) the roof is locked (closed with key).
    Use of <u>estar</u>, see No. 11
    cerrar(ie) con llave: to lock (to close with a key). $\qquad$ Dict(Idioms)

13. **El corredor está obscuro**: The hallway (corridor) is dark.
    Use of <u>estar</u> for a temporary condition.
    $\qquad$ XB1(estar)


### TRANSLATE

1. There is a fire in my apartment.
2. We will come right away.
3. Make everybody leave the apartment.
4. Don't come near here.
5. Watch out for the hose.
6. Who is your landlord?
7. The hallway is obstructed.
8. There is rubbish in the hall.

POLICE I                          POLICÍA I

BURGLARY                          ROBO

MRS. MARTÍN (ON THE PHONE): SRA. MARTÍN (AL
Hello, is this Police       TELÉFONO): Dígame,            1
Headquarters?               ¿Es esa la Comisaría          2
                            de Policía?

OFFICER: Yes.               POLICÍA: Sí.

MRS. MARTÍN: This is        SRA. MARTÍN: Soy
(I am) Mrs. Martin.         la señora Martin.
They robbed my apartment.   Me robaron en el
                            apartamento.

OFFICER: What is            POLICÍA: ¿Cuál es
your address?               su dirección?

MRS. MARTÍN: My             SRA. MARTÍN: ¿Mi
address? Yes. My            dirección? Sí. Mi
address is 320 East         dirección es
114th Street.               trescientos veinte,
Apartment 14.               Este, /de la/ calle
                            ciento catorce.
                            Apartamento número
                            catorce.

OFFICER: I am coming        POLICÍA: Iré en               3
(I will go) right           seguida.
away.

MRS. MARTÍN: Thank          SRA. MARTÍN: Muchas
you very much.              gracias. Adiós.
Good-bye.

(At the apartment)          (En el apartamento).

OFFICER: I am sergeant      POLICÍA: Soy /el/             4
Smith.                      sargento Smith.
You called us.              Vd. nos llamó.
Please tell me              Por favor, dígame             5
what happened.              qué pasó.

MRS. MARTÍN: I went         SRA. MARTÍN: Fui al
to the movies and I         cine y regresé
came back at about          aproximadamente
12:30.                      a las doce /y/ media.         6

| | | |
|---|---|---|
| The fire escape window was open. | La ventana /de la/ escalera /de/ incendios estaba abierta. | 7 |
| The robbers must have entered through it. | Los ladrones deben haber entrado por ella. | |
| OFFICER: Do you know what they took (away)? | POLICÍA: ¿Sabe Vd. qué /se/ llevaron? | 8 |
| MRS. MARTÍN: Yes, they took my TV and the radio. | SRA. MARTÍN: Sí. Se llevaron mi televisión y el radio. | |
| I am also missing my fur coat and some jewelry. | También me faltan mi abrigo /de/ piel y algunas joyas. | 9 |
| OFFICER: Is /this/ the first time that your apartment was robbed? | POLICÍA: ¿Es la primera vez que le robaron el apartamento? | 10 |
| MRS. MARTÍN: Yes, the first time. | SRA. MARTÍN: Sí, la primera vez. | |
| OFFICER: Did they rob anyone else on the floor? | POLICÍA: ¿Le robaron a alguien más en el piso? | |
| MRS. MARTÍN: No, I am the only /one/. | SRA. MARTÍN: No. Soy la única. | |
| OFFICER: Did you lock the windows and the door? | POLICÍA: ¿Cerró Vd. con llave las ventanas y la puerta? | 11 |
| MRS. MARTÍN: Yes, I always do it, before leaving. | SRA. MARTÍN: Sí. Antes /de/ salir lo hago siempre. | 12 |
| OFFICER: Can you give me a description of your coat and your jewels? | POLICÍA: ¿Puede Vd. darme una descripción de su abrigo y de sus joyas? | |

MRS. MARTÍN: Better than that. I have photos.
Here they are.

OFFICER: Thank you very much.
The photos are going to help us a lot.

MRS. MARTÍN: My husband engraved his social security number on the television and the radio.

Here it is.

OFFICER: Thank you. Did anyone see the robbers?

MRS. MARTÍN: My neighbor, María, says that she saw someone on the roof who seemed suspicious to her.
But she did not know what to do.

OFFICER: What is your name?

MRS. CRUZ: My name is María Cruz.

OFFICER: Can you describe him?

MRS. CRUZ: I think so.

OFFICER: Was he tall, taller than I?

SRA. MARTÍN: Mejor que eso. Tengo fotos.
Aquí están.

POLICÍA: Muchas gracias.
Las fotos nos ayudarán mucho.

SRA. MARTÍN: Mi marido grabó su número de seguro social en la televisión y en el radio.

Aquí está.

POLICÍA: Gracias. ¿Vio alguien a los ladrones?      13

SRA. MARTÍN: Mi vecina, María, dice que vio a alguien      13
en el tejado que le pareció sospechoso.
Pero ella no supo qué hacer.

POLICÍA: ¿Cuál es su nombre?

SRA. CRUZ: Me llamo María Cruz.

POLICÍA: ¿Puede Vd. describirlo?

SRA. CRUZ: Creo que sí.

POLICÍA: ¿Era alto, más alto que yo?

| | |
|---|---|
| MRS. CRUZ: Yes, he was, but he was younger.<br>He was about 17 years /old/. | SRA. CRUZ: Sí, /lo/ era, pero era más joven.<br>Tenía unos diez y siete años. 14 |
| OFFICER: And his clothes? | POLICÍA: Y, ¿<u>su ropa</u>? 15 |
| MRS. CRUZ: He wore blue jeans and a red shirt. | SRA. CRUZ: Llevaba <u>pantalones de vaquero</u> y una camisa roja. 16 |
| OFFICER: And his color? | POLICÍA: ¿Y su color? |
| MRS. CRUZ: He was white. | SRA. CRUZ: Era blanco. |
| OFFICER: At what time did you see him? | POLICÍA: ¿<u>A qué hora</u> le vio Vd? 17 |
| MRS. CRUZ: Around 11. | SRA. CRUZ: <u>Cerca de las once</u>. 18 |
| OFFICER: You never saw him before? | POLICÍA: ¿Nunca le vio antes? |
| MRS. CRUZ: No, I never saw him before. | SRA. CRUZ: No, nunca le vi antes. |
| OFFICER: Where was he when you saw him? | POLICÍA: ¿Dónde <u>estaba él cuando le vio</u>? 19 |
| MRS. CRUZ: Over there, on the roof.<br>Over there, where the light of that apartment is. | SRA. CRUZ: Allá, en el tejado.<br>Allá, donde está la luz de aquel apartamento. |
| OFFICER: Thank you very much, Mrs. Cruz. | POLICÍA: Muchas gracias, señora Cruz. |
| The numbers on the television and on the radio will help us a lot. | Los números en la televisión y en el radio nos ayudarán mucho. |

|  |  | |
|---|---|---|
| If we find out anything we will let you know (tell you). | Si nos enteramos de algo se lo diremos. | 20 |
| In the future, don't leave the fire escape window open. | En el futuro, no deje abierta la ventana /de la/ escalera /de/ incendios. | |
| You should have safety locks on the windows and doors. | Debe tener cerraduras /de/ seguridad en las ventanas y en las puertas. | 21 |
| MRS. MARTÍN: Thank you and good-bye. | SRA. MARTÍN: Gracias y adiós. | |
| OFFICER: Good-bye, ladies. | POLICÍA: Adiós, señoras. | |

## NOTES

1. **Dígame**: Hello.
   Literally: Tell me. Most Spanish speaking persons answer the phone either with **dígame** or **bueno**.   Dict(Idioms)

2. **/La/ Comisaría /de/ Policía**: Police Headquarters.    IA16 & Dict(Compound Nouns)

3. **Iré en seguida**: I am coming (I will go) right away.
   Iré: Future of **ir**.    XIVA1b(Future)
   Enseguida (en seguida): Right away.
                      Dict(Idioms)

4. **Soy /el/ sargento Smith**: I am Sergeant Smith.
   When speaking **about** someone, the definite article is used before titles.
   Here, Sgt. Smith is speaking about himself.
                      IIB4(Definite Article)

5. <u>Dígame qué pasó</u>: Tell me what happened.
   <u>Diga</u>: Command form of <u>decir</u>.
   pasar: to pass, to happen, to spend time.
        VIA2(Commands)

6. <u>A /las/ doce /y/ media</u>: At twelve thirty.
        XVF2(Time)

7. <u>La ventana /de la/ escalera /de/ incendios</u>
   <u>estaba abierta</u>: The fire escape window was
   open.    IA16 & Dict(Compound Nouns)

8. <u>¿Sabe Vd. que se llevaron?</u>: Do you know what
   they took (along)?
   llevarse algo: To take something away.
   cf. llevar ropa: To wear clothes.
        VIIE(Reflexive Verbs)

9. <u>Me faltan mi abrigo /de/ piel y algunas joyas</u>:
   I am missing my fur coat and some jewelry.
   Literally: My fur coat and some jewels are
   missing to me.
   <u>Joyas</u> (jewelry) is plural. The subject of
   <u>faltar</u> is what is missing.
   cf. Me gustan las joyas.
   <u>Mi abrigo /de/ piel</u>: My fur coat.
        XIL(faltar)
        IA16 & Dict(Compound Nouns)

10. <u>¿Le robaron el apartamento?</u>: Was your apartment
    robbed?
    The passive voice (was robbed) is used much
    less frequently in Spanish than in English.
    An active voice is substituted for the passive
    voice here.
    Literally: Did they rob the apartment for you?
         XXIVA(Substitution for
           Passive Voice)

11. <u>¿Cerró con llave las ventanas?</u>: Did you lock
    the windows?
    Cerrar (ie): To close.
    Cerrar con llave: To close with a key, i.e.
    to lock.    Dict(Idioms)

12. <u>Antes /de/ salir</u>: Before leaving.
    <u>Antes de</u>, like all prepositions in Spanish, is followed by the infinitive.
    XXIA(Infinitive after Preposition)

13. ¿<u>Vio alguien /a/ los ladrones</u>?: Did anyone see the robbers?
    Use of personal <u>a</u> before a direct object referring to persons.
    XVIA1m(Personal <u>a</u>)
    XIIA1(Preterite)

14. <u>Tenía unos diez y siete años</u>: He was about 17 years old.
    Tener...años: to be ...old
    XE1(tener)
    Use of Imperfect Tense (tenía) for description.
    XIIIB3
    Unos...años: about...years.
    XVD(about)

15. ¿<u>Su ropa</u>?: His clothes?
    <u>Ropa</u> is always used in the singular.
    IB9(Singular Nouns)

16. <u>Pantalones /de/ vaquero</u>: (Blue) jeans.
    Literally: Cowboy pants.
    IA16 & Dict(Compound Nouns)

17. ¿<u>A qué hora le vio</u>?: At what time did you see him?
    XVE(Time)

18. <u>Cerca /de las/ once</u>: Around (about) 11.
    XVD(About, around)

19. ¿<u>Dónde estaba él cuando le vio</u>?: Where was he when you saw him?
    Use of Imperfect Tense (estaba) for an action that was going on when another action started.
    XIIIB4(Use of Imperfect Tense)

20. Si /nos/ enteramos /de/ algo, /se/ lo diremos:
    If we find out anything, we will let you know.
    Enterarse /de/ algo: to find out something.
    VIIF(Reflexive Verbs)
    Se lo diremos: We will let you know.
    Literally: We will tell it to you.
    The indirect object pronoun (le - to you),
    changes to se if another pronoun beginning
    with l follows.    XIG2(Double Object
                              Pronouns)

21. Cerraduras /de/ seguridad: Safety locks.
    IA16 & Dict(Compound Nouns)


                    TRANSLATE


1.  I am Sergeant Smith.

2.  I am missing my fur coat.

3.  Is this Police Headquarters?

4.  Tell me what happened.

5.  What did they take?

6.  Is this the first time your apartment was robbed?

7.  Did anyone see the robbers?

8.  Did you lock the door?

9.  You should have safety locks on all windows.

10. If we find out anything, we will let you know.

## POLICE II

### ACCIDENT

MRS. GÓMEZ: My neighbor, Mrs. Vega slipped on the kitchen floor and can't get up.

Can you call an ambulance?

POLICE OFFICER: We will try.

At the apartment.

OFFICER: Good morning.

I am officer Brown.

You are Mrs. Gómez, aren't you?

The ambulance is coming right away.

(To Mrs. Vega):

Don't move till they arrive.

They will take you to the hospital.

Does /it/ hurt much?

MRS. VEGA: Not so much now, but I can't get /up/.

OFFICER: Who lives in the apartment with you?

MRS. VEGA: My two children, Pablo and María.

## POLICÍA

### ACCIDENTE

SRA. GÓMEZ: Mi vecina, /la/ Sra. Vega resbaló en el piso /de la/ cocina y no puede levantar/se/.  1

¿Puede Vd. llamar una ambulancia?

POLICÍA: Trataremos.

En el apartamento.

POLICÍA: Buenos días.

Soy /el/ policía Brown.  2

Vd. es /la/ Sra. Gómez, ¿verdad?  3

La ambulancia viene enseguida.  4

(A /la/ Sra. Vega):

No /se/ mueva hasta /que/ lleguen.  5

La llevarán al hospital.

¿Duele mucho?

SRA. VEGA: No tanto ahora, pero no puedo levantar/me/.  6

POLICÍA: ¿Quién vive en el apartamento con Vd.?

SRA. VEGA: Mis dos hijos, Pablo y María.

| | |
|---|---|
| They are at school now. | Están en /la/ escuela ahora. |
| OFFICER: When does your husband come back home? | POLICÍA: ¿Cuándo vuelve /a/ casa su marido? |
| MRS. VEGA: My husband died two years ago. | SRA. VEGA: <u>Mi marido murió hace dos años.</u> |
| OFFICER: Is there anyone who can take care of the children if you have to stay in the hospital? | POLICÍA: ¿<u>Hay alguien que pueda cuidar /a/ los niños</u> si Vd. tiene que permanecer en el hospital? |
| MRS. GÓMEZ: They can stay (be) with me. | SRA. GÓMEZ: <u>Pueden estar conmigo.</u> |
| OFFICER: How old are they? | POLICÍA: ¿<u>Qué edad tienen ellos</u>? |
| MRS. VEGA: Pablo is six years /old/ and María eight. | SRA. VEGA: <u>Pablo tiene seis años</u> y María ocho. |
| OFFICER: Do they come home /by/ themselves? | POLICÍA: ¿<u>Vuelven /a/ casa solos</u>? |
| MRS. VEGA: Yes. | SRA. VEGA: Sí. |
| MRS. GÓMEZ: I can pick them /up/ and tell them what has happened. | SRA. GÓMEZ: <u>Yo puedo recogerlos y decirles /lo/ que ha pasado.</u> |
| OFFICER: Before the ambulance arrives, let me ask you some questions. | POLICÍA: <u>Antes /de que/ llegue la ambulancia, déjeme hacerle unas preguntas.</u> |
| OFFICER: Are you epileptic? | POLICÍA: ¿<u>Es Vd. epiléptica</u>? |
| MRS. GÓMEZ: No. | SRA. GÓMEZ: No. |

7
8
9
10
11
12
13
14
15

| | |
|---|---|
| OFFICER: Have you ever used (taken) any drugs? | POLICÍA: ¿<u>Ha tomado</u> Vd. <u>algún narcótico alguna vez</u>? 16 |
| MRS. VEGA: No. | SRA. VEGA: No. |
| OFFICER: Do you have any heart ailment? | POLICÍA: ¿Tiene alguna <u>enfermedad /de/ corazón</u>? 17 |
| MRS. VEGA: No, but the doctor told me that I have high blood pressure. | SRA. VEGA: No, pero <u>el doctor me dijo que tengo /la/ presión alta</u>. 18 |
| OFFICER: What is the name of your family doctor? | POLICÍA: ¿Cuál es el nombre de su <u>médico /de/ cabecera</u>? 19 |
| MRS. VEGA: Doctor Franco. His office is at 320 East 110th Street. | SRA. VEGA: Doctor Franco. <u>Su consultorio está /en el/ trescientos veinte, Este, /de la/ calle ciento diez</u>. 20 |

### NOTES

1. <u>/La/ señora Vega resbaló en el piso /de la/ cocina</u>: Mrs. Vega slipped on the kitchen floor (the floor of the kitchen).
   /La/ señora Vega: Use of definite article before a title, when speaking <u>about</u> a person.
                   IIA2d (Use of Definite Article)
   cf. ¿Cómo está Vd, Sra. Vega?
   El piso /de la/ cocina: the kitchen floor.
                IA16 & Dict (Compound Nouns)

2. **Soy /el/ policía Brown**: I am (police) officer Brown.
Here again, officer Brown is speaking about himself.    IIA2d(Definite Article)
Soy: Use of the verb ser when speaking about a profession.    XAI(ser)

3. **Vd. es /la/ Sra. Gómez, ¿verdad?**: You are Mrs. Gómez, aren't you?
Use of definite article (See No. 1).
¿verdad?: Aren't you? (Also: isn't it? weren't you?, etc.) The English construction changes according to the preceding statement. The Spanish construction ¿(no es) verdad? literally means: Isn't it the truth? It, therefore, does not change.    Dict(Idioms)

4. **La ambulancia viene enseguida**: The ambulance is coming right away.
Here English uses a Present Progressive form for an immediate future. Spanish uses the Present Tense. Spanish never uses the Present Progressive form for verbs of motion (ir, venir, etc.).    IIIB2b(Spanish Present for
                                English Progressive)

5. **No /se/ mueva hasta /que/ lleguen**: Don't move until they arrive.
Moverse(ue): to move (oneself). o changes to ue in the singular and in the third person plural of the present tense.
              IIIB1b(Stem Changes)
hasta: until (preposition)
hasta que: until (conjunction)
The Subjunctive is used after the conjunction hasta que if future time is implied.
              XXVA3(Forms of Subjunctive)
              XXVD1d(Use of Subjunctive after
                        Conjunctions)

6. **No puedo levantar/me/**: I cannot get up.
Levantar/se/: to get /up/.
              VIIE(Reflexive Verbs)
cf. levantar algo: to lift something.

7. **Están en /la/ escuela:** They are at (in the) school.
   Use of *estar* for location.     XB2(estar)
   En /la/ escuela: At school.
                IIAs(Definite Article)

8. **Mi marido murió hace dos años:** My husband died two years ago.
   When used with the Preterite Tense, *hace* means *ago*.     XVG2(hace)

9. **¿Hay alguien que pueda cuidar /a/ los niños?:** Is there anyone who can take care of the children?
   Hay: is there? are there? there is, there are
                XD(hay)
   cuidar: to care for, to take care of.
   cuidar /a/ los niños: Use of personal *a* before a direct object referring to persons.
                XVIA1m(Personal *a*)
   Pueda: Present Subjunctive of *poder*.
                XXVA4(Subjunctive)
   The Subjunctive is used here because the speaker does not know if such a person exists or not.     XXVD1f

10. **Pueden estar conmigo:** They can stay (be) with me.
    conmigo: with me.
    The preposition *con* combines with *mí*: conmigo, contigo, but con él, con ella, etc.
                 XID2(Object of Preposition)

11. **¿Qué edad tienen ellos?:** How old are they (what is their age)?
    Use of *tener* for age.     XE1(tener)

12. **¿Vuelven /a/ casa solos?:** Do they come home alone (by themselves)?
    Volver(ue) a casa: to return home. *o* changes to *ue* in the singular and in the third person plural of the Present Tense.
                 IIIB1b(Stem Changes)
    sólo: alone (This is an adjective and is, therefore, pluralized here).
    cf. solo: only.

13. Yo puedo recogerlos y decirles /lo/ que ha pasado: I can pick them up and tell them (say to them) what has happened.
recoger (to pick up) takes a direct object (los)
decir (to tell something to someone) takes an indirect object of the person.
lo que ha pasado (what has happened) is the direct object of decir.
     XIB and C (Direct and Indirect
        Object Pronouns)
lo que: what. The relative pronoun what is translated by lo que when there is no antecedent. XXIIIB5(lo que)

14. Antes /de/ que llegue la ambulancia, déjeme hacerle unas preguntas: Before the ambulance arrives, let me ask you some questions (put some questions to you).
Antes de: before (preposition)
Antes de que: before (conjunction)
The subjunctive must be used after the conjunction antes de que when the action has not yet taken place.
     XXVAle(Subjunctive)
     XXVD1d(Subjunctive after
       Conjunction)

15. ¿Es Vd. epiléptica?: Are you epileptic?
Use of ser because epilepsy is a permanent condition. XA2(ser)

16. ¿Ha tomado Vd. algún narcótico alguna vez?: Have you ever (at any time) used (taken) any drugs (narcotics)?
algún: any      XXA3(algún)
alguna vez: ever, at any time. XVE3(vez)

17. Una enfermedad /de/ corazón: A heart ailment (disease).  IA16 & Dict(Compound Nouns)

18. El doctor me dijo que tengo /la/ presión alta: The doctor told me that I have high /blood/ pressure.
Use of definite article (la) for conditions of the body. English frequently uses the possessive adjective instead (My blood pressure is high). IIA2e(Definite Article) & XIIB2b
dijo: Preterite Tense of decir. (Preterite).

19. <u>El médico /de/ cabecera</u>: The family doctor.

                        Dict(Compound Nouns)

20. <u>Su consultorio está /en el/ 320 este /de la/ calle ciento diez</u>: His office is at 320 East 110th Street.
    Use of <u>estar</u> for location.     XB2(estar)
    Use of <u>definite</u> article (el, la) before numbers and streets.
                        IIA2p(Definite Article)


                    TRANSLATE


1. I am officer Brown.
2. The children are at school.
3. The ambulance is coming right away.
4. Don't move.
5. Who takes care of the children?
6. How old are they?
7. Have you ever used any drugs?
8. Do you have any heart ailment?
9. I have high blood pressure.
10. You are Mrs. Brown, aren't you?

## POLICE III

### DRUG ARREST

| English | Español | |
|---|---|---|
| OFFICER: I am detective Smith. | POLICÍA: Soy /el/ detective Smith. | 1 |
| I am arresting you for trying to sell heroin to me. | Le arresto por tratar de venderme heroína. | 2 |
| Keep your hands where I can see them. | Mantenga sus manos de manera que pueda verlas. | 3 |
| Lean against this car. I am going to search you. | Apóye/se/ contra este automóvil. Voy a registrarle. | 4 |
| I am taking this package to the police station. | /Me/llevo este paquete a la estación /de/ policía. | 5, 6 |
| Hold/out/your hands so that I can put the handcuffs /on/ you. | Ponga las manos de manera que pueda ponerle las esposas. | 7 |
| I am taking you to the station house. | Le llevo a la estación /de/ policía. | 8 |
| You will be placed in a detention cell until your trial comes up. | Vd. será colocado en una celda de detención hasta /que/ el juicio tenga lugar. | 9 |
| At the trial, you can get an attorney or, if you cannot pay the expenses, a lawyer will be assigned to you by the Court. | En el juicio, Vd. puede nombrar un abogado o si no puede pagar los gastos, un abogado le será asignado por la Corte. | 10, 11 |

NOTES

1. <u>Soy /el/ detective Smith</u>: I am detective Smith.
   Use of <u>ser</u> for professions.   XA1(ser)
   Use of <u>definite</u> article (el) before a title
   because detective Smith is talking <u>about</u>
   himself.       IIB4(Definite Article)

2. <u>Le arresto por tratar de venderme heroína</u>: I
   am arresting you for trying to sell me heroin.
   Use of Present Tense (arresto) in Spanish -
   Present Progressive Form in English. Spanish
   uses the Progressive form much less frequently
   than English.  IIIB2a(note)
   por: for, because of       XVIA7g(por)
   tratar de: to try to
   Use of infinitive after the preposition <u>de</u>
                XXIIA(Infinitive)

3. <u>Mantenga sus manos de manera que pueda verlas</u>:
   Keep your hands where (so that) I can (might be
   able to) see them.
   Mantenga: command form of <u>mantener</u>.
              VIA1(Command Forms)
   Use of Subjunctive (pueda) after the conjunction
   <u>de manera que</u> if future action is implied.
              XXVA2(Subjunctive Form)
              XXVD1(Use of Subjunctive)

4. <u>Apóyese contra este automóvil</u>: Lean against
   this car.
   Apoyarse contra: to lean against something
              VIIE(Reflexive Verbs)
   cf. apoyar: to support, protect.

5. <u>/Me/ llevo este paquete</u>: I am taking this
   package (along with me).
   Llevarse algo: to take something along.
   cf. llevar: to carry, wear.
              VII (Reflexive Verbs)

6. <u>La estación /de/ policía</u>: The police station.
              IA16 & Dict(Compound Nouns)

7. **Ponga las manos de manera que pueda ponerle las esposas**: Hold out (put) your (the) hands so that I can (may be able to) put the handcuffs on you.
   Ponga: Command form of **poner**
                       VIA3(Command Forms)
   Use of Subjunctive (pueda) after the conjunction **de manera que** with future time implied.
                       XXVD1(Subjunctive)

8. **Le llevo a la estación /de/ policía**: I am taking you to the police station.
   Llevar a alguien: to take someone somewhere.
   Use of Present Tense in Spanish, Present Progressive form in English.
                       IIIB2a(note)

9. **Hasta /que/ el juicio tenga lugar**: Until your (the) trial comes up (takes place).
   Hasta: until (preposition)
   Hasta que: until (conjunction)
   Use of Subjunctive (tenga) after the conjunction **hasta que**, when future time is implied.
                       XXVD1d(Subjunctive)

10. **Ud. puede nombrar un abogado**: You can appoint (name) an attorney.

11. **Un abogado le será asignado**: A lawyer will be assigned to you.
    Use of **ser** for passive voice.
                        XXIVB1(Passive Voice)

TRANSLATE

1. I am arresting you for trying to sell me narcotics.
2. You can get an attorney.
3. Keep your hands where I can see them.
4. I am going to put the handcuffs on you.

5. I am going to search you.
6. I am taking you to the police station.
7. You will stay in jail until your trial comes up.

## POLICE IV

### FAMILY DISPUTE I

ANTONIA (calling the police)

Please, send a policeman.
My brother and my father are fighting.

I am afraid that my father is going to kill my brother.

OFFICER: What is your address?

ANTONIA: 250 East Second Street.

OFFICER (arriving at the apartment) (Juan and Mr. Ruiz are fighting)

OFFICER: Break it up.

Mr. Ruiz, please come into the bedroom with me.

I want to talk to (with) you.

MR. RUIZ: I don't want him in my house any more.

He does not go to school and the truant officer comes every week.

## POLICÍA IV

### DISPUTA FAMILIAR I

ANTONIA (llamando /a/ la policía)  1

Por favor, manden un policía.
Mi hermano y mi padre están luchando.  2

Temo que mi padre va a matar /a/ mi hermano.  3

POLICÍA: ¿Cuál es su dirección?  4

ANTONIA: Doscientos cincuenta Este /de la/ calle segunda.

POLICÍA (llegando al apartamento) (Juan y /el/ señor Ruiz están luchando)  5

POLICÍA: Sepárense.  6

Sr. Ruiz, venga al dormitorio conmigo, por favor.  7

Quiero hablar con Vd.

SR. RUIZ: No le quiero más en mi casa.

No va a /la/ escuela y el vigilante escolar viene cada semana.  8

| | |
|---|---|
| Neither I nor the other children went to high school. | Ni yo ni los otros hijos fuimos a /la/ escuela secundaria.　9 |
| He can get an education, but he doesn't want to. | Él puede obtener una educación, pero no quiere. |
| Since my wife died ten years ago I have worked hard and taken care of him and the others. | Desde que mi esposa murió hace diez años　10 he trabajado duro y he cuidado de él　11 y /de/ los otros. |
| The others had to go to work but this one can go to school but he doesn't want to go and when I talk to him about that, he gets angry. | Los otros tuvieron　12 que ir a trabajar pero éste puede ir　13 a la escuela pero él no quiere ir y cuando le hablo de eso se enfada.　14 |
| OFFICER: How many other children do you have? | POLICÍA: ¿Cuántos otros hijos tiene Vd? |
| MR. RUIZ: Antonia, who lives here and Pablo and Carmen who are married. | SR. RUIZ: Antonia que vive aquí y Pablo y Carmen que están casados. |
| OFFICER: What happened? | POLICÍA: ¿Qué　15 pasó? |
| MR. RUIZ: I told him that the truant officer had come again and that if he didn't go to school, I would throw him /out/ of /the/ house. | SR. RUIZ: Yo le dije que el vigilante　16 escolar había venido otra vez y que si él no iba a /la/ escuela yo le echaría de casa.　17 |
| He got angry and threw a chair at me. | Él se enfadó y me tiró una　18 silla. |

| | |
|---|---|
| He nearly killed me. | Él casi me mató. |
| I still have the scar here on my head. | Todavía tengo la cicatriz aquí en la cabeza. |
| Then he ran away (escaped), and now he wants to come back again. | Entonces él escapó y ahora quiere volver otra vez. |
| Let him be /out/ in the street. | Déjele estar en la calle. |
| No son /of/ mine is going to act this way and stay in my house. | Ningún hijo mío va a actuar /de/ esta manera y permanecer en mi casa. | 19 |
| OFFICER: Now, look, he is your son. You don't really want him to leave, do you? | POLICÍA: Pues mire, él es su hijo. Vd. realmente no desea que /se/ vaya, ¿verdad? | 20 |
| MR. RUIZ: I don't want to have anything to do with him any more. | SR. RUIZ: No quiero tener nada más que ver con él. | 21 |
| OFFICER: Wait here. I will return in a little while. | POLICÍA: Espere aquí. Volveré en un rato. |
| OFFICER:(enters the living room to talk to Juan). | POLICÍA:(entra /en/ la sala para hablar con Juan). | 22 |
| OFFICER: Tell me what happened. | POLICÍA: Dime que pasó. |
| JUAN: I want to come (back) home but he doesn't let me. | JUAN: Quiero volver /a/ casa y él no me deja. |

| | | |
|---|---|---|
| OFFICER: Why did you run away? | POLICÍA: ¿Por qué escapaste? | 25 |
| JUAN: He yelled /at/ me and said to me that I had /to/ leave if I don't go to school when I am supposed /to/. | JUAN: Él me gritó y me dijo que tenía /que/ ir /me/ si no voy a /la/ escuela cuando debo. | 26 |
| So I got angry, and I threw the chair at him. | Entonces, me enfadé y le tiré la silla. | |
| I was sorry after I did it, and I ran away. | /Lo/ sentí después /de/ hacerlo y escapé. | 27 |
| I went to my sister Carmen's house and she got me a room near her. | Fui a casa /de/ mi hermana Carmen y ella me obtuvo un cuarto cerca /de/ ella. | 28 29 |
| I got a job (work) in a grocery store but I didn't like living alone. | Obtuve un trabajo en una bodega pero no me gustó vivir solo. | 30 |
| I guess my father is right. I should go back to school. | Creo que mi padre tiene razón. Debo volver a /la/ escuela. | 31 |
| Otherwise I'll never get a decent job. | De otro modo nunca obtendré un trabajo decente. | 32 |
| OFFICER (to the father): Mr. Ruiz, can you come here now? | POLICÍA (al padre): Sr. Ruiz, ¿Puede Vd. venir aquí ahora? | |
| Juan says that he is sorry and he wants to come back. | Juan dice que /lo/ siente y quiere regresar. | see 27 |

| | | |
|---|---|---|
| If you could talk things over calmly, instead of yelling at each other, and throwing things at each other, things could work out much better. | Si Vd. pudiera hablar /de las/ cosas con calma, en vez de gritarse y tirarse cosas, las cosas podrían ir mucho mejor. | 33 |
| Maybe you could let Juan stay let's say a month and see how things work out. | Tal vez Vd. podría dejar /a/ Juan permanecer, digamos un mes y ver como van las cosas. | 34 |
| (It) may be (that) he has learned a lesson. | Puede ser que él haya aprendido una lección. | 35 |
| If not, he will have to appear in Children's Court. | Si no /es así/, él tendrá /que/ comparecer ante el Tribunal /de/ Menores. | 36 |
| If you have any difficulty during this time, you can get in touch with the Family Crisis Unit at Police Headquarters. | Si Vd. tiene cualquier dificultad durante este tiempo, puede ponerse en contacto con la Unidad de problemas familiares en la Comisaría /de/ Policía. | 37 |
| Now, let me ask you some questions. | Ahora, déjeme hacerle algunas preguntas. | 38 |
| How old are you, Mr. Ruiz? | ¿Qué edad tiene Vd., Sr. Ruiz? | 39 |

MR. RUIZ: I am 45.

SR. RUIZ: Tengo cuarenta y cinco /años/.

OFFICER: And you, Juan?

POLICÍA: ¿Y tú, Juan?

JUAN: I am fifteen.

JUAN: Tengo quince.

OFFICER: And you, Antonia?

POLICIA: ¿Y Vd., Antonia?

ANTONIA: I am nineteen.

OFFICER: Where do you work, Mr. Ruiz?

MR. RUIZ: I work at ABC Construction Company.

OFFICER: Do you work, Miss Ruiz?

ANTONIA: No, I have to take care of the baby.

OFFICER: Are you on Welfare?

ANTONIA: Yes.

OFFICER: How long have you been living in this house?

MR. RUIZ: Six years.

OFFICER: Do Juan and Antonia have the same mother?

MR. RUIZ: Yes.

OFFICER: Did you ever before call the police, when you had an argument?

MR. RUIZ: No.

OFFICER: Where were you born, Mr. Ruiz?

MR. RUIZ: In San Germán, Puerto Rico.

ANTONIA: Tengo diecinueve.

POLICÍA: ¿Dónde trabaja Vd., Sr. Ruiz?

SR. RUIZ: Trabajo en /la/ ABC Construction Company. 40

POLICÍA: ¿Trabaja Vd., Srta. Ruiz?

ANTONIA: No, tengo que cuidar /al/ bebé. 41

POLICÍA: ¿Está Vd. en "welfare"?

ANTONIA: Sí.

POLICÍA: ¿Cuánto tiempo hace que viven Vds. en esta casa? 42

SR. RUIZ: Seis años.

POLICÍA: ¿Tienen Juan y Antonia la misma madre?

SR. RUIZ: Sí.

POLICÍA: ¿Llamaron Vds. /a/ la policía alguna vez antes, cuando tuvieron una disputa? 43

SR. RUIZ: No.

POLICÍA: ¿Dónde nació Vd., Sr. Ruiz? 44

SR. RUIZ: En San Germán, Puerto Rico.

| | | |
|---|---|---|
| OFFICER: And the children? | POLICÍA: ¿Y los hijos? | |
| MR. RUIZ: Antonia and the other children were born in Puerto Rico but Juan was born here. | SR. RUIZ: Antonia y los otros hijos nacieron en Puerto Rico pero Juan nació aquí. | |
| OFFICER: I am leaving now. Good-bye. | POLICÍA: <u>Ya me voy</u>. Adiós. | 45 |
| I hope that things will work /out/ among yourselves. | <u>Espero que /las/ cosas entre Vds. /se/ arreglen.</u> | 46 |

## NOTES

1. <u>Llamando /a/ la policía</u>: Calling the police.
   Llamando: Present participle of <u>llamar</u>.
   XVIIA(Present Participle)
   The personal <u>a</u> is used here because she is calling the people at the police station (not the building). XVIAlm(Personal <u>a</u>)

2. <u>Mi hermano y mi padre están luchando</u>: My brother and my father are fighting.
   Here, both Spanish and English use the Present Progressive Form since the action is going on right at the moment. XVIIB(Progressive Form)

3. <u>Va a matar /a/ mi hermano</u>: He is going to kill my brother.
   Use of personal <u>a</u> before a direct object referring to a person. XVIAlm(Personal <u>a</u>)

4. ¿<u>Cuál es su dirección</u>?: What is your address?
   Use of ¿<u>cuál</u>? for <u>what</u>? before the verb <u>ser</u>.
   VC3b(¿cuál?)

5. <u>Juan y /el/ señor Ruiz están luchando</u>: Juan and Mr. Ruiz are fighting.
   Use of definite article (el) before titles (señor), when talking <u>about</u> someone.
        IIA2d(Use of Definite Article)
   Use of Progressive Form (See No. 2).

6. <u>Sepárense: Break it up, separate</u>!
   Command form. The reflexive <u>se</u> is attached to the command form. A written accent mark must be placed on the originally stressed syllable.
       XIF3 & 4(Object Pronouns Attached to Command Forms)

7. <u>Sr. Ruiz, venga al dormitorio conmigo</u>: Mr. Ruiz, come to the bedroom with me.
   In direct address (Sr. Ruiz), no article is needed.
   conmigo: with me.
   cf. contigo - but: con Vd., con él, etc.
       XVIA2g(con)

8. <u>No va a /la/ escuela</u>: He does not go to school.
       IIA2s(Definite Article)

9. <u>Ni yo ni los otros hijos fuimos a /la/ escuela secundaria</u>: Neither I nor the other children went to high (secondary) school.
   ni...ni: neither...nor.
   fuimos: Preterite Tense of <u>ir</u>
       XIIA3e(Preterite Tense)
   <u>Yo y los otros hijos</u> is summed up by the pronoun <u>nosotros</u>. Therefore, the verb is <u>fuimos</u>.
   Ir a /la/ escuela: to go to school.
       IIA2s(Definite Article)

10. <u>Mi esposa murió hace diez años</u>: My wife died ten years ago.
    When used with the Preterite Tense, <u>hace</u> is translated into English <u>ago</u>.
        XVG2(hace)

11. <u>He cuidado de él</u>: I have taken care of him.
    <u>cuidar de</u>: to take care of someone.
    <u>cuidar</u> (to take care of) takes a direct object.
    <u>cuidar de</u> is followed by the stressed pronoun.
        XID2(Objects of Prepositions)

12. **Los otros tuvieron que ir a trabajar**: The others had to go to work.
    tuvieron: Preterite Tense of tener.
        XIIB1a (Preterites)
    tener que: to have to.

13. **éste**: this one.
    The demonstrative pronoun has the same form as the demonstrative adjective, except that there is an accent mark on the e.
        XVIIIB (Demonstrative Pronouns)

14. **Se enfada**: He gets angry.
    Enfadarse: to get angry.
        VIID4 (Reflexive Verbs)

15. **¿Qué pasó?**: What happened?
        Dict (Idioms)

16. **El vigilante escolar había venido otra vez**: The truant officer had come again.
    El vigilante escolar: the truant officer.
    había venido: he had come.
    Pluperfect Tense in English and Spanish.
        XXIC (Pluperfect Tense)
    otra vez: again    XVE3 (vez)

17. **Le dije que si él no iba a /la/ escuela, yo le echaría de casa**: I told him that if he didn't go to school, I would throw him /out/ of the house.
    Le dije: Preterite Tense of decir.
        XIIB3c (Irregular Preterite Tense)
    Si él no iba: If he didn't go. Use of Imperfect Tense. XIIIA3 (Imperfect Tense)
    le echaría de casa: I would throw him out. Spanish and English use the Conditional here.
        XIVB1a (Conditional)

18. **Me tiró una silla**: He threw a chair /at/ me.

19. Ningún hijo mío va a actuar /de/ esta manera: No son /of/ mine is going to act (in) this way.
Ningún: None, not any. When the negative begins the sentence, there is no need for the double negative. XXB4(Negatives)
un hijo mío: a son /of/ mine. Use of stressed possessive adjective.
     IXC(Possessive Adjectives)
/de/ esta manera: (in) this way.
     XVIA3h(Idioms with de)

20. Vd. no desea que se vaya, ¿verdad?: You don't want him to leave, do you?
Irse: to go away. VII(Reflexive Verbs)
When there is a change in subject (Vd., él), the infinitive cannot be used in Spanish after a verb of wishing. Instead, a dependent clause must be used. The verb in the dependent clause must be in the subjunctive.
Vd. no desea que se vaya: You don't want him to leave (You don't want that he should leave).
cf. Vd. quiere ir: You want to go.
     XXVD1(Use of Subjunctive)
     XXVA4(Irregular Subjunctive)
¿verdad?: do you? Also: don't you?, aren't you?, weren't you?, etc.
¿verdad? means literally: isn't it the truth? It, therefore, does not change according to what precedes. Dict(Idioms)

21. No quiero nada más que ver con él: I don't want to have anything to do with him any more.
tener que ver con: to have to do with.
     Dict(Idioms)
con él: with him. Use of stressed object pronoun after a preposition.
     XID1(Objects of Preposition)

22. El policía entra /en/ la sala para hablar con Juan: The policeman (enters) the living room (in order) to speak to (with) Juan.
Entrar en: to enter, to go into.
     XVID(Verbs & Prepositions)
Para: in order to  XVIA6a(Para)
hablar con alguien: to speak to (with) someone.

23. <u>Dime que pasó</u>: Tell me what happened.
    <u>Dime</u>: Familiar command form. Juan is a
    teenager. Therefore, the policeman uses the
    familiar form with him.
                VIB2(Familiar Commands)
    pasar: to pass, happen.
24. <u>Quiero volver /a/ casa</u>: I want to come (back)
    home.
    volver(ue) a casa: to come back (return),
    come.
    <u>Querer</u> is a stem changing verb.
                IIIB1b(Stem Changing Verbs)
25. <u>¿Por qué escapaste?</u>: Why did you run away
    (escape)?
    Use of familiar form (Preterite Tense)
                XIIB1(Preterite Tense)
26. <u>El me gritó y me dijo que tenía /que/ ir /me/
    si no voy a la escuela cuando debo</u>: He yelled
    /at/ me and said to me that I had to leave if
    I don't go to school when I am supposed to.
    Me gritó: He yelled /at/ me.
    tener /que/: to have to.
    Irse: to leave. Reflexive Construction
                VII(Reflexive Verbs)
    Ir a /la/ escuela: to go to school.
                IIA2s(Use of Definite Article)
    deber: to be supposed to, must.
    <u>Deber</u> is not as strong as <u>tener que</u>.
27. <u>Lo sentí después de hacerlo</u>: I was sorry
    (about it) after I did it (after doing it).
    Sentir: to feel or to be sorry. Dict(Idioms)
    Después de hacerlo: After doing it. After a
    preposition, the infinitive must be used in
    Spanish.    XXIIA(Infinitive)
    Object pronouns are attached to the infinitive.
                XIF(Position of Object Pronouns)
28. <u>Fui a casa /de/ mi hermana</u>: I went to my
    sister's house.
    Fui: Preterite Tense of <u>ir</u>.
                XIIB3e(Irregular Preterite)
    La casa de mi hermana: My sister's house.
                XVIA3e(de) and IXD(Possessives)

29. **Me obtuvo un cuarto cerca de ella**: She got (for) me a room near her.
    Obtuvo: Preterite Tense of <u>obtener</u> (to obtain, to get)     XIIB3(Irregular Preterite)

30. **No me gustó vivir solo**: I didn't like to live alone.
    The subject of the verb <u>gustar</u> is <u>vivir solo</u>.
                   XIJ(gustar)
    solo: alone
    cf. sólo: only.  Introd. G(Use of Accent Mark)

31. **Mi padre tiene razón**: My father is right.
    tener razón: to be right     XE2(tener)
    cf. tener calor: to be hot.

32. **De otro modo nunca obtendré un trabajo decente**: Otherwise, I will never get (obtain) a decent job.
    De otro modo: otherwise
                   XVIA3h(Idioms with <u>de</u>)
    Obtendré: I will get.  Future tense of <u>obtener</u>.     XIVAlb(Irregular Future).
    un trabajo (puesto): a job.

33. **Si Vd. pudiera hablar /de las/ cosas con calma en vez de gritarse y tirarse cosas, las cosas podrían ir mucho mejor**: If you could talk things over (talk about the things) calmly instead of yelling /at/ each other and throwing things at each other, things would work out (go) much better.
    Pudiera: Imperfect Subjunctive of <u>poder</u>.
                   XXVA3(Imperfect Subjunctive)
    The Subjunctive is used here in a contrary to fact clause, the Conditional is used in the result clause.  XXVC2b(Use of Imperfect Sub.)
    Con calma: calmly (with calm)    XVI2(con)
    gritarse y tirarse: to yell at each other and to throw things at each other. The reflexive construction is used here to indicate reciprocal action (each other).
                   VIIG(Reflexive Construction)

34. **Vd. podría dejar a Juan permanecer**: You could let Juan stay.
    podría: Conditional of <u>poder</u>.
                   XIVBlb(Irregular Conditional)

35. Puede ser que él haya aprendido la lección:
(It) may be (that) he has learned his lesson.
Puede ser: (it may be) is an expression of
uncertainty. Therefore, the subjunctive (haya
aprendido) must be used in the dependent clause.
XXVD1b(Use of Subjunctive)
haya: Subjunctive of haber (to have)
XXVA1g(Irregular Subjunctive)

36. Si no /es así/, él tendrá que comparecer ante
del Tribunal de Menores: If (it is) not (so),
he will have to appear at (in front of) the
Children's Court (Court for Minors).
tener que: to have to
tendrá: Future Tense of tener - XIVA1b
el Tribunal de Menores: The Children's Court
See Dict(Idioms)

37. Puede ponerse en contacto con...: You can get
in touch with...
Ponerse en contacto con: to get (put oneself)
in touch with          Dict(Idioms)

38. Déjeme hacerle algunas preguntas: Let me ask
you some questions.
Déjeme: Let me
The pronoun is attached to the command form.
An accent mark is necessary to maintain the
original stress. XIF(Position of Object
                           Pronouns)
hacer una pregunta: to ask, to pose a question
Dict(Idioms)

39. ¿Qué edad tiene Vd?: How old are you?
tener...años: to be...years old.
XE(tener)

40. Trabajo en /la/ ABC Construction Company: I
work for (the) ABC Construction Company.

41. Tengo /que/ cuidar al bebé: I have to take
care /of/ the baby.
cuidar: to take care of
XVIC(Verbs and Prepositions)
al bebé: Use of personal a
XVIA1m(Personal a)

42. ¿Cuánto tiempo hace que viven Vds. en esta casa?: How long have you been living in this house?
For an action which began in the past and is still going on, English uses the Past Progressive Form (have you been living), Spanish uses hace with the Present Tense.
IIIB2C(Present Tense)

43. ¿Llamaron Vds. /a/ la policía alguna vez antes?: Did you ever (at any time) before call the police?
Use of personal a (one calls the people in the building, not the building).
XVIA1m(Personal a)

44. ¿Dónde nació Vd?: Where were you born?
Nacer: to be born    XF(to be)

45. Ya me voy: I am leaving now.
Irse: to leave, to go away.
Use of Progressive Form (I am leaving) in English, Present Tense in Spanish. Spanish uses the Progressive Form much less frequently than English. IIIB2a(Present Tense)

46. Espero que /las/ cosas entre Vds. se arreglen: I hope that things will work /out/ among yourselves.
arreglarse: to work out.
VII(Reflexive Verbs)
Use of Subjunctive (arreglen) in the dependent clause, after a verb of hoping (espero) in the main clause. XXVA1a(Regular Subjunctive)
XXVD1a(Use of Subjunctive)


TRANSLATE


1. I am calling the police.
2. Break it up.
3. My husband died 5 years ago.

4. I had to go to work.
5. What happened?
6. Do you want him to leave?
7. I don't want to have anything to do with her.
8. He ran away.
9. I was sorry (about it).
10. I don't like to live alone.
11. He is right.
12. You can get in touch with me.
13. How long have you been living here?
14. I am leaving.

## POLICE V

### FAMILY DISPUTE II

#### ALCOHOLIC

MRS. MARTIN: Hello, police?
Will you please send an officer to 93 Front Street, Apartment 6H.

My husband is drunk.

OFFICER (at the apartment):
Good evening.
I am officer Brown.
What happened?

MRS. MARTIN:
I work all day and he is home and drinks.

He says that he is looking for work but he never makes it past the liquor store.

I have enough of this and I don't want him around any more.

MR. MARTIN: It is true, I was drinking but I promised not to drink any more.

## POLICÍA V

### DISPUTA FAMILIAR II

#### ALCOHÓLICO

SRA. MARTÍN: <u>Diga</u>, ¿policía?    1
Por favor, manden un policía <u>al noventa</u>   2
<u>y tres /de/ Front Street</u>, Apartamento seis hache.

<u>Mi marido está</u>   3
<u>borracho</u>.

POLICÍA (en el apartamento):
Buenas noches.
<u>Soy /el/ policía</u>   4
Brown.
<u>¿Qué pasó?</u>   5

SRA. MARTÍN:
Yo trabajo <u>todo el</u>   6
<u>día</u> y él está en casa y bebe.

Dice /que/ <u>busca</u>   7
<u>trabajo</u> pero <u>nunca</u>
<u>pasa /de/ la tienda</u>   8
<u>/de/ licores</u>.

Tengo bastante de esto y no le quiero más por aquí.

SR. MARTÍN: Es verdad, <u>estaba</u>   9
<u>bebiendo</u> pero prometí no beber más.

| | | |
|---|---|---|
| I am going to look /for a/ job. | Voy a buscar trabajo. | |
| She can't chase me out like this. | Ella no puede echarme como lo está haciendo. | 10 |
| OFFICER (to Mrs. Martín): It is now after two /o'clock/. | POLICÍA (a /la/ Sra. Martín): Ahora son más de /las/ dos. | 11 |
| He can't find any place to stay now. | Él no puede encontrar ahora ningún sitio /donde/ estar. | 12 |
| Why don't you leave things as they are and discuss them in the morning? | ¿Por qué no dejan las cosas como están y las discuten por la mañana? | 13 |

## NOTES

1. <u>Diga</u>: Hello (on the phone).
   Literally: Tell.   Dict(Idioms)

2. <u>Al noventa y tres /de/ Front Street</u>: At 93 Front Street.
   Use of definite article in addresses.
                IIA2p

3. <u>Mi marido está borracho otra vez</u>: My husband is drunk again.
   Use of <u>estar</u> for a temporary (!) condition.
                XB1(estar)
   otra vez:   again      XVE3(vez)

4. <u>Soy /el/ policía Brown</u>: I am officer Brown.
   Use of definite article (el) before titles.
   Officer Brown is speaking <u>about</u> himself.
                IIA2d(Definite Article)

5. <u>¿Qué pasó?</u>: What happened?
   pasar:  to happen.       Dict(Idioms)

6. <u>Todo el día</u>: All day (long).
VIIIA8(todo)
cf. todos los días: Every day.
VIIIB5(todos)
<u>Día</u> is masculine, although it ends in <u>a</u>.
IA3(Nouns ending in <u>a</u>)

7. <u>Dice que busca trabajo</u>: He says that he is looking for work.
buscar: to look for.
cf. mirar: to look at.
XVIC(Verbs and Prepositions)

8. <u>Nunca pasa /de/ la tienda /de/ licores</u>: He never gets past (passes) the liquor store.
La tienda /de/ licores: The liquor store.
IA16 & Dict(Compound Nouns)

9. <u>Estaba bebiendo</u>: I was (in the midst of) drinking.
Use of Past Progressive Form in English and Spanish.    XVIIB2b(Past Progressive)

10. <u>Como lo está haciendo</u>: Like this (like she is doing).
Use of Progressive Form because the action is going on right now.
XVIIB(Progressive Form)

11. <u>Son más de /las/ dos</u>: It is after (more than) two /o'clock/.
Son /las/ dos: It is two o'clock.
<u>Es</u> is used only with <u>la una</u>. Otherwise, the plural verb is used.    XVF1(Time)
Use of <u>de</u> for <u>than</u> before a numeral.
XVIA3e(de)

12. <u>No puede encontrar ahora ningún sitio /donde/ estar</u>: He can't find any place (where) to stay now.
No...ningún: not any. Use of double negative.
XXB1(Double Negative)

13. <u>Por la mañana</u>: In the morning.
cf. A /las/ once <u>de</u> la mañana: At 11 <u>in</u> the morning.    XVF4(<u>por</u> for time)

## TRANSLATE

1. My husband is drunk.
2. I am officer Brown.
3. What happened?
4. He does not go to look for a job.
5. It is after three o'clock.
6. I can't find any place to stay.
7. Discuss it again in the morning.

## POLICE VI

### HOLDUP

POLICE OFFICER: What happened?

MR. CASTRO: I was sitting in the park when a young man came towards me, pulled /out/ a knife and asked me /for/ my wallet.

I gave it to him but I had no money in it.

The man threw /away/ the wallet. Then some people came and he escaped.

OFFICER: What kind of knife did he have?

Can you describe it?

MR. CASTRO: It was short, with /a/ black handle.

OFFICER: Did he hurt you with the knife?

MR. CASTRO: He tried /to/.

OFFICER: How do you feel now?

Can you walk?

## POLICÍA VI

### ATRACO

POLICÍA: ¿Qué pasó?     1

SR. CASTRO: Estaba sentado en el parque cuando un joven vino hacia mí, sacó un cuchillo y me pidió mi billetera.     2, 3, 4, 5

Se la di pero no tenía dinero en ella.     6, 7

El hombre tiró la billetera. Entonces alguna gente vino y él escapó.     8, 9

POLICÍA: ¿Qué clase de cuchillo tenía?     10

¿Puede describirlo?

SR. CASTRO: Era corto, con puño negro.     11

POLICÍA: ¿Le hirió con el cuchillo?     12

SR. CASTRO: Trató.

POLICÍA: ¿Cómo /se/ siente ahora?     13

¿Puede caminar?

| | | |
|---|---|---|
| MR. CASTRO: Yes, I am all right (well) now. | SR. CASTRO: Sí, <u>estoy bien</u> ahora. | 14 |
| OFFICER: Can you describe the man who attacked you? | POLICÍA: ¿Puede Vd. <u>describir al hombre</u> que le atacó? | 15 |
| MR. CASTRO: Yes, he was white, about 25 years /old/, and he wore dirty old pants. | SR. CASTRO: Sí, <u>era blanco</u>, <u>tenía</u> see <u>unos veinticinco años</u> y <u>llevaba pantalones viejos</u> /y/ sucios. | 11 16 17 |
| He had a beard and dark hair. | Tenía barba y pelo negro. | |
| He was about 5 feet 5 (inches tall). | <u>Tenía como unos cinco pies</u> /y/ <u>cinco pulgadas</u>. | 18 |
| OFFICER: Would you know approximately how much he weighed? | POLICÍA: ¿<u>Sabría cuánto pesaba aproximadamente</u>? | 19 |
| MR. CASTRO: About 160 lbs. | SR. CASTRO: <u>Unas ciento sesenta libras</u>. | 20 |
| OFFICER: What was the color of his eyes? | POLICÍA: ¿Cuál era el color de sus ojos? | |
| MR. CASTRO: I think that they were brown, but I am not sure. | SR. CASTRO: <u>Creo que eran marrones pero no estoy seguro</u>. | 21 |
| OFFICER: Did he have any scar or tatoo? | POLICÍA: ¿Tenía alguna cicatriz o tatuaje? | |
| MR. CASTRO: I think that he had a scar on his cheek. | SR. CASTRO: Creo que <u>tenía una cicatriz</u> en la mejilla. | 22 |

| | |
|---|---|
| OFFICER: Did he use the right hand or was he left-handed? | POLICÍA: ¿Usó la mano derecha o era zurdo?  23 |
| MR. CASTRO: He was holding the knife in his (the) right hand. | SR. CASTRO: Sostenía el cuchillo en la mano derecha.  24 |
| OFFICER: What kind of shirt or jacket did he wear? | POLICÍA: ¿Qué clase de camisa o chaqueta llevaba?  25 |
| MR. CASTRO: He wore a red shirt. | SR. CASTRO: Llevaba una camisa roja. |
| OFFICER: In which direction did he run away (escape)? | POLICÍA: ¿En qué dirección escapó? |
| MR. CASTRO: This way. | SR. CASTRO: Por aquí.  26 |
| OFFICER: We will notify all the other precincts and we will call you if we know anything. You may have to help us identify the man. | POLICÍA: Notificaremos /a/ todos los otros precintos y le llamaremos si sabemos algo.  27<br>Puede ser que Vd. tenga que ayudarnos /a/ identificar al hombre.  28 |
| OFFICER: Were there any witnesses? | POLICIA: ¿Hubo algunos testigos?  29 |
| MR. CASTRO: No. | SR. CASTRO: No. |
| OFFICER: I have /to/ fill /out/ this report. | POLICÍA: Tengo /que/ llenar este informe.  30 |
| What is your name? | ¿Cómo se llama Vd?  31 |
| MR. CASTRO: Juan Castro. | SR. CASTRO: Juan Castro. |

| | |
|---|---|
| OFFICER: What is your address? | POLICÍA: ¿Cuál es su dirección? 32 |
| MR. CASTRO: 1260 Atlantic Avenue. | SR. CASTRO: Mil doscientos sesenta /de/ Atlantic Avenue. 33 |
| OFFICER: Your telephone number, please. | POLICÍA: Su número /de/ teléfono por favor. 34 |
| MR. CASTRO: 458-9264. | SR. CASTRO: Cuatro, cinco, ocho, nueve, dos, seis, cuatro. |
| OFFICER: All right. Go home now and calm /down/. | POLICÍA: Está bien. Ahora vaya /a/ casa y cálme/se/. 35 36 |
| We will call you if we hear (know) anything. | Le llamaremos si sabemos algo. |

## NOTES

1. ¿Qué pasó?: What happened?
   pasar: to happen.

2. Estaba sentado...cuando un joven vino: I was sitting (seated) when a young man came.
   Use of past Progressive form in English (was sitting) and Spanish (estaba sentado) for an action that was going on when something else happened. Use of simple past tense in English (came) and Preterite Tense in Spanish (vino) for the action that happened at a specific time.
           XVIIB1 (Formation of Progressive
               Forms)
           XVIIB2c (Use of Past Progressive
               Form)
           XIIB3b (Preterite Tense)

3. hacia mí: Towards me.
Use of stressed pronoun after prepositions.
XID(Stressed Pronouns)
Mí has an accent mark to differentiate it from the possessive adjective mi (my).
Introd. G (Accent Mark for Distinction of Words)

4. Sacó un cuchillo: He pulled /out/ a knife.
Sacar: to take out, pull out.
Use of Preterite Tense for an action that happened at a particular point.
XIIB4(Preterite Tense)

5. Me pidió mi billetera: He asked me /for/ my wallet.
Pedir algo: to ask /for/ something.
XVIC(Verbs and Prepositions)
XIIB2(Preterite)

6. Se la di: I gave it to him.
It refers to la billetera.
When two object pronouns of the third person are used, the indirect object is always se.
XIG(Double Object Pronouns)
XIIB3(Irregular Preterite)

7. No tenía dinero en ella: I had no money in it.
Use of Imperfect Tense for a description of a state.  XIIIB3(Imperfect)
En ella: stressed pronoun, used after the preposition en.  XID1

8. Tiró la billetera: He threw /away/ the wallet.
tirar: to throw, to throw away.

9. Alguna gente vino: Some people came.
La gente: people (in a group). Gente is always in the singular.
cf. el pueblo español: The Spanish people (nation).  IB9(Singular Nouns)

10. ¿Qué clase de cuchillo tenía?: What kind of knife did he have?
¿Qué clase de?: What kind of?  Dict(Idioms)
Since the verb tener usually describes something, it is generally used in the Imperfect Tense.  XIIIB3(Imperfect)

11. **Era corto:** He was short.
    **Era:** Imperfect Tense of **ser**
    XIIIA2(Irregular Imperfect)
    Use of Imperfect Tense for description.
    XIIIB3(Imperfect)

12. **¿Le hirió?:** Did he hurt you?
    **Herir** (hacer daño a): to hurt (wound) someone. **Herir** is a stem changing verb.
    XIIB2(Preterite of Stem Changing Verbs)
    Use of Preterite Tense for an action that took place at a specific time.

13. **¿Cómo /se/ siente ahora?:** How do you feel now?
    Sentirse(ie,i): to feel (good or bad)
    cf. sentir(ie,i): to feel, regret.
    **Sentir** is a stem changing verb.
    IIIB2b(Present Tense of Stem Changing Verbs)
    VIIE(Reflexive Verbs)

14. **Estoy bien:** I am all right (fine).
    Use of **estar** for health
    XB1(estar)
    IVA2(Present Tense)

15. **¿Puede Vd. describir al hombre?:** Can you describe the man?
    **Poder** (to be able to) is stem changing in the Present Tense.
    IIIB1b(Present Tense)
    Use of personal **a** before a direct object referring to a person.
    XVIA1m(Personal **a**)

16. **Tenía unos veinticinco años:** He was about 25 years /old/.
    Tener...años: to be...years /old/.
    Use of Imperfect Tense for a description in the past.    XIIIB3(Imperfect)

17. <u>Llevaba pantalones viejos /y/ sucios</u>: He wore dirty (and) old pants.
    Llevar ropa: to wear clothes.
    Use of Imperfect Tense for a description in the past.   XIIIB3(Imperfect Tense)

18. <u>Tenía como unos cinco pies /y/ cinco pulgadas</u>: He was about 5 feet (and) five (inches tall).
    Use of Imperfect Tense for description.
    XIIIB3(Imperfect Tense)

19. <u>¿Sabría cuánto pesaba?</u>: Would you know how much he weighed?
    Sabría: Conditional of <u>saber</u>. The conditional is used here both in English and Spanish.
          XIVB1b(Irregular Conditional)
          XIVB2(Use of Conditional)
    Use of Imperfect Tense (pesaba) for a description.   XIIIB3(Imperfect Tense)

20. <u>Unas 160 libras</u>: About 160 lbs.
    La libra: the pound.
    cf. el libro: the book.
              IA14(Gender of Nouns)
    uno(a)s: about   XVD(about)

21. <u>Creo que eran marrones pero no estoy seguro</u>: I believe that they were brown but I am not sure.
    Eran marrones: They were brown. Use of <u>ser</u> with colors (permanent quality).
          XA2(ser)
    Use of Imperfect Tense (eran) for description.
          XIIIA2 & XIIIB3(Imperfect Tense)
    No estoy seguro: I am not sure. Use of <u>estar</u> (the opinion may change).
          XB1(estar)

22. <u>Tenía una cicatriz</u>: He had a scar.
    Use of Imperfect Tense for description.
          XIIIB3(Imperfect Tense)

23. ¿Usó la mano derecha o era zurdo?: Did he use the right hand or was he left-handed?
Use of Preterite Tense (usó) for an action which happened at a specific time.
¿Era zurdo?: Was he left-handed?
When one is left-handed that is a permanent condition. Therefore, the verb ser is used.
It is used in the Imperfect Tense because this is a description. XA1(ser)
   XIIIB3(Imperfect for Description)
Although mano ends in o, it is feminine.
   IA2(note)

24. Sostenía el cuchillo en la mano derecha: He was holding the knife in the right hand.
sostener: to hold.
Use of Imperfect Tense for description (English Past Progressive Form)
   XIIIB3(Imperfect for English
      Past Progressive)

25. ¿Qué clase de camisa o chaqueta llevaba?: What kind of shirt or jacket was he wearing?
llevar ropa: to wear clothes.   Dict(Idioms)
¿Qué clase de?: What kind of?   Dict(Idioms)
Use of Imperfect Tense (llevaba) for description.   XIIIB3(Imperfect)

26. Por aquí: This way          Dict(Idioms)
   XVIA6(por)

27. Notificaremos /a/ todos los otros precintos: We will notify all the other precincts.
Notificaremos: Future Tense
   XIVA1a
Use of personal a because the staff in the precincts is being notified (not the precinct house).   XVIA1m(Personal a)

28. Puede ser que Vd. tenga que ayudarnos /a/ identificar al hombre: You may have to help us identify the man.
Puede ser: It may be.
Use of Subjunctive (tenga) after puede ser que (which is an expression of uncertainty).

XXVA5(Subjunctive of <u>tener</u>)
XXVD1b(Use of Subjunctive After Expression of Doubt)
ayudar <u>a</u> hacer algo: to help to do something.
al hombr<u>e</u>: Use of Personal <u>a</u>
XVIA1m(Personal <u>a</u>)

29. ¿<u>Hubo algunos testigos</u>?: Were there any witnesses?
<u>Hubo</u> is the Preterite of <u>hay</u> (there is, there are)    XD(haber)
Use of Preterite Tense because the action took place at a definite time.
XIIB3(Irregular Preterites)

30. <u>Tengo /que/ llenar este informe</u>: I have /to/ fill out this report.
Tener que: to have to. <u>Tener</u> is an irregular verb.        IVA1(Present Tense)
llenar: to fill, to fill out.
Dict(Idioms)

31. ¿<u>Cómo se llama Vd.</u>?: What is your name?
VIIE(Reflexive Verbs)

32. ¿<u>Cuál es su dirección</u>?: What is your address?
Use of ¿cuál? to express what? before the verb <u>ser</u>.   VC3b(¿cuál?)

33. <u>Mil doscientos sesenta /de/ Atlantic Avenue</u>: 1260 Atlantic Avenue.

34. <u>Su número /de/ teléfono</u>: Your telephone number.
IA16 and Dict(Compound Nouns)

35. <u>Está bien</u>: (It is) all right (fine).
Dict(Idioms)
The impersonal <u>it</u> as subject is not expressed.
XIA3(Omission of <u>it</u>)

36. <u>Vaya /a/ casa y cálmese</u>: Go home and calm /down/,(calm yourself).
Vaya: Command form of <u>ir</u>
VIA2(Irregular Command Forms)
Ir /a/ casa: to go home.
Cálmese: calm /down/, calm yourself.
VIID(Reflexive Verbs)

## TRANSLATE

1. Were you sitting when he came?
2. He pulled out a knife.
3. Did you have any money in it (la billetera)?
4. Did he hurt you?
5. Can you describe the man?
6. Did he have any scars?
7. What kind of a knife did he have?
8. What was the color of his eyes?
9. I have to fill out a report.
10. Go home and calm down.

## POLICE VII

### NARCOTICS OFFICER

OFFICER: How long have you been using (taking) heroin?

MR. VARGAS: For approximately two years.

OFFICER: Have you ever been under treatment in a narcotics program?

MR. VARGAS: No.

OFFICER: Have you ever been arrested on a narcotics charge?

MR. VARGAS: No.

OFFICER: What is your occupation?

MR. VARGAS: I am /a/ waiter but I have not worked for a long time.

OFFICER: You will be fingerprinted and photographed and lodged in a detention cell until the court disposes of your case.

You may get (name) a lawyer or the Court will assign one to you.

## POLICÍA VII

### OFICIAL DE NARCÓTICOS

POLICÍA: ¿Cuánto tiempo hace que toma heroína?   1

SR. VARGAS: Hace dos años, aproximadamente.

POLICÍA: ¿Ha estado Vd. alguna vez bajo tratamiento en un programa /de/ narcóticos?   2

SR. VARGAS: No.

POLICÍA: ¿Ha sido Vd. alguna vez arrestado por uso de narcóticos?   3

SR. VARGAS: No.

POLICÍA: ¿Cuál es su ocupación?   4

SR. VARGAS: Soy camarero pero hace mucho tiempo que no trabajo.   5
6

POLICÍA: Le tomarán las huellas digitales y una fotografía y será situado en una celda /de/ detención hasta que la Corte disponga de su caso.   7
8

Vd. puede nombrar un abogado o la Corte le asignará uno.

NOTES

1. ¿Cuánto tiempo hace que toma heroína?: How long have you been taking heroin?
   Use of hace with the Present Tense in Spanish, Past Progressive form in English, for an action that started in the past and is still going on.
       IIIB2c(Use of Present Tense)

2. ¿Ha estado Vd. alguna vez bajo tratamiento en un programa /de/ narcóticos?: Have you ever been under treatment in a narcotics program?
   Ha estado: Present Perfect Tense.
       XXIB1(form) and 2(Use of Present Perfect)
   Un programa de narcóticos: A narcotics program.
       IA16 & Dict(Compound Nouns)
   programa is masculine, although it ends in a.
       IA3(nouns in a)

3. ¿Ha sido Vd. arrestado alguna vez por uso de narcóticos?: Have you ever been arrested on a narcotics charge (for use of narcotics)?
   Ha sido arrestado?: Have you been arrested?
   Use of ser for passive voice.
   Sido: Past participle of Ser.
       XXIVB1(Use of Passive Voice)
       XXIVA(Formation of Passive Voice)

4. ¿Cuál es su ocupación?: What is your occupation?
   Use of ¿cuál? to translate what? before the verb ser.   VC3b(¿cuál?)

5. Soy camarero: I am /a/ waiter.
   Use of the verb ser for professions.
       XA1(Ser)
   Omission of indefinite article(a) before professions.   IIB2a(Indefinite Article)

6. <u>Hace mucho tiempo que no trabajo</u>: I have not worked for a long time (It has been a long time since I worked).
   Use of <u>hacer</u> with the Present Tense, to express an action that started in the past and is still going on. In English, the Perfect Tense is used.         IIIB2c(Present Tense)

7. <u>Le tomarán las huellas digitales</u>: They will fingerprint you (take your fingerprints).
   Tomarle las huellas digitales a alguien: to fingerprint someone.
                      Dict(Idioms)
   tomarán: Future Tense
                      XIVAla(Future)

8. <u>...hasta que la Corte disponga de su caso</u>: Until the court disposes of your case.
   disponga: Subjunctive form of dis<u>poner</u>.
                      XXVA5(Irregular Subjunctive)
   Use of Subjunctive after the conjunction <u>hasta que</u>, if the action has not already taken place.    XXVDle(Use of Subjunctive)


### TRANSLATE

1. How long have you been using this drug?
2. Have you been arrested on a narcotics charge before?
3. What is your occupation?
4. You will be fingerprinted and photographed.
5. You will be placed in a detention cell until the court disposes of your case.

## POLICE VIII

### INTOXICATED DRIVER

OFFICER: You are under arrest for drunken driving.

Please, get out of your car and get into the police car. Officer O'Neil will drive yours.

We are going to give you a drunkometer test.

You have a right to refuse if you don't want to take it.

However, if you refuse, your license may be suspended.

At the station House

OFFICER: Please, blow /up/ this balloon.

Return it to me without letting the air out.

Were you drinking?

MR. RUIZ: I took a few drinks.

## POLICÍA VIII

### CONDUCTOR INTOXICADO

POLICÍA: Vd. está bajo arresto por conducir intoxicado. 1

Por favor, salga de su automóvil y 2
monte en el automóvil /de la/ policía. 3
/El/ policía O'Neil conducirá el suyo. 4

Vamos a someterle a una prueba /con el/ medidor /de/ alcohol. 5

Vd. tiene el derecho de rehusar si no quiere tomarla.

Sin embargo si Vd. rehusa, su licencia puede ser cancelada. 6

En la estación /de/ policía 7

POLICÍA: Por favor, sople este balón. 8

Devuélvamelo sin dejar salir el aire. 9

¿Bebió Vd? 10

SR. RUIZ: Tomé unas bebidas.

| | |
|---|---|
| OFFICER: Just (exactly) how many did you have? | POLICÍA: Exactamente, ¿<u>Cuántas</u> tomó?   11 |
| MR. RUIZ: Three or four. | SR. RUIZ: Tres o cuatro. |
| OFFICER: When did you take the last drink? | POLICÍA: ¿Cuándo tomó Vd. la última bebida? |
| MR. RUIZ: Approximately half /an/ hour before leaving the bar. | SR. RUIZ: Aproximadamente <u>media hora antes</u> <u>/de/ salir del bar</u>.   12 |
| OFFICER: Please, stand /up/. | POLICÍA: Por favor, <u>póngase de pie</u>.   13 |
| Walk a straight line. | <u>Camine /en/ línea</u> <u>recta</u>.   14 |
| Pick these coins off the floor. | <u>Recoja estas monedas</u> <u>del suelo</u>.   15 |
| Stand on one leg | <u>Permanezca sobre</u> <u>una pierna</u>   16 |
| with eyes closed. | <u>con /los/ ojos</u> <u>cerrados</u>.   17 |
| Touch the tip of your nose with your finger. | <u>Tóquese la punta</u> <u>de la nariz</u> <u>con el dedo</u>.   18 |

                NOTES


1. <u>Vd. está bajo arresto por conducir intoxicado</u>:
   You are under arrest for drunken driving
   (driving drunk).
   Use of the verb <u>estar</u> before <u>bajo</u> (preposition
   of location)    XB2 (estar)
   por: for, because of
                       XVIA7g (por)

2. <u>Salga de su automóvil</u>: Get out of (leave) your car.
Salir: to leave (a place), to get out from (a place).
cf. deje la ropa aquí: leave your clothes here.
Salga: Command form of <u>salir</u>.
VIA1(Irregular Commands)

3. <u>Monte en el automóvil de la policía</u>: Get (climb) into the police car.
Montar: to climb, to step up (into).
El automóvil /de la/ policía: the police car.
IA16 & Dict(Compound Nouns)

4. <u>El suyo</u>: Yours.
Possessive pronoun. IXB(Possessive Pronouns)

5. <u>Vamos a someterle a una prueba /con el/ medidor /de/ alcohol</u>: We are going to give you (submit you to) a drunkometer test.
el medidor /de/ alcohol: the drunkometer.
IA16 & Dict(Compound Nouns)

6. <u>Su licencia puede ser cancelada</u>: Your license may be suspended (cancelled).
<u>Poder</u> (to be able to, may) is stem changing in the Present Tense. IIIB1b(Stem Changing Verbs)
Use of <u>ser</u> for Passive voice.
XXIV(Passive Voice)
Cancelar una licencia: to suspend a license.
Dict(Idioms)

7. <u>La estación /de/ policía</u>: the police station.
IA16 & Dict(Compound Nouns)

8. <u>Sople este balón</u>: Blow /up/ this balloon.
soplar: to blow, to blow up.
XVIC(Verbs & Prepositions)

9. <u>Devuélvamelo sin dejar salir el aire</u>: Return it to me without letting out the air (without letting the air get out).
Devolver algo: to return something.
cf. volver: to return, to come back.
<u>Devolver</u> (like <u>volver</u>) is a stem changing verb.
IIIB1b(Present)
Pronouns are attached to the command form. The indirect object precedes the direct.
XIF & G (Pos. of Obj. Pron.)

10. ¿Bebió Vd.?:  Were you drinking?  Did you drink?
    Use of Preterite Tense in Spanish. Spanish would use the Past Progressive Form only if he was in the midst of drinking when arrested.
    XVII2b(Progressive Forms)

11. ¿Cuántas?:  How many?
    ¿Cuánto(a)?: (How much?) and ¿Cuánto(a)s? (How many?) are adjectives. They, therefore, have to agree with the nouns they modify which, in this case, is bebidas.
    VC3g(¿cuántos?)

12. Media hora antes /de/ salir del bar:  Half /an/ hour before leaving the bar.
    Media hora:  half /an/ hour.
    IIB2b(Omission of Indefinite Article)
    The preposition antes de, like all Spanish prepositions, is followed by the Infinitive.
    XXII(Infinitive)

13. Pónga/se/ de pie:  Stand up.
    Ponerse de pie:  to stand up.
    VII(Reflexive Verbs)
    Dict(Idioms)

14. Camine /en/ línea recta:  Walk (on) a straight line.
    Dict(Idioms)

15. Recoja estas monedas del suelo:  Pick these coins off (up from) the floor.
    Recoger:  to pick up (something). g changes to j before a or o in order to maintain the original sound.
    VIA5(Spelling Changes in Commands)

16. Permanezca sobre una pierna:  Stand (stay) on one leg.
    Permanecer: to stay, to remain.
    c changes to zc in the first person Present Tense and in the Command Form.
    VIA3(Irregular Commands)

17. Con /los/ ojos cerrados:  With (the) eyes closed.

18. Tóque/se/ la punta de la nariz con el dedo:
Touch the tip of your (the) nose with your
(the) finger.
Tóquese:  Command form of reflexive verb.
Tocar:  to touch something.
A reflexive verb is used in Spanish when
referring to one's body (English uses a
possessive adjective).
            VIID2(Reflexive Verbs)
The c of the Infinitive changes to qu before e.
            VIA5(Commands)


TRANSLATE


1. You are under arrest for drunken driving.
2. Get out of your car and get into the police car.
3. We are going to give you a drunkometer test.
4. Blow up this balloon.
5. Return it to me without letting the air out.
6. How many drinks did you have?
7. Stand up, please.
8. Walk a straight line.
9. Stand on one leg, with eyes closed.
10. Touch the tip of your nose with your finger.

## POLICE IX

### TRAFFIC ACCIDENT

|  |  | |
|---|---|---|
| POLICE OFFICER: Are you all right? | POLICÍA: ¿<u>Está Vd. bien</u>? | 1 |
| MR. GÓMEZ: I don't know. | SR. GÓMEZ: <u>No sé</u>. | 2 |
| My right leg is hurt. | <u>Tengo herida la pierna</u> derecha. | 3 |
| POLICE OFFICER: Stay in the car. | POLICÍA: <u>Permanezca en el automóvil</u>. | 4 |
| We will call an ambulance. | Vamos a llamar una ambulancia. | |
| (to Mr. Padró, the other driver). | (al Sr. Padró, el otro conductor). | 5 |
| In what direction were you going? | ¿<u>En qué dirección iba</u>? | 6 |
| MR. PADRÓ: I was going to turn to the right when the light changed. | SR. PADRÓ: <u>Iba a torcer a la derecha cuando la luz cambió</u>. | 7 |
| The other car continued /straight/ ahead. | <u>El otro automóvil siguió derecho</u>. | 8 |
| POLICE OFFICER: Let me see your license and registration certificate, please. | POLICIA: <u>Déjeme ver su licencia y el registro /del/ automóvil</u>, por favor. | 9 |
| The accident will be reported and you will have to appear in Court. | <u>Se dará parte del accidente y Vd. tendrá que comparecer en la Corte</u>. | 10 |
| You are lucky. Nobody is seriously hurt. | <u>Tiene suerte</u>. Nadie está herido gravemente. | 11 |

NOTES

1. ¿Está Vd. bien?: Are you all right (well)?
2. No sé: I don't know.
   Sé: First person Present Tense of saber
                 IVA(Irregular Present Tense)
   An accent mark is placed on the sé. Se without the accent mark is the reflexive pronoun meaning oneself, himself, etc.
                 Introd. G(Accents)
3. Tengo herida la pierna: My leg is hurt.
4. Permanezca: Stay.
   Command form of permanecer.
                 VIA1(Irregular Commands)
5. Al Sr. Padró: to Mr. Padró.
   Use of definite article (el), when talking about someone. The preposition a combines with the article to form al.
                 IIA2d(Use of Definite Article)
                 IIAf(Contraction a plus el)
6. ¿En qué dirección iba?: In what direction were you going?
   Use of Imperfect Tense for an action that went on when something else happened.
                 XIIIB4(Use of Imperfect Tense)
   iba: Imperfect Tense of ir.
                 XIIIA2(Irregular Imperfect Tense)
7. Iba a torcer a la derecha cuando la luz cambió: I was going to turn to the right when the light changed.
   Use of Imperfect Tense (iba) for an action that was going on. Preterite Tense (cambió) for the action that happened at a specific time.
                 XIIIB4(Imperfect and Preterite Tense)

8. El otro automóvil siguió derecho: The other car continued /straight/ ahead.
seguir(i, g) derecho: to continue straight ahead.
Seguir is a stem changing verb.
    XIIIB2b(Preterite Tense)

9. Déjeme ver su licencia y el registro /del/ automóvil: Let me see your license and registration certificate (certificate of the registration).
Déjeme: The object pronoun is attached to the command form. A written accent mark is needed to maintain the original stress.
    XIF(Position of Object Pronouns)
el registro del automóvil: the car registration. IA16 & Dict(Compound Nouns)

10. Se dará parte del accidente y Vd. tendrá que comparecer en la Corte: The accident will be reported and you will have to appear in Court.
dar parte de: to report (something)
    Dict(Idioms)
Se dará parte del accidente: The accident will be reported.
Use of Passive Voice in English - Reflexive Construction in Spanish. Spanish makes much less use of the Passive Voice than English.
    VIID3(Reflexive for Passive)
tendrá: future tense of tener.
    XIVA1b(Irregular Future)

11. Tiene suerte: You are lucky (have luck).
    XE2(tener)

## TRANSLATE

1. Are you all right?
2. Stay here.
3. In what direction were you going when the light changed?
4. Let me see your license and registration.
5. The accident will be reported.
6. You are lucky.

POLICE X

TRAFFIC TICKET

POLICE OFFICER: Pull over to the curb, please.
Your license, please.

MR. VEGA: Why? What is the matter?

POLICE OFFICER: You did not stop at the stop sign.

I am going to give you a ticket.

MR. VEGA: I am sorry. I did not see the sign.

POLICE OFFICER: That is no excuse.
You will have /to/ appear in Court.

If you want, you may plead not guilty.

POLICÍA X

MULTA

POLICÍA: <u>Arrímese a la acera, por favor</u>.   1
Su licencia, por favor.

SR. VEGA: ¿Por qué? ¿<u>Qué pasa</u>?   2

POLICÍA: Vd. no paró en <u>la señal /de/ stop</u>.   3

<u>Voy a ponerle una multa</u>.   4

SR. VEGA: <u>Lo siento</u>.  5
No vi el letrero.

POLICÍA: Eso no es excusa.
<u>Tendrá /que/ comparecer en la Corte</u>.   6

Si Vd. quiere, <u>puede declararse no culpable</u>.   7

NOTES

1. <u>Arrímese a la acera</u>: Pull over to the curb.
   Arrimarse a: to get close to, to pull over to.
                          Dict(Idioms)
   Arrímese: Command form. The reflexive pronoun (like all other object pronouns) is attached to the command form.    XIF(Pos. of Object
                                  Pronouns)

2. ¿Qué pasa?: What is the matter, what is going on?  Dict(Idioms)
3. La señal /de/ stop: The stop sign.
   IA16 &Dict(Compound Nouns)
4. Voy a ponerle una multa: I am going to give you a ticket (fine).
   Poner una multa a alguien: to give someone a ticket (fine).  Dict(Idioms)
5. Lo siento: I am sorry (about it).
   Sentir (stem changing verb): To feel, to be sorry.  IIIB1b(Stem Changing Verbs)
   Dict(Idioms)
6. Tendrá /que/ comparecer en /la/ Corte: You will have to appear in Court.
   Tener que: to have to.  Dict(Idioms)
   Tendrá: Future Tense of tener. XIVA1b(Future)
7. Puede declararse no culpable: You may plead (declare yourself) not guilty.
   declararse no culpable: to plead not guilty.
   Dict(Idioms)

## TRANSLATE

1. Pull over to the curb.
2. What happened?
3. I am going to give you a ticket.
4. You may plead not guilty.

## POLICE XI

### MISSING PERSONS

MRS. ROSADO: My son left early this morning to go to school but he has not come back.

POLICEMAN: How old is he?

MRS. ROSADO: 15.

POLICEMAN: At what time does he usually come home?

MRS. ROSADO: He is usually at home by 6 o'clock the latest.

POLICEMAN: Did you call the school?

MRS. ROSADO: We tried, but there isn't anyone there now.

We looked for him all over the neighborhood, but no-one knows anything.

POLICEMAN: Do you have a photograph of your son?

MRS. ROSADO: Yes, here /it/ is.

## POLICÍA XI

### PERSONAS PERDIDAS

SRA. ROSADO: Mi hijo salió temprano esta mañana para ir a la escuela pero no ha regresado.

POLICÍA: ¿Cuántos años tiene?    1

SRA. ROSADO: Quince.

POLICÍA: ¿A qué hora vuelve usualmente a casa?    2

SRA. ROSADO: Usualmente está en casa a las seis a más tardar.    3

POLICÍA: ¿Llamó Vd. a la escuela?    4

SRA. ROSADO: Tratamos, pero no hay nadie allí ahora.    5

Le buscamos por toda la vecindad,    6
pero ninguno sabe nada.    7

POLICÍA: ¿Tiene Vd. una fotografía de su hijo?

SRA. ROSADO; Sí, aquí está.

| | | |
|---|---|---|
| POLICEMAN: What clothes was he wearing? | POLICÍA: ¿Qué <u>ropa llevaba</u>? | 8 |
| MRS. ROSADO: Blue dungarees and a red shirt. | SRA. ROSADO: <u>Pantalones de vaquero azules</u> y una camisa roja. | 9 |
| POLICEMAN: Does he have any scars or identifying marks? | POLICÍA: ¿Tiene él algunas cicatrices o <u>señas especiales por las que puede ser identificado</u>? | 10 |
| MRS. ROSADO: He is approximately 5 feet 3 inches tall and weighs 120 lbs. | SRA. ROSADO: Él <u>es</u> aproximadamente <u>/de/ cinco pies y tres pulgadas /de/ alto</u> y pesa ciento veinte libras. | 11 |
| He has black hair and dark eyes. | Tiene pelo negro y ojos obscuros. | |
| POLICEMAN: We will notify all the other precincts and will notify you when we hear anything. | POLICÍA: <u>Notificaremos /a/ todos los otros precintos</u> y <u>les comunicaremos cuando oigamos algo</u>. | 12<br>13 |
| Go home and don't worry too much. | <u>Vaya /a/ casa y no se preocupe</u> demasiado. | 14 |

### NOTES

1. ¿<u>Cuántos años tiene</u>?: How old is he?
<u>Tener</u>...años: To be...old    XE1(tener)
<u>Tener</u> is irregular and stem changing.
                      IVA1c(tener)

2. ¿A qué hora vuelve usualmente a casa?: At what time does he usually come (return) home?
¿A qué hora?: At what time? XVE(Time)
Volver is a stem changing verb.
              IIIB1b(Present Tense)
Volver (ir) a casa: to go home.
cf. Estar en casa: to be at home.
              Dict(Idioms)
              XVIA1(a) and XVIA4(en)

3. Está en casa a /las/ seis a más tardar: He is at home by six, the latest.
Estar for location.    XB2(estar)
En casa: at home.     XVIA4(en)
A /las/ seis: At six.   XVE2(Time)
A más tardar: At the latest. Dict(Idioms)

4. ¿Llamó Vd. /a/ la escuela?: Did you call the school?
She called the people in the school, not the building. Therefore, the personal a is needed.
              XVIA1m(Personal a)

5. No hay nadie: There isn't anyone.
Hay: there is, there are   XD(hay)
No...nadie: Double negative
              XXB1(Double Negative)

6. Le buscamos por todo la vecindad: We looked for him all over the neighborhood.
Buscar: to look /for/.
              XVIC(Verbs and Prepositions)
cf. mirar: to look /at/
Le here is the direct object pronoun.
              XIB(Direct Object Pronouns)
Por toda la vecindad: all over (through the whole) neighborhood.

7. Ninguno sabe nada: No-one knows anything.
Double Negative construction.
              XXB1(Double Negative)
saber: to know (about something.
cf. conocer: to be familiar with a person or thing.      Dict(Idioms)

8. **¿Qué ropa llevaba?**: What clothes was he wearing?
   **Ropa** (clothes) is always used in the singular.
           IB9(Singular Nouns)
   Use of Imperfect Tense (llevaba) in Spanish, Past Progressive form in English (was he wearing), for a description.
           XIIIB3(Imperfect)

9. **Pantalones de vaquero azules**: Bluejeans (blue cowboy pants). IA16 & Dict(Compound Nouns)

10. **Señas /especiales por las que puede ser/ identificado**: Identifying marks.
    (Special marks by which he can be identified.)
    Ser identificado: to be identified. Use of **ser** for Passive Voice.
            XXIVB1 & XA7(Passive Voice)

11. **Es aproximadamente /de/ cinco pies /y/ tres pulgadas /de/ alto**: He is approximately 5 feet 5 inches tall.

12. **Notificaremos /a/ todos los precintos**: We will notify all the precincts.
    Use of Personal **a** before precintos (the people in the precincts will be notified).
            XVIA1m(Personal **a**)

13. **Les comunicaremos cuando oigamos algo**: We will notify (communicate with) you when we hear anything.
    **Les** (indirect object pronoun). What is communicated is the direct object. The people who are being notified (**to whom** something is communicated), are the indirect object.
    Use of Subjunctive (oigamos) after **cuando**, because the action has not yet taken place and may never take place.
            XXVA5(Subjunctive of **oír**)
            XXVD1d(Use of Subjunctive)

14. **Vaya /a/ casa y no se preocupe:** Go home and don't worry.
    Ir /a/ casa: to go home.
    cf. Estar en casa: to be at home.
    Vaya: Command form of _ir_     VIA2(Commands)
    preocuparse: to worry     VIIE(Reflexive Verbs)
    No se preocupe: Command form. In the negative command, pronouns precede the verb.
                 XIF(Position of Object Pronouns)

## TRANSLATE

1. At what time does your son usually come home?
2. We looked for him all over the neighborhood.
3. No-one knows anything.
4. What kind of clothes was he wearing?
5. Does he have any identifying marks?
6. We will notify you when we hear anything.
7. Don't worry.

## SOCIAL SERVICE I
## FAMILY

MRS. JIMÉNEZ: Good morning. Is this the Welfare office?

SOCIAL WORKER: Yes. What can I do for you?

MRS. JIMÉNEZ: What do I have to do in order to get help?

SOCIAL WORKER: In /the/ first place, we have /to/ fill /out/ the form.

What is your name?

MRS. JIMÉNEZ: Concepción Jiménez.

SOCIAL WORKER: Where do you live?

MRS. JIMÉNEZ: At 246 Atlantic Avenue, Brooklyn.

SOCIAL WORKER: Do you have a telephone?

MRS. JIMÉNEZ: Yes. The number is 704-8632.

SOCIAL WORKER: Is /it/ a house or an apartment?

## AUXILIO SOCIAL I
## FAMILIA

SRA. JIMÉNEZ: Buenos días. ¿Es esta la oficina /del/ Auxilio Social?

TRABAJADOR SOCIAL: Sí. ¿En qué puedo servirla?     1

SRA. JIMÉNEZ: ¿Qué debo hacer para recibir ayuda?     2

TRABAJADOR SOCIAL: En primer lugar tenemos /que/ llenar el formulario.     3, 4

¿Cómo se llama Vd?     5

SRA. JIMÉNEZ: Concepción Jiménez.

TRABAJADOR SOCIAL: ¿Dónde vive Vd?

SRA. JIMÉNEZ: En /el/ doscientos cuarenta y seis /de/ Atlantic Avenue, Brooklyn.     6

TRABAJADOR SOCIAL: ¿Tiene Vd. teléfono?     7

SRA. JIMÉNEZ: Sí. El número es siete, cero, cuatro, ocho, seis, tres, dos.

TRABAJADOR SOCIAL: ¿Es una casa o un apartamento?

MRS. JIMÉNEZ: An apartment.

SOCIAL WORKER: On what floor do you live?

MRS. JIMÉNEZ: On the fourth floor.

SOCIAL WORKER: How many rooms do you have?

MRS. JIMÉNEZ: Four.

SOCIAL WORKER: How many people live in your apartment?

MRS. JIMÉNEZ: Six. My husband, I and four children.

SOCIAL WORKER: How many people sleep in every room?

MRS. JIMÉNEZ: My husband, I and the baby sleep in the bedroom and the other children in the other room.

SOCIAL WORKER: Is there /a/ bathroom in your apartment?

MRS. JIMÉNEZ: No. The toilet is in the hall. We share it with /another/ family.

SRA. JIMÉNEZ: Un apartamento.

TRABAJADOR SOCIAL: ¿En qué piso vive Vd?

SRA. JIMÉNEZ: En el cuarto piso.

TRABAJADOR SOCIAL: ¿Cuántos cuartos tiene?

SRA. JIMÉNEZ: Cuatro.

TRABAJADOR SOCIAL: ¿Cuántas personas viven en su apartamento?

SRA. JIMÉNEZ: Seis. Mi esposo, yo y cuatro niños.

TRABAJADOR SOCIAL: ¿Cuántas personas duermen en cada cuarto?

SRA. JIMÉNEZ: Mi esposo, yo y el bebé dormimos en el dormitorio y los otros niños en el otro cuarto.

TRABAJADOR SOCIAL: ¿<u>Hay cuarto /de/ baño en su apartamento</u>?    8

SRA. JIMÉNEZ: No. <u>El retrete está en el pasillo.</u>    9
Lo compartimos con otra familia.

| | |
|---|---|
| SOCIAL WORKER: Do you have hot and cold water in your apartment? | TRABAJADOR SOCIAL: ¿Tiene agua caliente y fría en su apartamento? |
| MRS. JIMÉNEZ: Yes. | SRA. JIMÉNEZ: Sí. |
| SOCIAL WORKER: Do you have heat in your apartment? | TRABAJADOR SOCIAL: ¿Tiene calefacción en su apartamento? |
| MRS. JIMÉNEZ: Yes, but in winter it is often cold. | SRA. JIMÉNEZ: Sí, pero <u>en /el/ invierno hace frío</u> muchas veces.  10 |
| SOCIAL WORKER: Do you have any savings? | TRABAJADOR SOCIAL: ¿Tiene algunos ahorros? |
| MRS. JIMÉNEZ: No. We spent them last year when I was sick. | SRA. JIMÉNEZ: No. Los gastamos<u>/el/</u>  11 <u>año pasado cuando yo estuve enferma</u>.  12 |
| SOCIAL WORKER: How old are your children? | TRABAJADOR SOCIAL: <u>¿Cuántos años</u>  13 <u>tienen sus niños</u>? |
| MRS. JIMÉNEZ: The oldest is 16, John 12, Elena 8 and the baby 2. | SRA. JIMÉNEZ: La mayor dieciséis, Juan doce, Elena ocho, y el bebé dos. |
| SOCIAL WORKER: Does your husband work? | TRABAJADOR SOCIAL: ¿Trabaja su marido? |
| MRS. JIMÉNEZ: No. He has been sick for four weeks. | SRA. JIMÉNEZ: No. <u>Hace cuatro semanas</u>  14 <u>que está enfermo</u>. |
| SOCIAL WORKER: Do you work? | TRABAJADOR SOCIAL: ¿Trabaja Vd? |
| MRS. JIMÉNEZ: No. I can't work because I have to take care of the children. | SRA. JIMÉNEZ: No, no puedo trabajar porque <u>tengo que cuidar a los niños</u>. |

My older daughter
works a few hours
as /a/ saleslady.
She earns about
twenty dollars
a week.

SOCIAL WORKER:
How much do you pay
for rent?

MRS. JIMÉNEZ: Ninety
dollars a month.

SOCIAL WORKER: Do
you belong to any
/church/ parish?

MRS. JIMÉNEZ: Yes.
We belong to the
parish of San Juan
Bautista.

SOCIAL WORKER: Are
you /a/ member of
any community
organization or
club?

MRS. JIMÉNEZ: No,
we don't belong to
any.

SOCIAL WORKER: Is
any religious
organization
helping you?

MRS. JIMÉNEZ: No.
We do not get any
help.

SOCIAL WORKER: When
did you enter the
United States?

MRS. JIMÉNEZ: Six
years ago.

Mi hija mayor
trabaja unas horas
como vendedora.
Gana <u>unos veinte</u>      16
<u>dólares a /la/</u>
<u>semana.</u>

TRABAJADOR SOCIAL:
¿Cuánto paga de
alquiler?

SRA. JIMÉNEZ: Noventa
dólares al mes.

TRABAJADOR SOCIAL:
¿Pertenece Vd. a
alguna parroquia?

SRA. JIMÉNEZ: Sí.
Pertenecemos a la
parroquia de San
Juan Bautista.

TRABAJADOR SOCIAL:
¿Es Vd. miembro de
alguna sociedad o
club en la comunidad?

SRA. JIMÉNEZ: No,
<u>no pertenecemos a</u>
<u>ninguna.</u>                17

TRABAJADOR SOCIAL:
¿Le ayuda alguna
organización
religiosa?

SRA. JIMÉNEZ: No.
<u>No recibimos ninguna</u>
<u>ayuda.</u>         see 17

TRABAJADOR SOCIAL:
¿Cuándo entró /en/
<u>los Estados Unidos?</u>  18

SRA. JIMÉNEZ: <u>Hace</u>
<u>seis años.</u>

| | | |
|---|---|---|
| SOCIAL WORKER: Since when have you been living in New York? | TRABAJADOR SOCIAL: ¿Desde cuándo vive Vd. en Nueva York? | 20 |
| MRS. JIMÉNEZ: I have been living in New York since I arrived in the United States. | SRA. JIMÉNEZ: Vivo en Nueva York desde see /que/ llegué a los Estados Unidos. | 20 |
| SOCIAL WORKER: Fine. That is all. You will receive answers within two weeks. | TRABAJADOR SOCIAL: Bueno. Eso es todo. Vd. recibirá contestaciones dentro /de/ dos semanas. | 21 |
| MRS. JIMÉNEZ: Thank you. | SRA. JIMÉNEZ: Gracias. | |
| SOCIAL WORKER: You are welcome, Mrs. Jiménez. Good-bye. | TRABAJADOR SOCIAL: De nada, señora Jiménez. Adiós. | 22 |

## NOTES

1. ¿En qué puedo servirla?: What can I do for you? Literally: With what can I serve you?
   Dict(Idioms)
2. Para recibir ayuda: In order to receive help. Para: in order to. XVIA6(para)
3. En primer lugar: In /the/ first place, first of all. Dict(Idioms)
4. Llenar el formulario: to fill out the form.
   XVIC(Verbs & Prepositions)
   Dict(Idioms)
5. ¿Cómo se llama Vd?: What is your name? Llamarse: to be called.
   VIIE(Reflexive Constructions)

6. En /el/ doscientos cuarenta y seis /de/ Atlantic Avenue: At 246 Atlantic Avenue.
   IIA2p(Use of Definite Article)

7. ¿Tiene Vd. teléfono?: Do you have /a/ telephone? In questions and negative statements the indefinite article (a) is left out before nouns referring to types.
   IIB2e(Omission of Indefinite Article)

8. ¿Hay cuarto /de/ baño en su apartamento?: Is there /a/ bathroom in your apartment?
   Hay: Is there?, there is.   XD(hay)
   un cuarto /de/ baño: a bathroom.
   IA16 & Dict(Compound Nouns)
   Omission of indefinite article (a). See No. 7.

9. El retrete está en el pasillo: The toilet is in the hall.
   Use of estar for location.   XB2(estar)

10. En /el/ invierno, hace frío muchas veces: In winter it is often cold.
    Use of definite article (el) before the names of the seasons.   IIA2f(Use of Definite Article)
    Hace frío: it is cold.   XC(hacer)
    Muchas veces: Many times, often.   XVE3(vez)

11. El año pasado: last year.
    Use of definite article before año.
    IIA2r(Use of Definite Article)

12. Cuando estuve enferma: When I was sick.
    Use of estar for health.   XB1(estar)
    Use of Preterite Tense for a condition that lasted a limited time (last year).
    XIIA(Use of Preterite Tense)
    XIIB3d(Preterite of estar)

13. ¿Cuántos años tienen sus hijos?: How old are your children?
    tener...años: to be...old.   XE1(Tener)
    Tener is a stem changing verb.
    IIIB1b(Stem Changing Verbs)

14. <u>Hace cuatro semanas que está enfermo</u>: He has been sick for four weeks.
Use of <u>hace</u> with the Present Tense for an action that started in the past and is still going on. English uses the Present Perfect Tense.   IIIB2c(<u>hace</u> with Present Tense)
XVG1

15. <u>Tengo que cuidar /a/ los niños</u>: I have to take care /of/ the children.
Tener que: to have to. <u>Tener</u> is an irregular and stem changing verb.   IVA1c(tener)
cuidar: to take care of
Use of Personal <u>a</u> before a direct object referring to a person.
XVIA1m(Personal <u>a</u>)

16. <u>Unos veinte dólares /a la/ semana</u>: About twenty dollars /a/ (per) week.
Unos: about
a la (por) semana: a (per) week.

17. <u>No pertenecemos a ninguna</u>: We do not belong to any.
Use of Double Negative (no...ninguna) is required in Spanish unless the sentence begins with the negative expression.
XXB1(Double Negative)

18. <u>¿Cuándo entró Vd. / a/ los Estados Unidos?</u>: When did you enter the United States?
Entrar <u>a</u> : to enter (a place)
XVID(Verbs and Prepositions)
cf. salir <u>de</u>: to leave (a place)

19. <u>Hace seis años</u>: Six years ago.
In this construction, <u>hace</u> takes the place of the English <u>ago</u>.   XVG2(hace)

20. <u>¿Desde cuándo vive Vd. en Nueva York?</u> <u>Vivo en Nueva York desde....</u>: Since when have you been living in New York? I have been living in New York since...
Use of Present Tense for an action that started in the past and is still going on. English uses the Present Perfect Progressive form.   IIIB2c(Use of Present Tense)

21. <u>Dentro /de/ dos semanas</u>: Within two weeks.
    dentro de: within          Dict(Idioms)

22. <u>De nada</u>: You are welcome.  Dict(Idioms)

## TRANSLATE

1. What do I have to do to get help?
2. You have to fill out the form.
3. Is there a bathroom (telephone) in your apartment?
4. In summer, it is often hot.
5. How old are your children?
6. I have to take care of the children.
7. We do not get any help.
8. How long have you been living in New York?
9. You will receive an answer within a week.
10. I was sick last year.

## SOCIAL SERVICE II
## ABANDONED WIFE

SOCIAL WORKER: Why are you applying /for/ public assistance?

MRS. AYALA: My husband left (abandoned) me.

SOCIAL WORKER: Do you have /any/ children?

MRS. AYALA: Yes, three.

SOCIAL WORKER: Do they live with you?

MRS. AYALA: Yes.

SOCIAL WORKER: How have you supported yourself up /to/ now?

MRS. AYALA: My husband was working.

SOCIAL WORKER: Do you have /any/ debts?

MRS. AYALA: I owe last month's electric bill.

SOCIAL WORKER: How much is /it/?

MRS. AYALA: Here /it/ is. It is /for/ $9.85.

## SERVICIO SOCIAL II
## MUJER ABANDONADA

TRABAJADOR SOCIAL: ¿Por qué solicita ayuda pública?   1

SRA. AYALA: Mi marido me abandonó.

TRABAJADOR SOCIAL: ¿Tiene Vd. niños?   2

SRA. AYALA: Sí, tres.

TRABAJADOR SOCIAL: ¿Viven con Vd?

SRA. AYALA: Sí.

TRABAJADOR SOCIAL: ¿Cómo se ha mantenido hasta ahora?

SRA. AYALA: Mi marido trabajaba.   3

TRABAJADOR SOCIAL: ¿Tiene Vd. deudas? see 2

SRA. AYALA: Debo la cuenta /de/ electricidad /del/ mes pasado.   4

TRABAJADOR SOCIAL: ¿Cuánto es?

SRA. AYALA: Aquí está. Es nueve ochenta y cinco.   5

| | |
|---|---|
| SOCIAL WORKER: Were you receiving public assistance or food stamps? | TRABAJADOR SOCIAL: ¿Recibía Vd. ayuda pública o sellos /para/ alimentos? 6 |
| MRS. AYALA: They gave us forty dollars worth in food stamps every month. | SRA. ALAYA: Nos daban /el valor de/ cuarenta dólares en sellos para alimentos todos los meses. 7 |
| SOCIAL WORKER: Do you have Medicaid? | TRABAJADOR SOCIAL: ¿Tiene Vd. Medicaid? |
| MRS. AYALA: Yes. | SRA. AYALA: Sí. |
| SOCIAL WORKER: What is the number of your Medicaid card? | TRABAJADOR SOCIAL: ¿Cuál es el número de su tarjeta /de/ Medicaid? 8 |
| MRS. AYALA: 73,898,87,47 | SRA. AYALA: Setenta y tres, ochocientos noventa y ocho, ochenta y siete, cuarenta y siete. |
| SOCIAL WORKER: Does /any/ other person besides your three children live with you? | TRABAJADOR SOCIAL: ¿Vive otra persona con Vd. además /de/ sus tres niños? 9 |
| MRS. AYALA: No-one. | SRA. AYALA: Nadie. |
| SOCIAL WORKER: How old are your children? | TRABAJADOR SOCIAL: ¿Cuántos años tienen sus niños? 10 |
| MRS. AYALA: They are six, nine and fifteen years /old/. | SRA. AYALA: Tienen seis años, nueve y quince. |
| SOCIAL WORKER: Are /they/ all well or is anyone blind, sick or disabled? | TRABAJADOR SOCIAL: ¿Están todos bien o hay alguno ciego, enfermo o inválido? 11 |

| | |
|---|---|
| MRS. AYALA: All are well. | SRA. AYALA: Todos están bien. |
| SOCIAL WORKER: Are you or any of your children drug addicts or have you attended any drug treatment program? | TRABAJADOR SOCIAL: ¿Es Vd. o /son/ algunos de sus hijos adictos /a las/ drogas o han asistido /a/ algún programa para cura de adictos /a las/ drogas? |
| MRS. AYALA: No. | SRA. AYALA: No. |
| SOCIAL WORKER: Do you know where your husband lives? | TRABAJADOR SOCIAL: ¿Sabe Vd. dónde vive su esposo? |
| MRS. AYALA: No, I don't know (it). | SRA. AYALA: No, no /lo/ sé. |
| SOCIAL WORKER: Do you know the address of his last /place of/ employment? | TRABAJADOR SOCIAL: ¿Sabe Vd. la dirección de su último empleo? |
| MRS. AYALA: Yes, he was working as elevator operator at 185 East 33rd Street, in Manhattan. | SRA. AYALA: Sí, trabajaba como ascensorista en /el número/ ciento ochenta /y/ cinco, Este, /de la/ calle treinta y tres, de Manhattan |
| SOCIAL WORKER: Do you know what his social security number is? | TRABAJADOR SOCIAL: ¿Sabe Vd. cuál es el número de su seguro social? |
| MRS. AYALA: Yes, it is 187-61-3916. | SRA. AYALA: Sí, es /el/ ciento ochenta y siete, sesenta y uno, treinta y nueve, dieciseis. |

Numbered markers in right margin: 12, 13, 14, 15, 16

SOCIAL WORKER: Please, tell me the names of your children.

MRS. AYALA: Antonia, Paco and Alberto.

SOCIAL WORKER: When did your husband leave (abandon) you?

MRS. AYALA: Last month.

SOCIAL WORKER: Have you tried to get support (money) from him?

MRS. AYALA: How can I do it if I don't know where he is?

SOCIAL WORKER: Do you or your husband have /any/ other children who do not live in your house?

MRS. AYALA: I don't have /any/ other children and I think neither /has/ my husband.

SOCIAL WORKER: Have you or any of your children been in a psychiatric hospital, jail, school for mentally retarded or in a foster home during the last six months?

TRABAJADOR SOCIAL: Por favor, dígame los nombres de sus hijos.

SRA. AYALA: Antonia, Paco y Alberto.

TRABAJADOR SOCIAL: ¿Cuándo la abandonó su esposo?

SRA. AYALA: /El/ mes pasado.

TRABAJADOR SOCIAL: ¿Ha tratado de conseguir dinero de él?    17

SRA. AYALA: ¿Cómo puedo hacerlo si no sé dónde está?    18

TRABAJADOR SOCIAL: ¿Tiene Vd. o su esposo otros hijos que no vivan en su casa?    19

SRA. AYALA: Yo no tengo otros hijos y creo que mi marido tampoco.    20

TRABAJADOR SOCIAL: ¿Ha estado Vd. o alguno de sus hijos en un hospital de psiquiatría, cárcel, escuela para atrasados mentales, o en un hogar /de/ adopción durante los últimos seis meses?    21

| | |
|---|---|
| MRS. AYALA: No. | SRA. AYALA: No. |
| SOCIAL WORKER: Do you live in an apartment or in a private house? | TRABAJADOR SOCIAL: ¿Vive Vd. en un apartamento o en una casa privada? |
| MRS. AYALA: In an apartment. | SRA. AYALA: En un apartamento. |
| SOCIAL WORKER: Who is the landlord of the building where you live? | TRABAJADOR SOCIAL: ¿Quién es el dueño del edificio donde vive? |
| MRS. AYALA: Smith Corporation. Their address is 589 Atlantic Avenue. | SRA. AYALA: /La/ corporación Smith. Su dirección es /el número/ quinientos ochenta /y/ nueve /de la/ avenida Atlantic.    22 |
| SOCIAL WORKER: Do you have a lease? | TRABAJADOR SOCIAL: ¿Tiene Vd. un contrato de arrendamiento?    23 |
| MRS. AYALA: No. | SRA. AYALA: No. |
| SOCIAL WORKER: Do any of your children work? | TRABAJADOR SOCIAL: ¿Trabajan algunos de sus hijos? |
| MRS. AYALA: Alberto makes deliveries for the grocery store on the corner, but all that they give him is tips. | SRA. AYALA: Alberto reparte mercancías para la bodega /que está/ en la esquina, pero todo lo que le dan son propinas.    24 |
| SOCIAL WORKER: Did you work at any time? | TRABAJADOR SOCIAL: ¿Trabajó Vd. alguna vez? |
| MRS. AYALA: Yes, I worked before I had Antonia and also last year until they fired me. | SRA. AYALA: Sí, trabajé antes /de/ tener a Antonia y también /el/ año pasado hasta /que/ me despidieron.    25<br>   26 |

SOCIAL WORKER: Do you get any help from anyone?

MRS. AYALA: No. The only person in my family who lives in New York is my brother Juan, and he can hardly support his own family.

SOCIAL WORKER: Do you have any bank account or safe deposit box?

MRS. AYALA: I have twenty dollars in my account at the Lincoln Savings Bank.

SOCIAL WORKER: Are you a citizen of the United States?

MRS. AYALA: Yes. I was born in Puerto Rico and my children were born here.

SOCIAL WORKER: Do you swear that the information you gave me is correct and that you will inform us in case there should be any change in your situation?

MRS. AYALA: I swear that what I said is the truth.

TRABAJADOR SOCIAL: ¿Recibe Vd. alguna ayuda de alguien?

SRA. AYALA: No. La única persona en mi familia que vive en Nueva York es mi hermano Juan, y él casi no puede mantener /a/ su propia familia.   27

TRABAJADOR SOCIAL: ¿Tiene Vd. alguna cuenta /de/ banco   28 o caja /de/ seguridad?   29

SRA. AYALA: Tengo veinte dólares en mi cuenta del Lincoln Savings Bank.

TRABAJADOR SOCIAL: ¿Es Vd. ciudadana de los Estados Unidos?

SRA. AYALA: Sí, nací en Puerto   30 Rico y mis hijos nacieron aquí.

TRABAJADOR SOCIAL: ¿Jura Vd. que la información que me dio es correcta y que nos informará en caso /de que/ haya algún cambio en su   31 situación?

SRA. AYALA: Juro   32 que lo dicho es la verdad.

NOTES

1. ¿Por qué solicita Vd. ayuda pública?: Why are you applying /for/ public assistance?
   solicitar: to apply for
       XVIC(Verbs and Prepositions)
   Use of Progressive Form (are you applying) in English, Present Tense in Spanish. The Progressive Form is used much more rarely in Spanish than in English.
       XVIIC2b and IIIB2a(note)

2. ¿Tiene Vd. niños?: Do you have /any/ children?
   The indefinite any is not used in questions and in negative statements unless it is stressed, in which case it is translated by alguno(a)s.
       XXA1(Omission of any)

3. Mi marido trabajaba: My husband was working.
   Use of Imperfect Tense in Spanish, Past Progressive in English, for an action of indefinite duration.
       XIIIB1(Use of Imperfect Tense)

4. Debo la cuenta /de/ electricidad /del/ mes pasado: I owe last month's electric bill.
   Deber (as main verb): to owe.
   La cuenta /de/ electricidad /del/ mes pasado: Last month's electric bill (the bill for electricity for the past month).
   The preposition de is used in Spanish in lieu of the possessive ('s) in English.
       IA16 & Dict (Compound Nouns)
       XVIA3a & IXD(de for
            possessive)

5. Aquí está: Here /it/ is.
   Use of estar for location.
       XB2(estar)

6. ¿Recibía Vd. ayuda pública o sellos /para/ alimentos?: Did you receive (were you receiving) public assistance or food stamps? They received (or did not receive) food stamps for an indefinite time. Therefore, the Imperfect Tense must be used in Spanish.
      XIIIB1 and
      B3(Use of Imperfect Tense)
Sellos /para/ alimentos: food stamps.
      IA16 & Dict(Compound Nouns)

7. Nos daban /el valor de/ cuarenta dólares en sellos /para/ alimentos todos los meses: They gave (used to give) us $40 worth (the value of $40) in food stamps every month. Use of Imperfect Tense (daban) for a repeated action.  XIIIB2(Use of Imperfect Tense)
todos los meses: every month.
Expressions like siempre, todos los meses, etc. are generally followed by the Imperfect Tense.

8. ¿Cuál es el número de su tarjeta /de/ Medicaid?: What is the number of your Medicaid card?
Use of ¿cuál? for what? before the verb ser.
     VC3b(¿cuál?)

9. ¿Vive otra persona con Vd. además /de/ sus tres niños?: Does /any/ other person besides your three children live with you?
Omission of any in questions and negative statements.   XXA1(Omission of any)
además de: besides.

10. ¿Cuántos años tienen sus niños? How old are your children?
Tener...años: to be...years old.
     XE1(tener)

11. ¿Están todos bien o hay alguno ciego, enfermo o inválido?: Are /they/ all well or is anyone blind, sick or disabled?
Estar bien: to be well. Use of estar for health.    XB1(Estar)
Hay: is there, are there?  XD(hay)
alguno: someone, anyone.

12. ¿Es Vd. o /son/ algunos de sus hijos adictos /a las/ drogas?: Are you or (are) any of your children drug addicts?
In English are is used for both you and the children. Therefore, the verb does not have to be repeated. However, in Spanish it is ¿Es Vd? and ¿Son ellos? Therefore, the verb has to be repeated.
adictos /a las/ drogas: drug addicts.
IA16 & Dict(Compound Nouns)

13. ¿Han asistido /a/ algún programa /para cura de/ adictos /a las/ drogas?: Have you attended any drug treatment program (a program for the cure of people addicted to drugs)?
IA16 & Dict(Compound Nouns)
asistir a: to attend (school, a program, etc.)
XVID(Verbs & Prepositions)

14. ¿Sabe Vd. dónde vive su esposo?: Do you know where your husband lives?
saber: to know (about something)
cf. ¿Conoce Vd. al señor Brown?: Do you know Mr. Brown?

15. Trabajaba como ascensorista en /el número/ ciento ochenta /y/ cinco, este, /de la/ calle treinta /y/ tres, de Manhattan: He was working as elevator operator at 185 East 33rd Street, in Manhattan.
Use of Imperfect Tense (trabajaba) for a past action of indefinite duration. English uses the Past Progressive form here (he was working). XIIIB1(Use of Imperfect Tense)

16. ¿Sabe Vd. cuál es el número /de/ su seguro social?: Do you know what his social security number is?
Use of ¿cuál? for what? after the verb ser.
VC3b(¿cuál?)
El número /de/ seguro social: The social security number. IA16 & Dict(Compound Nouns)

17. ¿Ha tratado de conseguir dinero de él?:  Have you tried to get (obtain) money from him?
de él:  from him.
Use of stressed pronoun after a preposition.
XD1(Object of Preposition)

18. No sé dónde está:  I don't know where he is.
Sé is the first person present tense of saber. The accent is necessary to distinguish the word from the reflexive pronoun se.
IVA3(Present Tense of saber)
Intr. G(Accent marks)
Use of estar for location.   XB1(estar)

19. ¿Tiene Vd. o su esposo otros hijos que no vivan en su casa?:  Do you or your husband have (any) other children who do (may) not live in your house?
Use of subjunctive (vivan) because the speaker does not know if such other children exist or not (uncertainty). XXVB1f(Use of Subjunctive)

20. Yo no tengo otros hijos:  I don't have /any/ other children.
Any is not translated in questions or negative expressions.     XXA1(Omission of any)

21. Un hogar /de/ adopción:  a foster home.
IA16 & Dict(Compound Nouns)

22. Es /el número/ quinientos ochenta y nueve /de la/ avenida Atlantic:  It is 589 Atlantic Avenue.     IIA2p(Use of Definite Article)

23. Un contrato /de/ arrendamiento:  A lease (rental contract).
IA16 & Dict(Compound Nouns)

24. Alberto reparte mercancías para la bodega /que está/ en la esquina:  Alberto makes deliveries for the grocery store (which is) on the corner.
La bodega:  grocery store (in the Caribbean area).
repartir mercancías:  to make deliveries, to deliver merchandise.

25. Antes /de/ tener /a/ Antonia: Before I had Antonia. XVIA1m(Personal a)
Use of infinitive after a preposition in Spanish. XXIIA(Use of Infinitive)

26. Hasta /que/ me despidieron: Until they fired me. Dict(Idioms)
despedir a alguien: to fire someone.
Despidieron: Preterite Tense of despedir.
XIIB2b(Preterite Tense)

27. Casi no puede mantener /a/ su propia familia: He can hardly (he nearly cannot) support his own family.
Use of personal a before a direct object referring to persons (la familia).
XVIA1m(Personal a)

28. Una cuenta /de/ banco: a bank account.
IA16 & Dict(Compound Nouns)

29. Una caja /de/ seguridad: a safe deposit box.
IA16 & Dict(Compound Nouns)

30. Nací en Puerto Rico: I was born in Puerto Rico.
nacer: to be born. XF & Dict(Idioms)

31. Nos informará en caso /de que/ haya algún cambio: You will inform us in case there is (might be) any change.
Use of subjunctive (haya) after the conjunction en caso de que, which indicates uncertainty.
XXVA1f(Irregular Subjunctive)
XXVD1e(Use of Subjunctive)

32. Juro que /lo dicho/ es la verdad: I swear that /what I said/ is the truth.
Lo dicho: what was (is) said.
IIA1d(Use of lo)

## TRANSLATE

1. I am applying for assistance.
2. My wife was working.
3. We owe last month's gas bill.
4. We received food stamps.
5. What is your social security number?
6. Is one of your children a drug addict?
7. My husband was working as an elevator operator.
8. Have you tried to get money from them?
9. Has he ever been in a foster home?
10. I cannot support my family.
11. Do you swear that what you said is the truth?

HOUSING I

LOOKING FOR AN APARTMENT

MR. BROWN: Good morning, madam. What can I do for you?

MRS. GÓMEZ: I am looking /for/ an apartment.

MR. BROWN: Why are you looking for /an/other apartment?

MRS. GÓMEZ: Because the one I have is too small.

MR. BROWN: All right. We are going to fill /out/ the forms. What is your name?

MRS. GÓMEZ: María Gómez.

MR. BROWN: Are you single married separated divorced or widowed?

MRS. GÓMEZ: I am married. I have two children. One is seven years old, and the other thirteen. And in a few months we are expecting /an/other one.

MR. BROWN: Where do you live now?

VIVIENDA I

BUSCA DE UN APARTAMENTO

SR. BROWN: Buenos días, señora. ¿En qué puedo servirla?  1

SRA. GÓMEZ: Busco un apartamento.  2

SR. BROWN: ¿Por qué busca otro apartamento?  3

SRA. GÓMEZ: Porque el que tengo es demasiado pequeño.  3

SR. BROWN: Pues, vamos a llenar los formularios. ¿Cómo se llama Vd?  4

SRA. GÓMEZ: María Gómez.

SR. BROWN: ¿Es Vd. soltera casada separada divorciada o viuda?  5

SRA. GÓMEZ: Estoy casada. Tengo dos niños. Uno tiene siete años y el otro trece. Y en algunos meses esperamos otro.  5 6 7

SR. BROWN: ¿Dónde vive ahora?

MRS. GÓMEZ: I live at 130 East 110th Street, in a three-room apartment.

MR. BROWN: How much rent do you pay each month?

MRS. GÓMEZ: I pay $100.

MR. BROWN: Is there /a/ toilet in the apartment?

MRS. GÓMEZ: Yes, there is one.

MR. BROWN: Is there /a/ bathtub or shower?

MRS. GÓMEZ: There is a shower.

MR. BROWN: On what floor do you live?

MRS. GÓMEZ: I live on the third floor.

MR. BROWN: Is there /an/ elevator in the building?

MRS. GÓMEZ: No, there isn't /any/ elevator.

MR. BROWN: Does every room have an outside window?

MRS. GÓMEZ: No, only two, the living room and the children's room.

SRA. GÓMEZ: <u>Vivo en /el/ ciento treinta Este /de la/ calle ciento diez</u>, en un <u>apartamento de tres cuartos</u>.    8

   9

SR. BROWN: ¿Cuánto paga /de/ alquiler cada mes?

SRA. GÓMEZ: Pago cien dólares.

SR. BROWN: ¿<u>Hay retrete en el apartamento</u>?    10

SRA. GÓMEZ: Sí, hay uno.

SR. BROWN: ¿Hay bañera o ducha?

SRA. GÓMEZ: Hay una ducha.

SR. BROWN: ¿En qué piso vive Vd?

SRA. GÓMEZ: Vivo en el tercer piso.

SR. BROWN: ¿Hay ascensor en el edificio?

SRA. GÓMEZ: <u>No, no hay ascensor</u>.    10

SR. BROWN: ¿Tiene cada cuarto una <u>ventana /al/ exterior</u>? 11

SRA. GÓMEZ: No, solamente dos, la sala y <u>el cuarto /de los/ niños</u>.    12

| | |
|---|---|
| MR. BROWN: Do you have heat? | SR. BROWN: ¿Tiene calefacción? |
| MRS. GÓMEZ: Yes, but sometimes the heat does not work. | SRA. GÓMEZ: Sí, pero <u>a veces la calefacción no funciona</u>.   13 |
| MR. BROWN: And hot water? | SR. BROWN: ¿Y agua caliente? |
| MRS. GÓMEZ: Yes, the landlord has to provide it, too. | SRA. GÓMEZ: Sí, el casero tiene que proveerla también. |
| MR. BROWN: How long have you been living in New York City? | SR. BROWN: <u>¿Cuánto tiempo hace que vive en /la/ ciudad /de/ Nueva York</u>?   14 |
| MRS. GÓMEZ: About two years. | SRA. GÓMEZ: <u>Como dos años</u>.   15 |
| MR. BROWN: How long has your husband been living here? | SR. BROWN: ¿Cuánto tiempo hace que su esposo vive aquí?   see 14 |
| MRS. GÓMEZ: He has been living here for about six or seven years. | SRA. GÓMEZ: Hace como seis o siete años que vive aquí. |
| MR. BROWN: Where did you live during the last two years? Begin with the present address. | SR. BROWN: ¿Dónde vivió Vd. durante los dos ultimos años? Empiece por <u>la dirección actual</u>.   16 |
| MRS. GÓMEZ: The first year I lived in a friend's house and then where I am now. | SRA. GÓMEZ: El primer año viví <u>en casa /de/ un amigo</u> y después donde estoy ahora.   17 |

MR. BROWN: Did you or any person included in this application ever live in a Housing Authority site or in a Project?

MRS. GÓMEZ: No, never.

MR. BROWN: When and where were you born?

MRS. GÓMEZ: I was born on September 15th, 1942, in Cuba.

MR. BROWN: Do you work?

MRS. GÓMEZ: No, but my husband does.

MR. BROWN: Where does he work?

MRS. GÓMEZ: He works at Macy's, on 34th Street.

MR. BROWN: Since when does he work there?

MRS. GÓMEZ: Since March of last year.

MR. BROWN: Where was your husband born?

SR. BROWN: ¿Vivió Vd. o cualquier persona incluída en esta solicitud alguna vez en algún sitio perteneciente al Departamento de Viviendas o en algún proyecto?

SRA. GÓMEZ: No, nunca.

SR. BROWN: ¿Cuándo y dónde nació? 18

SRA. GÓMEZ: Nací /el/ quince /de/ 19 septiembre /de/ mil novecientos cuarenta y dos, en Cuba.

SR. BROWN: ¿Trabaja Vd?

SRA. GÓMEZ: No, pero mi esposo, sí. 20

SR. BROWN: ¿Dónde trabaja él?

SRA. GÓMEZ: Trabaja en Macy's en /la/ calle treinta y cuatro.

SR. BROWN: ¿Desde cuándo trabaja él allí?

SRA. GÓMEZ: Desde marzo del año pasado.

SR. BROWN: ¿Dónde nació su esposo? see 18

MRS. GÓMEZ: He was
born in Puerto Rico,
in San Juan, on
March 3rd, 1940.

SRA. GÓMEZ: Nació
en Puerto Rico, en
San Juan, el tres
/de/ marzo /de/ mil
novecientos cuarenta.  21

MR. BROWN: Is your
husband /a/ soldier
or veteran?

SR. BROWN: ¿Es su
marido soldado o
veterano del ejército?

MRS. GÓMEZ: Yes,
/he/ is /a/ veteran.

SRA. GÓMEZ: Sí,
es veterano.

MR. BROWN: Does he
receive any Veterans
or Disability
payments?

SR. BROWN: ¿Recibe    22
él alguna paga /por
ser/ veterano o
/por/ invalidez?

MRS. GÓMEZ: No,
nothing.

SRA. GÓMEZ: No,
nada.

MR. BROWN: How much
did your husband earn
in the last twelve
months?

SR. BROWN: ¿Cuánto
ganó su esposo
en los doce últimos
meces?

MRS. GÓMEZ: About
$400 a month.

SRA. GÓMEZ: Unos
cuatrocientos
dólares al mes.      23

MR. BROWN: Does any
other member
of your family
work?

SR. BROWN: ¿Hay       24
algún otro miembro
de su familia que
trabaja?

MRS. GOMEZ: I
used to work but
not now since
I am pregnant.

SRA. GOMEZ: Yo        25
solía trabajar pero
no ahora ya que
estoy embarazada.

MR. BROWN: Is your husband or any of the persons who will live with you receiving income from any other source, like the Veterans Administration, Welfare, or Social Security?

MRS. GÓMEZ: No.

MR. BROWN: Do you swear that the statements made in this application are true (the truth)?

MRS. GÓMEZ: Yes.

MR. BROWN: Sign here, please.

MRS. GÓMEZ: Thank you. When will we receive answers?

MR. BROWN: In one or two weeks, by mail.

MRS. GÓMEZ: Thank you, sir.

MR. BROWN: Good-bye, madam.

SR. BROWN: ¿Está su esposo o alguna de las personas que vivirán con Vd. recibiendo paga de algún otro sitio, como la Administración /de/ Veteranos, /el/ Auxilio Social Público, o /el/ Seguro Social?

SRA. GÓMEZ: No.

SR. BROWN: ¿Jura Vd. que las declaraciones hechas en esta solicitud son verdad?

SRA. GÓMEZ: Sí.

SR. BROWN: Firme aquí, por favor.

SRA. GÓMEZ: Gracias. ¿Cuándo recibiremos contestaciones?

SR. BROWN: En una o dos semanas, por correo.

SRA. GÓMEZ: Gracias, señor.

SR. BROWN: Adiós, señora.

## NOTES

1. ¿En qué puedo servirla? What can I do for you?
   Literally: In (with) what can I serve you?
           Dict(Idioms)

2. Busco un apartamento: I am looking /for/ an apartment.
   Buscar: to look for
   cf. mirar: to look at. XVIC(Verbs & Prepos.)
   Although Spanish has a Progressive Form, it is used much less frequently than in English. Use of the Progressive Form in Spanish indicates that the action is going on right at the time described. Otherwise, the Present Tense is used, as is the case here.
           IIIB2a(note)

3. ¿Por qué?: Why?
   cf. porque: because.
           Vb3(Interrogatives)

4. ¿Cómo se llama Vd?: What is your name?
   Literally: How do you call yourself?
           VIID1(Reflexive Verbs)
           Dict(Idioms)

5. ¿Es Vd. soltera?: Are you single?
   Estoy (soy) casada: I am married.
   Ser or estar may be used for soltero(a), casado(a), divorciado(a)
           XA and B (ser & estar)

6. Tiene siete años: He is seven years old.
   Literally: He has seven years.
           XE1(tener)
           IIIB1b(Stem Changing Verbs)

7. Esperamos otro: We expect /an/other.
   Esperar: to hope, to expect.
   otro: /an/other

8. Vivo en /el/ ciento treinta Este /de la/ calle ciento diez:  I live at 130 East 110th Street.
    IIB16(Definite Article)
    la calle ciento diez:  110th Street.
    XVB4(Ordinal Numbers)
    Use of ordinal number after the number 10.
9. Un apartamento /de/ tres cuartos:  A three-room apartment (An apartment of three rooms).
    IA16 & Dict(Compound Nouns)
10. ¿Hay retrete en el apartamento?:  Is there /a/ toilet in the apartment?
    No hay ascensor:  There isn't /any/ elevator.
    A or any are often left out in questions or negative statements in Spanish.  Only if any or not any are stressed, algún or ningún are used.    IIB5(Omission of Indef. Art.)
11. Una ventana al exterior:  An outside window (a window to the outside).
    IA16 & Dict(Compound Nouns)
12. El cuarto /de/ los niños:  The children's room (the room of the children).
    The possessive ('s or s') is always expressed by the preposition de in Spanish.
    IXD and XVIA3(de)
13. A veces la calefacción no funciona:  Sometimes the heat does not work (function).
    A veces:  sometimes.    XVE3(vez)
    funcionar:  to work, to function
    cf. El hombre trabaja:  the man works.
14. ¿Cuánto tiempo hace que vive en la ciudad /de/ Nueva York?:  How long have you been living in New York City (the city of New York)?
    For an action that began in the past and is still going on, Spanish uses hace with the Present Tense (hace...que vive) - English uses the Past Progressive Form (have you been living).
    IIIB2c(hace & Present Tense)
15. Como dos años:  About two years.
    XVD(time)

16. <u>La dirección actual</u>: The present address.
    actual: present
    cf. English <u>actual</u>: efectiva, efectivamente.
17. <u>En casa de un amigo</u>: In a friend's house (in the house of a friend).
    IXD and XVIA3(de)
18. <u>¿Dónde nació?</u>: Where were you born?
    Nacer: to be born.      XF
19. <u>/El/ quince /de/ septiembre /de/ mil novecientos cuarenta y dos</u>: On September 15th, 1942.      XVC(dates)
20. <u>No, pero mi esposo, sí</u>: No, but my husband does (yes).
21. <u>¿Es su marido soldado?</u>: Is your husband /a/ soldier?
    Use of <u>ser</u> for professions    XA1(ser)
    Omission of indefinite article before professions      IIB1
22. <u>¿Recibe él alguna paga /por ser/ veterano o /por/ invalidez?</u>: Does he receive any Veterans or Disability Payment (payment for being /a/ veteran or for disability)?
    IA16 & Dict(Compound Nouns)
23. <u>Al mes</u>: a (per) month.    XVIA1c(a)
24. <u>¿Hay algún otro miembro de su familia que trabaja?</u>: Does any other member of your family work?
    Literally: Is there any other member of your family who works:
    Hay: there is, is there?    XD(hay)
25. <u>Yo solía trabajar</u>: I used to work.
    Soler(ue): to do something usually, to be accustomed to do something.
    Dict(Idioms)

## TRANSLATE

1. I live at 145 West 96th Street.
2. I am looking for an apartment.
3. Are you single, married, separated, divorced or widowed?
4. Is there a bathtub or shower in your apartment?
5. I have been living here for about two years.
6. There isn't any elevator in the building.
7. Give me your present address, please.
8. Is your husband a veteran?
9. When and where were you born?
10. I used to work.

HOUSING II

COMPLAINTS

A. Heat

MISS BROWN: Come in,
(enter) please.
Take a seat.
What can I do
for you?

MRS. GÓMEZ: The
landlord does not
give us /any/ heat.

MISS BROWN: Did
you speak to (with)
him about this?

MRS. GÓMEZ: Yes,
several times, but
without result.

MISS BROWN: Does
he collect the
rent himself?

MRS. GÓMEZ: Yes.

MISS BROWN: The
first of the
month is Monday.
Speak to him again
then.

MRS. GÓMEZ: What
do we gain by that?
He always promises
but we still have
no heat.
We have /to/
wear our coats
in the house.
My son was
hospitalized with
pneumonia.

VIVIENDA II

QUEJAS

A. Calefacción

SRTA. BROWN: Entre,
por favor.
Tome un asiento.
¿En qué puedo                1
servirla?

SRA. GÓMEZ: El
casero no nos da
calefacción.

SRTA. BROWN: ¿Habló
con él de eso?

SRA. GÓMEZ: Sí,
varias veces, pero
sin resultado.

SRTA. BROWN: ¿Cobra
él mismo el alquiler?        2

SRA. GÓMEZ: Sí.

SRTA. BROWN: El
primero del mes
es lunes.
Háblele otra vez             3
entonces.

SRA. GÓMEZ: ¿Qué
ganamos con eso?
Él siempre promete
pero todavía no
tenemos calefacción.
Tenemos que llevar           4
los abrigos en
casa.
Mi hijo fue
hospitalizado con
neumonía.

MISS BROWN: The
temperature of
the house must be
68 degrees.

If not, you can
report (denounce)
the landlord to
the Health Department.

I will call your
landlord and I
will tell you
what happens.

Do you have /a/
telephone?

MRS. GÓMEZ: No,
but my neighbor,
Mrs. Goya, has a
telephone.
The number is
136-5978.

MISS BROWN: I think
that /it/ will be
possible /to/ settle
this matter with
the landlord.

B. <u>A leak in
the ceiling</u>

MISS BROWN: Next,
please

MRS. RUIZ: I have a
leak in the ceiling
and all the furniture
is getting ruined.

SRTA. BROWN: La
temperatura de la
casa debe estar
/en los/ sesenta y
ocho grados.

Si no, <u>pueden
denunciar al casero</u>   5
al Departamento de
Salubridad Pública.

<u>Llamaré /a/ su</u>   6
<u>casero</u> y le diré
/a/ usted /lo/ que
pasa.

¿Tiene Vd.
teléfono?

SRA. GÓMEZ: No,
pero mi vecina,
<u>/la/ Sra. Goya</u>,   7
tiene teléfono.
El número es uno-
tres-seis-cinco-
nueve-siete-ocho.

SRTA. BROWN: Creo
que será posible
arreglar este
asunto con el
casero.

B. <u>Una gotera en
el techo</u>

SRTA. BROWN: /El/
siguiente, por
favor.

SRA. RUIZ: Tengo
una gotera en el
techo y <u>todos los</u>   8
<u>muebles están
arruinándose.</u>

MISS BROWN: I will call the landlord to fix the leak within a week.

If he does not do it, call me.

MRS. RUIZ: Do I come back here if he does not fix it?

MISS BROWN: You can call me by phone or make an appointment to come.

MRS. RUIZ: What can we do if he does not do anything?

MISS BROWN: Then we will file (formulate) a complaint.

C. Light

MRS. RODRÍGUEZ: They cut /off/ our electric light.

MISS BROWN: Did you pay all the bills?

MRS. RODRÍGUEZ: Not during the last two months, because I had to buy clothes for the children.

MISS BROWN: Do you have the money to pay /for/ the light now?

SRTA. BROWN: Llamaré al casero para arreglar la gotera dentro /de/ una semana.

Si no lo hace, llámeme.

SRA. RUIZ: ¿Vuelvo /a/ aquí si no la arregla?

SRTA. BROWN: Puede llamarme por teléfono, o hacer una cita para venir.

SRA. RUIZ: ¿Qué podemos hacer si él no hace nada?   9

SRTA. BROWN: Entonces formularemos una queja.

C. Luz

SRA. RODRÍGUEZ: Nos cortaron las luz   10 eléctrica.

SRTA. BROWN: ¿Pagó Ud. todas las cuentas?

SRA. RODRÍGUEZ: No durante los dos   11 últimos meses porque tuve que comprar ropa para los niños.   12

SRTA. BROWN: ¿Tiene el dinero para pagar la luz ahora?   13

MRS. RODRÍGUEZ: No. I still don't have it.

MISS BROWN: Do you have the last two bills?

MRS. RODRÍGUEZ: Yes, here they are.

MISS BROWN: The Welfare Department is going to pay them now, but they will deduct the amount from your next check.

D. Fire

MRS. LÓPEZ: We had a fire in our apartment last night.

We had to abandon the house.

MISS BROWN: I am sorry. Was anyone hurt?

MRS. LÓPEZ: No, thank God. Everybody was able to leave in time.

The firemen had /to/ get the baby.

Now everything is burnt and we can't return to the apartment.

SRA. RODRÍGUEZ: No. Todavía no lo tengo.

SRTA. BROWN: ¿Tiene las dos últimas cuentas? see 11

SRA. RODRÍGUEZ: Sí. Aquí están.

SRTA. BROWN: El departamento de servicio social va a pagarlas ahora, pero deducirán el importe de su próximo cheque.

D. Fuego (Incendio)

SRA. LÓPEZ: Tuvimos un incendio en nuestro apartamento anoche. 14
Todos tuvimos /que/ abandonar la casa.

SRTA. BROWN: Lo siento. 15
¿Resultó alguien herido? 16

SRA. LÓPEZ: No, gracias /a/ Dios.
Todos pudieron salir a tiempo. 17

Los bomberos tuvieron /que/ recoger al bebé. 18

Ahora todo está quemado y no podemos regresar al apartamento. 19

| | | |
|---|---|---|
| We spent the night at my sister's house. | Pasamos la noche en /la/ casa /de/ mi hermana. | 20 |
| MISS BROWN: We are going to find /an/other apartment for you. | SRTA. BROWN: Vamos a encontrar otro apartamento para ustedes. | |
| In the meantime, you can stay (be) at the Hotel San José. | Entretanto, pueden ustedes estar en el Hotel San José. | |
| MRS. LÓPEZ: Where is /it/? | SRA. LÓPEZ: ¿Dónde está? | |
| MISS BROWN: 110 East 117th Street. | SRTA. BROWN: /En el/ ciento diez, Este /de la/ calle ciento diecisiete. | 21 |
| MRS. LÓPEZ: And my furniture? Everything was burnt. | SRA. LÓPEZ: ¿Y mis muebles? Todo se quemó. | 22 |
| MISS BROWN: You will get some money for furniture and clothing. | SRTA. BROWN: Recibirá algún dinero para muebles y ropa. | |

NOTES

1. ¿En qué puedo servirla?: What can I do for you?
   Literally: In (with) what can I serve you?
                    Dict(Idioms)

2. ¿Cobra él mismo el alquiler?: Does he collect the rent himself?
   él mismo: he, himself.
   Himself here is not a reflexive pronoun and must, therefore, be expressed by mismo.

3. Otra vez: again          XVE3(vez)

4. <u>Tenemos /que/ llevar los abrigos</u>   We have to
   wear our (the) coats.
   Tener que: to have to
   llevar ropa: to wear clothes     Dict(Idioms)
   <u>ropa</u> is always in the singular.
                     IB9(Singular Nouns)

5. <u>Pueden denunciar al casero</u>: You can report
   (denounce) the landlord.
   al casero: Use of personal <u>a</u> before a direct
   object referring to a definite person.
                     XVIA1m(Personal <u>a</u>)

6. <u>Llamaré /a/ su casero y le diré /a usted lo/</u>
   <u>que pasa</u>: I will call your landlord and will
   tell you what (that which) happens.
   a su casero: Use of personal <u>a</u>
                     XVIA1m(Personal <u>a</u>)
   a usted: this clarifies the indirect pronoun
   <u>le</u> (<u>decir</u> takes an indirect object), which
   could mean to him, to her, to you, to them.
                     XIC1(Indirect Object Pronouns)
   lo que: Use of compound relative pronoun,
   since there is no antecedent.
   cf. la palabra <u>que</u> uso: The word <u>which</u> I use.
   Le diré <u>lo que</u> dice: I will tell you <u>what</u>
   he says.       XXIIIB5(Compound Relative Pronoun)

7. <u>La Sra. Goya</u>: Mrs. Goya.
   Use of definite article with titles, except in
   direct address.
   cf. Buenos días, Sra. Goya.
                     IIB4(Use of Definite Article)

8. <u>Todos los muebles están arruinándose</u>: All the
   furniture is getting ruined.
   Spanish reflexive construction (arruinarse) -
   English use of the verb <u>to get</u>.
   Los muebles: the furniture. <u>Muebles</u> is always
   used in the plural.
                     VIID3(Use of Spanish Reflexive
                           Verb)
                     IB8(Plural Nouns)

9. <u>Si él no hace nada</u>: If he doesn't do anything.
   Use of double negative (no...nada)
                     XXB1

10. /Nos/ cortaron la luz eléctrica: They cut
    /off/ /our/ electric light.
    (They cut the electric light off for us).
    Use of indirect object pronoun (nos) in
    Spanish - possessive adjective in English
    (our).          XIC4(Indirect Object Pronouns)

11. Durante los dos últimos meses: During the
    last two months.
    Notice the word order:
    los dos ultimos meses:  The last two months.

12. Tuve que comprar ropa para los niños: I had
    to buy clothes for the children.
    Tener que:  to have to.
    Tuve:  Preterite of tener.
                    XIIB3(Preterite)
    la ropa:  the clothes.  Ropa is always used in
    the singular.   IB9(Singular Nouns)
    para los ninos:  (meant) for the children.
                    XVIA5(para)

13. ¿Tiene el dinero para pagar la luz?: Do you
    have the money to pay /for/ the light?
    pagar:  to pay, to pay for.
                    XVIC(Verbs & Prepositions)

14. Tuvimos un incendio: We had a fire.
    Tuvimos:  Preterite of tener
                    XIIB3(Preterite)

15. Lo siento:  I am sorry about it.
                    Dict(Idioms)

16. ¿Resultó alguien herido?: Was anyone hurt?
                    Dict(Idioms)

17. Todos pudieron salir a tiempo: Everybody was
    (all were) able to leave in time.
    Poder:  to be able to.  Pudieron:  Preterite
    of poder.           XIIB3(Preterite)
    a tiempo:  on time   XVIAla(Prepositions)

18. Tuvieron /que/ recoger al bebé: They had /to/
    get (pick up) the baby.
    Tuvieron:  Preterite of tener XIIB3(Preterite)
    Tener que:  to have to
    al bebé:  Use of personal a
                    XVIAlm(Personal a)

19. <u>Todo está quemado</u>: Everything is burnt.
    Use of <u>estar</u> for a condition which is the result of an action (quemar).
    XB3
20. <u>En la casa de mi hermana</u>: In my sister's house (in the house of my sister).
    XVIA3a(de)
21. <u>/En el/ ciento diez este /de la/ calle ciento diez y seis</u>: 110 East 117th Street.
    Use of cardinal numbers, (ciento diez y seis) after the number 10.
    XVB4(Cardinal Numbers)
22. <u>Todo se quemó</u>: Everything was burnt.
    Use of reflexive verb in Spanish (se quemó), passive voice in English (was burnt).
    VIID3(Reflexive Verbs)

TRANSLATE

1. What can I do for you?
2. Does the landlord collect the rent himself?
3. We still don't have any heat.
4. We have to wear our coats.
5. I will call your landlord and tell you what happens.
6. It will be possible to settle this matter.
7. The landlord has to fix the leak.
8. We will file a complaint.
9. They cut off the electric light.
10. No-one was hurt.
11. Do you have the last two bills?
12. We spent the night in my brother's house.
13. You will receive some money for furniture and clothes.

| FOOD STAMPS | SELLOS (ESTAMPILLAS) /PARA/ ALIMENTOS | |
|---|---|---|
| MR. CASTILLO: Good morning. I would like to apply /for/ food stamps. | SR. CASTILLO: Buenos días. Me gustaría solicitar estampillas /para/ alimentos. | 1 |
| CLERK: Fine. Sit down. What is your name? | EMPLEADO: Bueno. Siénte/se/. ¿Cómo se llama Vd? | 2<br>3 |
| MR. CASTILLO: My name is Hector Castillo. | SR. CASTILLO: Me llamo Hector Castillo. | 3 |
| CLERK: Are all unemployed members of your family between the ages of 18 and 65 here with you? | EMPLEADO: ¿Están todos los miembros desempleados de su familia, entre las edades de dieciocho y sesenta y cinco /años/, aquí con Vd? | 4 |
| MR. CASTILLO: No, my wife is working. She works a few hours a week and my oldest son goes to college (the university). | SR. CASTILLO: No, mi esposa está trabajando. Trabaja algunas horas /a/ la semana, y mi hijo mayor va a la universidad. | 5 |
| CLERK: What is the total net monthly income of your family? | EMPLEADO: ¿Cuál es el total neto mensual de ingresos de su familia? | 6 |
| MR. CASTILLO: I am unemployed. They are giving me sixty dollars a week. My wife works part-time. She earns about fifty dollars a week. | SR. CASTILLO: Estoy desempleado. Me dan sesenta dólares /a/ la semana. Mi esposa trabaja tiempo parcial. Gana aproximadamente cincuenta dólares /a/ la semana. | 7<br>8 |

| | |
|---|---|
| CLERK: How many are you in your family? | EMPLEADO: ¿Cuántos son Vds. en su familia? |
| MR. CASTILLO: My wife and I and 3 children.<br>My mother-in-law also lives with us. | SR. CASTILLO: Mi esposa, yo y tres niños.<br>Mi suegra también vive con nosotros. |
| CLERK: How old is your mother-in-law? | EMPLEADO: ¿Qué edad tiene su suegra?    9 |
| MR. CASTILLO: She is 72. | SR. CASTILLO: Tiene setenta y dos /años/. |
| CLERK: Do you have any assets, that is to say, savings, stocks, bonds, etc.? | EMPLEADO: ¿Tiene Ud. cualquier clase de valores, es decir, ahorros, acciones, bonos, etc.? |
| MR. CASTILLO: We have two hundred dollars in the bank and I have a government bond for (of) fifty dollars. | SR. CASTILLO: Tenemos doscientos dólares en el banco y yo tengo un bono del    10 gobierno de cincuenta dólares. |
| CLERK: Do you have your wife's pay stubs or pay envelopes? | EMPLEADO: ¿Tiene    11 Vd. los talonarios o sobres /de/ pago /de/ su esposa? |
| MR. CASTILLO: Yes, here is her last pay envelope. It is for (of) forty six dollars. However, since she does piece work, her pay varies. Sometimes she earns a little more and at other times a little less. | SR. CASTILLO: Sí, aquí está el sobre del último pago. Es de cuarenta y seis dólares. Sin embargo, dado que ella trabaja a    12 destajo, su paga varía. Algunas veces gana un poco más y otras veces un poco menos. |

| | |
|---|---|
| Here is also the bank book and the bond, and here is my unemployment card. | Aquí está también el libro /del/ banco y el bono, y aquí está mi tarjeta /de/ desempleo. |
| | 13 |
| | 14 |
| CLERK: Do you have last month's electric, gas and telephone bills? | EMPLEADO: ¿Tiene Vd. las cuentas /de/ electricidad, gas y teléfono del último mes? |
| | 15 |
| MR. CASTILLO: Yes, I have them all. | SR. CASTILLO: Sí, las tengo todas. |
| | 16 |
| CLERK: Have you had any medical expenses recently? | EMPLEADO: ¿Ha tenido Vd. algunos gastos médicos recientemente? |
| MR. CASTILLO: I belong to HIP. I don't have /any/ medical expenses but I had to pay thirty dollars for some fillings for (of) my daughter, Lourdes. Here is the bill for that. | SR. CASTILLO: Pertenezco al HIP. No tengo gastos médicos pero tuve que pagar treinta dólares por algunos empastes de mi hija Lourdes. Aquí está la cuenta de eso. |
| | 17 |
| | 18 |
| CLERK: How old are your children? | EMPLEADO: ¿Qué edades tienen sus hijos? |
| MR. CASTILLO: Ten, twelve and eighteen. | SR. CASTILLO: Diez, doce y dieciocho. |
| CLERK: Does the eighteen year old work or does he attend school? | EMPLEADO: ¿Trabaja el /de/ dieciocho años o asiste /a/ la escuela? |
| | 19 |
| | 20 |
| MR. CASTILLO: He attends classes at Staten Island Community College. | SR. CASTILLO: El asiste /a/ clases en Staten Island Community College. |

147

CLERK: Does he pay anything there?

MR. CASTILLO: Forty eight dollars per semester. Here is the receipt.

CLERK: Does he get any financial aid?

MR. CASTILLO: No.

CLERK: Did he work /at/ any time?

MR. CASTILLO: Yes, he worked last summer in a department store.

CLERK: Please give me the social security numbers of everyone in the family.

MR. CASTILLO: Mine is 069-48-4976.

My wife's is 780-56-8643.

and Carlos' is 654-97-865.

My mother-in-law never worked here.

EMPLEADO: ¿Paga él algo allí?

SR. CASTILLO: Cuarenta y ocho dólares por semestre. Aquí está el recibo.

EMPLEADO: ¿Recibe él alguna <u>ayuda</u> económica?      21

SR. CASTILLO: No.

EMPLEADO: ¿<u>Trabajó</u>      22
<u>él alguna vez</u>?

SR. CASTILLO: Sí, el trabajó el verano pasado en un almacén.

EMPLEADO: Por favor, déme <u>los números del</u>      23
<u>Seguro Social de</u>
<u>cada uno de la</u>
<u>familia</u>.

SR. CASTILLO: <u>El</u>
<u>mío</u> es cero-sesenta      24
y nueve-cuarenta y ocho-cuarenta y nueve setenta y seis.

<u>El de mi esposa</u> es      24
siete-ocho-cero-
cincuenta y seis-
ochenta y seis-
cuarenta y tres,
y <u>el de Carlos</u> es      24
seis-cincuenta y cuatro-noventa y siete-ocho-sesenta y cinco.

Mi suegra nunca trabajó aquí.

| | |
|---|---|
| CLERK: You will receive by mail an authorization to purchase food stamps. | EMPLEADO: Ud. recibirá por correo una autorización para comprar estampillas /para/ alimentos. |
| You can get the stamps at most banks. | Ud. puede obtener las estampillas en <u>la major parte de los bancos</u>.    25 |
| MR. CASTILLO: How much will I have? | SR. CASTILLO: ¿<u>Cuánto tendré</u>?    26 |
| CLERK: I cannot tell (it to) you right now but we will notify you as soon as (it is) possible. | EMPLEADO: <u>No se lo puedo decir</u> ahora mismo pero <u>le notificaremos</u> tan <u>pronto como sea posible</u>.    27<br><br>   28 |

                    NOTES

1. <u>Me gustaría solicitar estampillas /para/ alimentos</u>: I would like to apply /for/ food stamps.
    Me gustaría: I would like to. Use of Conditional for politeness.
                    XIJ(gustar)
                    XIVB1(Conditional)
    estampillas /para/ alimentos: food stamps
                    IA16 (Compound Nouns)
    solicitar: to apply for
                    XVIC(Verbs & Prepositions)

2. <u>Siénte/se/</u>: Sit down.
    sentarse: to sit down.
                    VIIE(Reflexive Const.)
                    VIA4(Command Forms)

3. ¿Cómo /se/ llama?: What is your name?
   Llamarse: to be called.
   Literally: to call oneself.
                        VIIE(Reflexive Constructions)
4. ¿Están todos los miembros desempleados de su familia...aquí?: Are all the unemployed members of your family here?
   Use of estar for location.  XB2(estar)
5. Mi esposa está trabajando: My wife is working.
   Use of estar with the present participle of the main verb to form the progressive tense (in the midst of).  XVIIB1 & 2(Progr.) & XB3(estar)
6. ¿Cuál es el total...de ingresos?: What is the total income?
   ¿Cuál? Is used to translate what? before the verb to be, except when a definition is called for.  VC3b(¿Cuál?)
7. Estoy desempleado: I am unemployed.
   Use of estar for what is (hopefully) a temporary condition.  XB1(estar)
8. Sesenta dólares /a/ la semana: Sixty dollars a week.
9. ¿Qué edad tiene su suegra?: How old is (what is the age of) your mother-in-law?
   Use of tener for age.  XE1(tener)
10. Un bono del gobierno: a government bond.
                        IA16 and Dict(Compound Nouns)
11. ¿Tiene Vd. los talonarios o sobres /de/ pago de su esposa?: Do you have your wife's stubs or pay envelopes (the pay stubs of your wife)? The possessive in Spanish is expressed by the preposition de.  XVIA3a(de) and IXD(de)
12. Ella trabaja a destajo: She does piece work.
                        Dict(Idioms)
13. El libro /del/ banco: The bank book.
                        IA16 and Dict(Compound Nouns)
14. La tarjeta /de/ desempleo: The unemployment card.  IA16 and Dict(Compound Nouns)

15. <u>Las cuentas /de/ electricidad, gas y teléfono
    del último mes</u>: Last month's electric, gas
    and telephone bills (the bills <u>of</u> last month).
                          IA16 and Dict(Compound Nouns)

16. <u>Las tengo todas</u>: I have them all.
    <u>Las</u> refers to <u>las cuentas</u>.
                              XIB4(Object Pronouns)
    <u>Todas</u> is an adjective and, therefore, has to
    agree with the noun (las cuentas).
                            VIIIB5(todos)

17. <u>Pertenezco al HIP</u>: I belong to (the) HIP
    (Health Insurance Plan).
    Pertenecer a: to belong to.
                        XVIA1a(Verbs and Prepositions)
    In the <u>yo</u> form the <u>c</u> changes to <u>zc</u>
    cf. conocer.       IIIB1c(Present Tense)

18. <u>No tengo gastos médicos</u>: I don't have /any/
    medical expenses.    XXB1(Double Negative)

19. <u>¿Trabaja /el de/ dieciocho años?</u>: Does the
    18 year old (the one who is 18) work?

20. <u>Asiste a la escuela</u>: He attends school.
    Asistir a la escuela: to attend school.
                              Dict(Idioms)

21. <u>Ayuda económica</u>: Financial (economic) aid.

22. <u>¿Trabajó él alguna vez?</u>: Did he work at any
    time?
    alguna vez: any time, some time.
                          XVE3(vez)

23. <u>Los números del Seguro Social de cada uno de
    la familia</u>: The social security numbers of
    everyone in the family.
    El número del seguro social: the social
    security number. IA16 & Dict(Compound Nouns)
    cada uno: each one, every one.

24. <u>El mío,...el /de/ mi esposa...el /de/ Carlos</u>:
    El mío: mine. Possessive pronoun
                        IXB(Possessive Pronouns)
    El /de/ mi esposa...el /de/ Carlos: my wife's
    and Carlos'.
    Literally: the one of my wife and the one of
    Carlos.       IXD & XVIA3a(<u>de</u> for possessive)

25. **La mayor parte de los bancos:** Most (the greatest part of the) banks.   Dict(Idioms)

26. **¿Cuánto tendré?:** How much will I have?
    **tendré:** Future of **tener**. XIVAb(Future)

27. **No se lo puedo decir:** I cannot tell (it to) you.
    **It** (lo) is the direct object. **To you** is the indirect object. When the indirect object pronoun (le) is followed by another pronoun of the third person (lo), it changes to **se**.
    The indirect object precedes the direct object.
    XIF(Pos. of Object Pronouns)

28. **Le notificaremos tan pronto como sea posible:** We will notify you as soon as (it is) possible.
    **Sea:** is the subjunctive of **ser**.
    XXVA1h(Subjunctive Forms)
    Use of Subjunctive (sea) after the conjunction **tan pronto como**, when future time is implied.
    XXVD1d(Subjunctive after conjunctions)

## TRANSLATE

1. I would like to apply for food stamps.
2. What is the total net monthly income of your family?
3. How old is your father-in-law?
4. Do you have any government bonds?
5. Show me your unemployment card, please.
6. Do you have last month's electric, gas and telephone bills?
7. Did you ever work?
8. My daughter attends school.
9. We belong to HIP.
10. What is your social security number?
11. You can get food stamps at most banks.

UNEMPLOYMENT INSURANCE	SEGURO DE DESEMPLEO

MR. JIMÉNEZ: I am out of work and I want to apply /for/ Unemployment Insurance benefits.

SR. JIMÉNEZ: <u>Estoy sin trabajo y quiero solicitar beneficios</u> /del/ seguro /de/ desempleo.   1  2

CLERK: Did you leave your work or were you dismissed?

DEPENDIENTE: Dejó Vd. su trabajo o <u>le despidieron</u>?   3

MR. JIMÉNEZ: They dismissed everybody.

SR. JIMÉNEZ: <u>Despidieron /a/ todos</u>.   4

CLERK: For whom did you work?

DEPENDIENTE: <u>Para quién trabajó Vd</u>?   5

MR. JIMÉNEZ: For ABC Construction Company.

SR. JIMÉNEZ: Para /la/ ABC Construction Company.

CLERK: What is their address?

DEPENDIENTE: <u>Cuál es su dirección</u>?   6

MR. JIMÉNEZ: 864-8th Avenue, New York City.

SR. JIMÉNEZ: Ochocientos sesenta y cuatro /de la/ octava avenida /en/ New York City.

CLERK: How long did you work for this firm?

DEPENDIENTE: Cuánto tiempo trabajó Vd. para esta firma?

MR. JIMÉNEZ: Three years.

SR. JIMÉNEZ: Tres años.

CLERK: How much did you earn on the average?

DEPENDIENTE: Cuánto ganó <u>de promedio</u>?   7

MR. JIMÉNEZ: I earned $150 /a/ week and a little more when there was overtime.

SR. JIMÉNEZ: Gané ciento cincuenta dólares /a la/ semana y un poco más <u>cuando había horas extra</u>.   8

| | |
|---|---|
| CLERK: Have you /ever/ collected unemployment insurance before? | DEPENDIENTE: ¿Ha cobrado Vd. seguro /de/ desempleo antes? |
| MR. JIMÉNEZ: Yes, when I was out of work 4 years ago. | SR. JIMÉNEZ: Sí, cuando <u>estuve sin trabajo hace cuatro años</u>.   9 |
| CLERK: Do you have your social security card, your unemployment insurance book, your claim card, and the calendar insert? | DEPENDIENTE: ¿Tiene su tarjeta /de/ seguro social, su libro /del/ seguro de desempleo su tarjeta /de/ reclamación y el calendario-adjunto? |
| MR. JIMÉNEZ: Here they are. | SR. JIMÉNEZ: Aquí están. |
| CLERK: When was the last day on which you worked? | DEPENDIENTE: ¿Cuándo fue el último día en que trabajó Vd? |
| MR. JIMÉNEZ: Last Friday. | SR. JIMÉNEZ: /El/ viernes pasado. |
| CLERK: Are you ready, willing and able to work? | DEPENDIENTE: <u>¿Está listo, deseoso y capacitado para trabajar</u>?   10 |
| MR. JIMÉNEZ: Yes, I am. | SR. JIMÉNEZ: Sí, /lo/ estoy. |
| CLERK: You will not receive any benefit(s) for the first week of unemployment. | DEPENDIENTE: <u>Vd. no recibirá ningún beneficio</u> por la primera semana de desempleo.   11 |

MR. JIMÉNEZ: How much
am I going to receive
in unemployment
benefits?

SR. JIMÉNEZ: ¿Cuánto
voy a obtener
de beneficios /de/
desempleo?

CLERK: Your
weekly payments
are generally
about half of
your average
weekly salary
during the past
fifty two
weeks.
The maximum you can
get is
$95

per week.

DEPENDIENTE: Sus
pagos semanales
son generalmente
<u>cerca /de la/ mitad</u>   12
<u>del promedio</u> de su
sueldo semanal
durante las pasadas
cincuenta y dos
semanas.
El máximo que puede
obtener es /de/
noventa y cinco
dólares
por semana.

MR. JIMÉNEZ: For
how long can I
get the
benefits?

SR. JIMÉNEZ: ¿<u>Por</u>   13
<u>cuánto tiempo</u> puedo
obtener los
beneficios?

CLERK: The
regular period
is twenty six
weeks, but
it can be extended
for another thirteen
weeks.

DEPENDIENTE: El
período regular
es /de/ veintiséis
semanas, <u>pero</u>   14
<u>puede alargarse</u>
por otras trece
semanas.

MR. JIMÉNEZ: What
happens if I get
some work
during this time?

SR. JIMÉNEZ: ¿Qué
pasa si yo obtengo
cualquier trabajo
durante este tiempo?

| | |
|---|---|
| CLERK:  If you work one day, you will receive three quarters of your weekly payment. If you work two days, you will receive half the pay and if you work three days, a quarter. | DEPENDIENTE: Si Vd. trabaja un día recibirá tres cuartos de su pago semanal. Si trabaja dos días, recibirá /la/ mitad del pago, y si trabaja tres días, un cuarto. |
| You cannot earn more than ninety five dollars and you must be available to work the rest of the days of the week. | No puede ganar <u>más de noventa y cinco dolares</u> y tiene que estar estar disponible para trabajar el resto de los días de la semana.   15 |
| MR. JIMÉNEZ:  How do I get my checks? | SR. JIMÉNEZ: ¿Cómo obtengo mis cheques? |
| CLERK:  They will be sent to you by mail. | DEPENDIENTE:  <u>Le serán mandados</u> por correo.   16 |
| MR. JIMÉNEZ:  When am I going to get my first check? | SR. JIMÉNEZ: ¿Cuándo voy a recibir mi primer cheque? |
| CLERK:  You will receive your first check in three or four weeks. | DEPENDIENTE: Recibirá su primer cheque en tres o cuatro semanas. |
| MR. JIMÉNEZ:  Why am I not going to receive a check for the first week? | SR. JIMÉNEZ: ¿Por qué no voy a recibir un cheque por la primera semana? |

CLERK: The
week in which
you initiate your
claim is
considered a
waiting period.

Your first check
will be for the
second week.

You sign for it
in the third
week and you get it
by mail a
week later.

After this,
if your claim
is in order,
you will receive
your checks weekly.

## WEEKLY REPORT

CLERK: Good
morning.
You are here
for your weekly
report.

Have you had any
work including
work for your
own account
during this week?

MR. JIMÉNEZ: No,
I couldn't find
any work.

DEPENDIENTE: La
semana en que
inicia su
reclamación <u>se</u>       17
<u>considera un período</u>
<u>/de/ espera</u>.

Su primer cheque
será por la
segunda semana.

Vd. firma por él
en la tercera
semana y lo recibe
por correo una
semana más tarde.

Después de esto,
si su reclamación
está en orden,
recibirá sus cheques
semanalmente.

## REPORTE SEMANAL

DEPENDIENTE: Buenos
días.
Vd. está aquí
para su reporte
semanal.

¿Ha tenido algún
trabajo incluyendo
trabajo por su
propia cuenta
durante esta semana?

SR. JIMÉNEZ: No,
no pude encontrar
ningún trabajo.

CLERK: Were you ready, willing and able to work every day during the week for which you are applying /for/ benefits?

DEPENDIENTE: ¿Estuvo Vd. listo, deseoso, y capaz de trabajar cada día durante la semana para la cual solicita beneficios? 18

MR. JIMÉNEZ: Yes.

SR. JIMÉNEZ: Sí.

CLERK: Have you received any job offer?

DEPENDIENTE: ¿Ha recibido alguna oferta /de/ trabajo? 19

MR. JIMÉNEZ: No, I have not received any.

SR. JIMÉNEZ: No, no he recibido ninguna.

CLERK: Have you claimed benefits from any other state or federal unemployment law for this week?

DEPENDIENTE: ¿Ha reclamado beneficios de alguna otra ley estatal del seguro /contra/ desempleo por esta semana?

MR. JIMÉNEZ: No.

SR. JIMÉNEZ: No.

CLERK: Sign here, please.

DEPENDIENTE: Firme aquí, por favor.

Any person who gives false information or abstains from giving any information, in order to be able to collect unemployment insurance may lose up to twenty weeks of benefits.

Cualquier persona que dé información falsa o se abstenga de dar cualquier información, para poder cobrar el seguro contra desempleo puede perder hasta veinte semanas de beneficios. 20

| | | |
|---|---|---|
| Any person | Cualquier persona | see 20 |
| who receives payments | que reciba pagos | |
| as a result | como resultado | |
| of such | de tal | |
| false information, | información falsa | |
| must return | tiene que devolver | 21 |
| all the money collected | todo el dinero | |
| and may receive | y puede recibir | |
| a fine of | una multa de | |
| up to | hasta | |
| five hundred dollars | quinientos dólares | |
| or be sent | o ser enviado | 22 |
| to jail | a /la/ cárcel | |
| for a year | por un año | |
| or both | o ambas /cosas/ | 23 |
| at the same time. | a la vez. | |

## NOTES

1. **Estoy sin trabajo**: I am out of work (without work).
   Use of **estar** for what is (he hopes) a temporary condition. XB1(estar)

2. **Quiero solicitar beneficios /del/ seguro /de/ desempleo**: I want to apply /for/ Unemployment Insurance Benefits.
   solicitar: to apply for
                           XVIC(Verbs & Prepositions)
   beneficios /del/ seguro /de/ desempleo:
   Unemployment Insurance Benefits.
                      IA16 and
                      Dict(Compound Nouns)

3. ¿Le despidieron?: Were you dismissed? Did they dismiss you?
Spanish often avoids use of Passive Voice by substituting an active construction.
Despedir (to dismiss) is a stem changing verb.
      XXIVA2(Substitute for Passive Voice)
      XIIB2b(Preterite of stem changing verbs)

4. Despidieron /a/ todos: They dismissed everybody.
Use of personal a before a pronoun referring to persons (todos)  XVIA1m(Personal a)

5. ¿Para quién trabajó Vd.?: For whom did you work?
trabajar para: to work for.
      XVIA6f(para)

6. ¿Cuál es su dirección?: What is your address?
Use of ¿cuál? for what? before the verb ser.   VC3b(¿cuál?)

7. De promedio: on /the/ average. Dict(Idioms)

8. Cuando había horas extra: When there was (used to be) overtime (extra hours).
Había is the Imperfect Tense of hay (there is)
      XD(hay)
      XIIIB2(Use of Imperfect Tense)

9. Estuve sin trabajo hace cuatro años: I was out of work (without work) four years ago.
Use of Preterite Tense for a past action at a definite time (hace cuatro años).
Estuve: Preterite Tense of estar
      XIIB1a(Preterite of estar)
Hace cuatro años: Four years ago.
      XVG2(hace with Preterite Tense)

10. ¿Está listo, deseoso y capacitado para trabajar?: Are you ready, willing and able to work?
Use of estar to express a condition.
      XB1(estar)

11. <u>Vd. no recibirá ningún beneficio</u>: You will not receive any benefit(s).
    No...ningún: not any. Use of double negative.
    XXB1(Double Negative)

12. <u>Cerca /de la/ mitad del promedio</u>: About half of the average.

13. <u>¿Por cuánto tiempo?</u>: For how long (how much time)?

14. <u>Puede alargarse</u>: It can be extended.
    Use of reflexive construction in Spanish in lieu of English passive voice.
    VIID3(Reflexive for Passive)

15. <u>Más de noventa /y/ cinco dólares</u>: More than $95.
    Use of <u>de</u> to translate <u>than</u> before a numeral.
    XVIA3e(de)

16. <u>Le serán mandados</u>: They will be sent to you.
    Use of <u>ser</u> for passive voice.
    XXIVB(Passive Voice)
    Serán: Future tense of <u>ser</u>.
    XIVA1a(Future Tense)

17. <u>Se considera un período /de/ espera</u>: It is considered a waiting period.
    Use of reflexive construction (se considera) in lieu of English passive voice.
    VIID3(Reflexive for Passive)
    Un período /de/ espera: a waiting period.
    IA16 & Dict(Compound Nouns)

18. <u>La semana para la cual solicita beneficios</u>: The week for which you are applying for benefits.
    la cual: Relative pronoun used after a preposition.      XXIIIB5(la cual, etc.)
    solicitar: to apply for
    XVIC(Verbs & Prepositions)
    Use of present tense in Spanish, progressive form in English. Spanish uses the progressive form much less than English.
    IIIB2a(note) &
    XVIIC2b(Present Tense for Progressive Construction)

19. **Alguna oferta /de/ trabajo**: Any job offer (offer of work).
    IA16 & Dict(Compound Nouns)
20. **Cualquier persona que dé... o se abstenga de...**: Any person who gives (may give)...or abstains (may abstain) from...
    Use of Subjunctive because **cualquier persona** is indefinite.    XXVD1f(Use of Subjunctive)
21. **Tiene que devolver el dinero**: He has to return the money.
    devolver(ue): to return (something)
    cf. volver(ue): to return, to come back.
22. **ser enviado a /la/ cárcel**: To be sent to jail.
    Use of **ser** for passive voice.
    XXIVB(Passive Voice)
23. **ambas /cosas/ a la vez**: Both (things) at the same time.
    XVE3(vez) & Dict(Idioms)

## TRANSLATE

1. I want to apply for Unemployment Insurance Benefits.
2. I was dismissed.
3. How much did you earn on the average?
4. I was out of work three years ago.
5. Are you ready, willing and able to work?
6. The checks will be sent to you by mail.
7. The first week is a waiting period.
8. Did you get any job offer?
9. Sign here, please.
10. For whom did you work?

| WORKMEN'S COMPENSATION | COMPENSACIÓN OBRERA | |
|---|---|---|
| MRS. PACE: What type (class) of work do you do? | SRA. PACE: ¿Qué clase de trabajo hace usted? | |
| MR. RIVERA: I am /a/ welder. | SR. RIVERA: <u>Soy soldador</u>. | 1 |
| MRS. PACE: What were you doing when you were injured? | SRA. PACE: ¿Qué <u>estaba haciendo usted cuando /se/ hirió</u>? | 2 |
| MR. RIVERA: I was soldering a piece of metal. | SR. RIVERA: Estaba soldando una pieza de metal. | |
| MRS. PACE: How much do you earn on /the/ average per day or week? | SRA. PACE: ¿<u>Cuánto gana usted de promedio por día o /por/ semana</u>? | 3 |
| MR. RIVERA: About /a/ hundred /and/ fifty dòllars per week. | SR. RIVERA: <u>Unos ciento cincuenta dólares por semana</u>. | 4 |
| MRS. PACE: When did the accident occur? | SRA. PACE: ¿Cuándo ocurrió el accidente? | |
| MR. RIVERA: Last (past) Wednesday, May 15th. | SR. RIVERA: <u>/El/ miércoles pasado, /el/ quince /de/ mayo</u>. | 5 |
| MRS. PACE: Did they pay you /for/ the whole day on which you were injured? | SRA. PACE: ¿<u>Le pagaron completo el día en que resultó herido</u>? | 6 |
| MR. RIVERA: Yes. | SR. RIVERA: Sí. | |

MRS. PACE: What is the name and address of your employer?

MR. RIVERA: Ace Welding Company, 160 East, Tenth Street, New York City.

MRS. PACE: What is the name of your foreman?

MR. RIVERA: John O'Neil.

MRS. PACE: Have you returned to (the) work?

MR. RIVERA: No, the doctor says that I can't work until next week.

MRS. PACE: Did you do any other work during the period of disability?

MR. RIVERA: No. Until today I could not get /out/ of bed.

MRS. PACE: Did you receive any wages since you were injured?

MR. RIVERA: No, I did not receive anything and I have to pay the rent this week.

SRA. PACE: ¿Cuál es el nombre y la dirección de su patrono?   7

SR. RIVERA: Ace Welding Company, Ciento sesenta Este, calle diez, Nueva York.

SRA. PACE: ¿Cuál es el nombre de su capataz?

SR. RIVERA: John O'Neil.

SRA. PACE: ¿Ha regresado Vd. al trabajo?

SR. RIVERA: No, el doctor dice que no puedo trabajar hasta   8 la semana que viene.

SRA. PACE: ¿Hizo usted algún otro trabajo durante el período de invalidez?

SR. RIVERA: No. Hasta hoy no pude   9 levantar/me de la/ cama.

SR. PACE: ¿Recibió usted algún sueldo desde /que/ resultó herido?

SR. RIVERA: No, no recibí nada y tengo   10 que pagar el alquiler esta semana.

MRS. PACE: Are you under medical treatment?

MR. RIVERA: Yes.

MRS. PACE: What is the name and address of the physician who treats you?

MR. RIVERA: Dr. Greene. His address is 235 Sixth Avenue.

MRS. PACE: Did you receive any Workmen's Compensation Benefits?

MR. RIVERA: No. I came here for that.

MRS. PACE: Please, fill /out/ this application.

MR. RIVERA: Are they going to pay the doctor's bills?

MRS. PACE: Yes. If you present the bills, your employer or your employer's insurance company, will pay /for/ them.

MR. RIVERA: I had to take a taxi to go to the doctor's office. Are they going to pay /for/ that?

SRA. PACE: ¿Está usted bajo trata- miento médico?

SR. RIVERA: Sí.

SRA. PACE: ¿Cuál es el nombre y la dirección del médico que le trata?    see 7

SR. RIVERA: Dr. Greene. Su dirección es dos- cientos treinta /y/ cinco /de la/ Sexta Avenida.

SRA. PACE: ¿Recibió usted cualquier beneficio de Compensación Obrera?

SR. RIVERA: No. Vine aquí por eso.

SRA. PACE: Por favor, llene esta solicitud.    11

SR. RIVERA: ¿Van a pagar las cuentas del médico?    12

SRA. PACE: Sí. Si usted presenta las cuentas, su patrono o el seguro /de/ su patrono, las pagará.    13

SR. RIVERA: Tuve que tomar un taxi para ir a la consulta del médico.    14
¿Van a pagar eso?

| | |
|---|---|
| MRS. PACE: Yes. | SRA. PACE: Sí. |
| MR. RIVERA: How much will they pay me for compensation? | SR. RIVERA: ¿Cuánto me pagarán por compensación? |
| MRS. PACE: I cannot tell (it to) you exactly. The limit is two-thirds of your weekly wage. | SRA. PACE: No puedo decírselo exactamente. El límite es dos tercios de su paga semanal.　　15 |

NOTES

1. Soy soldador: I am /a/ welder.
   No article is used before professions, except when they are modified.
   cf. Soy un buen soldador.
   　　　　　　　　IIB1(Omission of Indefinite
   　　　　　　　　　　　Article)
2. ¿Qué estaba haciendo cuando se hirió?: What were you doing when you were injured (hurt)? Here Spanish, like English, uses the Progressive Form, which is formed with the verb estar plus the present participle of the main verb. The Progressive Form is used because the meaning is: What were you in the midst of doing?
   　　　　　　　　XVIIB1(Formation of
   　　　　　　　　　　　Progressive Form)
   　　　　　　　　XVIIB2d(Use of Past
   　　　　　　　　　　　Progressive)
   se hirió: you were injured. Use of Preterite Tense for an action which happened at a particular time. XIIA(Use of Preterite Tense) herir (to wound) is a stem changing verb.
   　　　　　　　　XIIB2b(Preterite of Stem
   　　　　　　　　　　　Changing Verbs)
   A reflexive construction is used in Spanish (se hirió), the passive voice (you were hurt) in English.　　　VIID3(Reflex. Const. in Span.,
   　　　　　　　　passive voice in English)

3. ¿Cuánto gana de promedio por día o por semana?: How much do you earn on the average per day or per week?
de promedio: on the average.
           XVIA3h & Dict(Idioms)
por día (semana): per day (week)
           XVIA7h(por)

4. Unos ciento cincuenta dólares por semana: About /a/ hundred /and/ fifty dollars per week.

5. /El/ miércoles pasado, /el/ quince /de/ mayo: Last Wednesday, May 15th.
           XVC(dates)

6. ¿Le pagaron completo el día en que resultó herido?: Did they pay you /for/ the whole day on which you were injured?
Literally: Did they pay you completely for the day...
pagar: to pay, to pay for.
           XVIC(Verbs and Prepositions)
resultar (ser) herido: to be injured.
           Dict(Idioms)

7. ¿Cuál es el nombre de su patrono?: What is your employer's name?
Use of ¿cuál? to translate what? when followed by ser. VC3b(¿Cuál?)
Use of de in lieu of the English possessive ('s)
           XVIA3a &
           IXD(de for possessive)

8. No puedo trabajar hasta la semana que viene: I can't work until next week (the week which is coming). Dict(Idioms)

9. No pude levantar/me de la/ cama: I could not get /out/ of (from the) bed.
Levantar/se/: to get up
           VIIE(Reflexive Construction)
cf. levantar algo: to lift something.
Pude: Preterite Tense of poder
           XIIB3a(Preterite of poder)

10. <u>No recibí nada</u>: I did not receive anything. Use of double negative unless the negative word begins the sentence.
     XXBI(Double Negative)

11. <u>Llene esta solicitud</u>: Fill /out/ this application.
    llenar: to fill, to fill out.
     XVIC(Verbs and Prepositions)

12. <u>¿Van a pagar las cuentas del médico?</u>: Are they going to pay /for/ the doctor's bills?
    pagar: to pay, to pay for
     XVIC(Verbs and Prepositions)
    las cuentas /del/ médico: the doctor's bills.
    Use of <u>de</u> in lieu of English possessive ('s).
     XVIA3a & IXD(<u>de</u>)

13. <u>El seguro /de/ su patrono</u>: Your employer's insurance.
    Use of <u>de</u> in lieu of English possessive ('s).
     XVIA3a & IXD(<u>de</u>)

14. <u>Para ir a la consulta del médico</u>: (In order) to go to the doctor's office (the office of the doctor).
    Para: in order to.
     XVIA6a(Para)
    la consulta /del/ médico: the doctor's office.
    Use of <u>de</u> (see No. 13)
     Dict(Compound Nouns)

15. <u>No puedo decírselo</u>: I cannot tell (it to) you. The direct object of decir is what one is saying (lo). The person to whom one says something is the indirect object. Where there are two object pronouns of the third person, i.e. both beginning with <u>l</u>, the indirect object pronoun changes from <u>le</u> or <u>les</u> to <u>se</u>.
     XIG(Double Object Pronouns)
    Object pronouns are attached to the infinitive. When two object pronouns are added to the infinitive, a written accent mark must be placed on the last syllable of the infinitive, in order to maintain the original stress.
     XIF(Pos. of Object Pronouns)

TRANSLATE

1. What were you doing when you were injured?
2. How much do you earn per week (month)?
3. Are they going to pay me for the whole day?
4. I can't work until next month.
5. I could not get out of bed.
6. Please, fill out this application.

| BANKING | BANCO | |
|---|---|---|
| MISS GONZÁLEZ: Good morning. Are you the teller? | SRTA. GONZÁLEZ: Buenos días. ¿Es Vd. el cajero? | |
| MR. BROWN: No, madam. The tellers are over there. What can I do for you? | SR. BROWN: No, señora. Los cajeros están allá. ¿En qué puedo servirla? | 1 |
| MISS GONZÁLEZ: I want to cash this check, please. | SRTA. GONZÁLEZ: Quiero cambiar este cheque, por favor. | |
| MR. BROWN: Excuse me, madam, but without an account in our bank, we cannot change your check. | SR. BROWN: Dispénseme, señora, pero sin una cuenta en nuestro banco, no podemos cambiar su cheque. | |
| MISS GONZÁLEZ: Oh, what /a/ pity. It is already nearly three. | SRTA. GONZÁLEZ: ¡Ay! ¡Qué lástima! Ya son casi las tres. | 2 |
| MISS BROWN: I am sorry, madam. But, (just) a moment. Why don't you open an account in our bank today? | SRTA. BROWN: Lo siento, señora. Pero, un momento. ¿Por qué no abre Vd. una cuenta en nuestro banco hoy /mismo/? | 3 |
| MISS GONZÁLEZ: Is /it/ easy? | SRTA. GONZÁLEZ: ¿Es fácil? | |
| MR. BROWN: Of course. Sit /down/ please. Well. What kind of account do you prefer? | SR. BROWN: Por supuesto. Siénte/se/, por favor. Bueno. ¿Qué clase de cuenta prefiere Vd? | 4 5 6 |

MISS GONZÁLEZ: What kind of accounts do you have?

MR. BROWN: Well, we have different kinds.
The two most popular /ones/ are savings accounts and checking accounts.

MISS GONZÁLEZ: What is the difference?

MR. BROWN: On (with) a savings account, we pay you interest of nearly 6% per year.

MISS GONZÁLEZ: Interest? Six percent?

MR. BROWN: Yes. And at the /same/ time, you save your money for purchases or for going on vacation.

MISS GONZÁLEZ:* I like vacations.

MR. BROWN: The other /one/ is a checking account. With this account you receive checks for ordinary purchases.

SRTA. GONZÁLEZ: ¿Qué tipo de cuentas tienen Vds?

SR. BROWN: Bueno, tenemos varias clases.
Las dos más populares son /las/ cuentas /de/ ahorros    7
y /las/ cuentas corrientes.

SRTA. GONZÁLEZ: ¿Cuál es la diferencia?

SR. BROWN: Con una cuenta de ahorros, le pagamos interés de casi seis por    8
ciento al año.

SRTA. GONZÁLEZ: ¿Interés? ¿Seis por ciento, eh?

SR. BROWN: Sí.
Y a la vez    9
Vd. ahorra su dinero para /hacer/ compras o para ir de vacaciones.

SRTA. GONZÁLEZ: Me gustan /las/    10
vacaciones.

SR. BROWN: La otra es una cuenta corriente. Con esta cuenta recibe cheques para /hacer/ compras ordinarias.

171

MISS GONZÁLEZ: Does a checking account produce interest?

MR. BROWN: Unfortunately not.

MISS GONZÁLEZ: Do I have to pay anything for this service?

MR. BROWN: Every check costs you ten cents. We also charge you fifty cents extra per month.

MISS GONZÁLEZ: With a savings account, I can save my money, and with a checking account I can pay by check my ordinary purchases, is that so?

MR. BROWN: Yes, that's it.

MISS GONZÁLEZ: Then I think that it is worthwhile to have both kinds of accounts.

MR. BROWN: Many people do that. Do you want to open them right now?

MISS GONZÁLEZ: Yes, please.

SRTA. GONZÁLEZ: ¿Produce interés una cuenta corriente?

SR. BROWN: Desgraciadamente, no.

SRTA. GONZÁLEZ: ¿Debo pagar algo por este servicio?

SR. BROWN: Cada cheque le cuesta diez centavos. También le cobramos cincuenta centavos extra al mes.

11
12

SRTA. GONZÁLEZ:¿Con una cuenta /de/ ahorros, puedo ahorrar mi dinero, y con una cuenta corriente, puedo pagar con cheque mis compras ordinarias, ¿verdad?

SR. BROWN: Sí, eso es.

13

SRTA. GONZÁLEZ: Entonces creo que vale la pena tener las dos clases de cuenta.

14

SR. BROWN: Muchas personas hacen eso. ¿Quiere Vd. abrirlas ahora mismo?

SRTA. GONZÁLEZ: Sí, por favor.

MR. BROWN: We are going to fill /out/ these cards in order to open your accounts.

What is your name?

MISS GONZÁLEZ: Rosa González.

MR. BROWN: Your address, please.

MISS GONZÁLEZ: 88 West 75th Street.

MR. BROWN: What is your husband's name?

MISS GONZÁLEZ: I don't have (one). I am single.

MR. BROWN: Your telephone number?

MISS GONZÁLEZ: 981-5303.

MR. BROWN: What kind of work do you do?

MISS GONZÁLEZ: I work in an office.

That is, I am /a/ secretary.

MR. BROWN. Where do you work?

SR. BROWN: Vamos a llenar estas tarjetas para abrir sus cuentas.

¿Cómo se llama Vd?   15

SRTA. GONZÁLEZ: Rosa González.

SR. BROWN: Su dirección, por favor.

SRTA. GONZÁLEZ: Ochenta y ocho, calle setenta y cinco, oeste.

SR. BROWN: ¿Cómo se llama su esposo?   15

SRTA. GONZÁLEZ: No tengo. Soy soltera.

SR. BROWN: ¿Su número /de/ teléfono?

SRTA. GONZÁLEZ: Nueve, ochenta y uno, cincuenta y tres, cero, tres.

SR. BROWN: ¿En qué trabaja Vd?   16

SRTA. GONZÁLEZ: Trabajo en una oficina.
Es decir, soy   17
secretaria.

SR. BROWN: ¿Dónde trabaja Vd?

MISS GONZÁLEZ: I
work in the office
of Mr. Renaldo,
a lawyer.
The address is
1, Pennsylvania
Plaza.
I started yesterday.

MR. BROWN: How much
do you earn per year?

MISS GONZÁLEZ: I
earn $7,500.

MR. BROWN: Whom do
you want to name
as beneficiary?

MISS GONZÁLEZ: My
sister,
Maruja.
She lives with me.

MR. BROWN: Fine.
Do you want to sign
these cards here
and here, please?

MR. BROWN: Do you
have any signed
identification?
Your driver's
license, for
instance.

MISS GONZÁLEZ: Yes,
here in my wallet.

MR. BROWN: Thank
you. Fine.
Everything is in order.
I need your signature
on these cards.
The rest I will
fill out afterwards.

SRTA. GONZÁLEZ:
Trabajo en la
oficina <u>del señor</u>   18
<u>Renaldo,</u> un abogado.
La dirección es
/número/ uno,
Pennsylvania Plaza.
Empecé ayer.

SR. BROWN: ¿Cuánto
gana Vd. <u>al año</u>?   19

SRTA. GONZÁLEZ:
Gano siete mil
quinientos dólares.

SR. BROWN: ¿A quién
quiere Vd. nombrar
como beneficiario?

SRTA. GONZÁLEZ:
/A/ mi hermana,
Maruja.
Ella vive conmigo.

SR. BROWN: Bueno.
¿Quiere Vd. firmar
estas tarjetas aquí
y aquí, por favor?

SR. BROWN: ¿Tiene
Vd. alguna identi-
ficación firmada?
Su licencia /de/
conducir, por
ejemplo.

SRTA. GONZÁLEZ: Sí,
aquí en la cartera.

SR. BROWN: Gracias.
Bueno.
Todo está en orden.
Necesito su firma
en estas tarjetas.
El resto /lo/
llenaré después.

| | |
|---|---|
| What color check do you prefer? Red, yellow or blue? | ¿Qué color /de/ cheque prefiere Vd? ¿Rojo, amarillo o azul? |
| MISS GONZÁLEZ: I like yellow. | SRTA. GONZÁLEZ: Me gusta /el/ amarillo.   20 |
| MR. BROWN: Yellow. Fine. Within a week, you will receive a package of checks. You will also receive deposit slips. | SR. BROWN: Amarillo. Bueno. Dentro /de/ una semana Vd. recibirá un paquete de cheques. También recibirá impresos para depositar su dinero. |
| MISS GONZÁLEZ: Thank you. | SRTA. GONZÁLEZ: Gracias. |
| MR. BROWN: And today, how much money do you want to deposit in your accounts? | SR. BROWN: Y hoy, ¿cuánto dinero quiere depositar en sus cuentas? |
| MISS GONZÁLEZ: A hundred dollars in each one, and the rest I will take out. | SRTA. GONZÁLEZ: Cien dólares en cada una, y lo demás me lo llevaré. |
| MR. BROWN: /One/ hundred dollars in your savings account and one hundred dollars in your checking account. | SR. BROWN: Cien dólares en su cuenta de ahorros y cien dólares en su cuenta corriente. |
| MISS GONZÁLEZ: Yes, I want to save as much as possible. | SRTA. GONZÁLEZ: Sí, quiero ahorrar lo más posible.   21 |
| MR. BROWN: Fine. Now, take this check and the papers to the teller. He will give you your money. | SR. BROWN: Bueno. Pues, lleve este cheque y los papeles al cajero. Él le dará su dinero. |

MISS GONZÁLEZ:
Thank you, Mr. Brown.

SRTA. GONZÁLEZ:
Gracias, señor Brown.

MR. BROWN: You are welcome, Miss González.

SR. BROWN: <u>De nada</u>, señorita González.     22

And if you have any problem, come to see me.

Y si tiene algún <u>problema</u>, venga a verme.     23

MISS GONZÁLEZ:
Thank you, and Good-bye.

SRTA. GONZÁLEZ:
Gracias, y adiós.

MR. BROWN: Good-bye, Miss González.

SR. BROWN: Adiós, señorita González.

## NOTES

1. <u>¿En qué puedo servirla?</u>: What can I do for you?
   Literally: With (in) what can I serve you?
   Dict(Idioms)

2. <u>¡Qué lástima!</u>: What /a/ pity!
   Dict(Idioms)

3. <u>/Lo/ siento</u>: /I/ am sorry (about it).
   Dict(Idioms)

4. <u>Por supuesto</u>: Of course.
   Dict(Idioms)

5. <u>Siénte/se/</u>: Sit /down/.
   Reflexive construction in Spanish.
   The reflexive pronoun is attached to the command form.     VII(Reflexive Verbs)
   XIF3(Pos. of Object Pronoun)

6. <u>¿Qué clase de cuenta prefiere Vd?</u>: What kind of account do you prefer?
   ¿Qué clase de?: What kind of?     Dict(Idioms)
   prefe<u>r</u>ir:
   e changes to <u>ie</u> in the singular and in the third person plural of the present tense.
   IIIB1b(Stem Changing Verbs)

7. <u>Cuentas /de/ ahorros y cuentas corrientes</u>:
   Savings accounts and checking accounts.
   					IA16 & Dict(Compound Nouns)
8. <u>Seis por ciento al año</u>: Six percent per (a) year.
9. <u>A la vez</u>: At the /same/ time.
   					XVE3(vez)
10. <u>Me gustan /las/ vacaciones</u>: I like vacations.
    Literally: The vacations are pleasing to me.
    The subject of <u>me gustan</u> is <u>las vacaciones</u>.
    Therefore, the verb has to be in the plural.
    					XIJ(gustar)
    					IIA2a(Use of Definite Article)
11. <u>Le cobramos</u>: We charge you (make a charge to you).			XIC1(Indirect Object)
12. <u>al mes</u>: a (per) month.
    					IIB17(Use of Definite Article)
13. <u>Eso es</u>: That's it.
    					Dict(Idioms)
14. <u>Vale la pena</u>: It is worthwhile.
    Literally: it is worth the trouble.
    					Dict(Idioms)
15. <u>¿Cómo se llama su esposo?</u>: What is your husband's name?
    Literally: How does your husband call himself?
    Use of reflexive construction in Spanish.
    					VIIE(Reflexive Verbs)
    					Dict(Idioms)
16. <u>¿En qué trabaja Vd?</u>: What kind of work do you do?
    Literally: In what do you work?
    					Dict(Idioms)
17. <u>Es decir, soy secretaria</u>: /That/ is, I am /a/ secretary.
    Es decir: that is (Literally: that is to say)
    					Dict(Idioms)
    The indefinite article (a) is not used after the verb <u>ser</u>, when referring to professions.
    					IIB2a(Omission of Indefinite Article)

18. En la oficina del señor Renaldo:  In Mr. Renaldo's office (in the office of Mr. Renaldo).
    The definite article (el) is used before titles (señor), when one speaks about a person.
          IIA2d(Use of Definite Article)
19. Al año:  per year.
          IIA2q(Definite Article)
20. Me gusta el amarillo:  I like yellow.
    Literally: (the) yellow is pleasing to me. Use of definite article (el) when speaking about something in general.
          IIA2b(Definite Article)
21. Lo más posible:  As much as possible.
          IIA1 (lo)
          Dict(Idioms)
22. De nada:  You are welcome.  Literally: of nothing.  Dict(Idioms)
23. Algún problema:  Any problem.
    Although problema ends in a, it is masculine. cf. el programa, el mapa, etc.
          IA3(gender)
    algún: any  XXA3(alguno, algún)


      TRANSLATE


1. What can I do for you?
2. We have savings account and checking accounts.
3. I am sorry.
4. What kind of account do you prefer?
5. We charge you 50¢ per month.
6. It is worthwhile.
7. What is your name?
8. What kind of work do you do?

9. I am a secretary.
10. I work in the office of Mr. Brown.
11. As much as possible.
12. Do you have a problem?
13. You are welcome.

| TRAVEL AGENT | AGENTE DE VIAJES |
|---|---|
| MRS. DÍAZ: Good morning. | SRA. DÍAZ: Buenos días. |
| CLERK: Good morning. What can I do /for/ you? | DEPENDIENTE: Buenos días. ¿En qué puedo <u>servirla</u>?    1 |
| MRS. DÍAZ: Can tickets be bought here? | SRA. DÍAZ: <u>¿Se pueden comprar boletos aquí</u>?  2 |
| CLERK: Yes, madam. Where do you want to go (to)? | DEPENDIENTE: Sí, señora. <u>¿A dónde quiere ir Vd</u>?   3 |
| MRS. DÍAZ: I want two tickets to Bogotá. | SRA. DÍAZ: Quiero dos pasajes para Bogotá. |
| CLERK: You want to go to Bogotá. Who is going to accompany you? | DEPENDIENTE: Vd. quiere ir a Bogotá. ¿Quién va a acompañarla? |
| MRS. DÍAZ: My husband, Mr. Díaz. We are going to visit our parents in Bogotá. | SRA. DÍAZ: Mi esposo, /el/ <u>señor Díaz</u>.   4<br><u>Vamos /a/ visitar</u>   5<br><u>/a/ nuestros padres</u> en Bogotá. |
| CLERK: Do you want round trip tickets? | DEPENDIENTE: ¿Quiere Vd. <u>pasajes /de/</u>   6<br><u>ida y vuelta</u>? |
| MRS. DÍAZ: Yes, round trip, please. | SRA. DÍAZ: Sí, /de/ ida y vuelta, por favor. |
| CLERK: Tourist or first class? | DEPENDIENTE: ¿Turista o /de/ primera clase? |
| MRS. DÍAZ: Tourist. | SRA. DÍAZ: Turista. |

| | |
|---|---|
| CLERK: Do you want to make a reservation right now? | DEPENDIENTE: ¿Quiere Vd. hacer <u>una reserva</u> ahora mismo?  7 |
| MRS. DÍAZ: Yes, we want to leave next Tuesday. | SRA. DÍAZ: Sí, queremos salir /el/ próximo martes.  8 |
| CLERK: Do you want to go with LAN CHILE, Pan American or /an/ other line? | DEPENDIENTE: ¿Quiere Vd. ir por LAN CHILE, Pan American <u>u otra</u> línea?  9 |
| MRS. DÍAZ: /It/ doesn't matter. I prefer a direct flight. | SRA. DÍAZ: <u>No importa.</u> Prefiero un vuelo directo.  10 |
| CLERK: A direct flight to Bogota. That would be LAN CHILE. | DEPENDIENTE: Un vuelo directo para Bogotá. <u>Este sería</u> LAN CHILE.  11 |
| The other lines make a stop in Miami or México. | Las otras líneas <u>hacen escala</u> en Miami o /en/ México.  12 |
| MRS. DÍAZ: No, we do not want to make a stop. | SRA. DÍAZ: No, no queremos hacer escala. |
| CLERK: (on phone): LAN CHILE? This is "Viajes al Sur". I need two passages for Bogotá next Tuesday. Do you have them? In the name of Mr. & Mrs. Díaz. Tourist. Round trip. When do you want to return? | DEPENDIENTE: (al teléfono): ¿LAN CHILE? Aquí habla "Viajes al Sur". Necesito dos pasajes para Bogotá /el/ próximo martes. ¿Los tienen? A nombre del Sr. y de la Sra. Díaz. Turista. /De/ ida y vuelta. ¿Cuándo quiere Vd. Volver? |
| MRS. DÍAZ: Within three weeks. | SRA. DÍAZ: <u>Dentro de</u> tres semanas.  13 |

| | |
|---|---|
| CLERK: Three weeks later.<br>Thank you. Good-bye. | DEPENDIENTE: Tres semanas más tarde.<br>Gracias. Buenos días. |
| The flights are confirmed. | Los pasajes están confirmados. 14 |
| MRS. DÍAZ: That's it.<br>How much do the tickets cost? | SRA. DÍAZ: Eso es. 15<br>¿Cuánto cuestan los pasajes? |
| CLERK: Let's see. | DEPENDIENTE: Vamos 16<br>a ver. |
| Two round trip tickets in tourist class, from New York to Bogotá:<br>The two tickets (will) cost you seven hundred dollars.<br>Do you want to pay by (with) check or credit card? | Dos pasajes /de/ ida y vuelta en clase /de/ turista, desde Nueva York a Bogotá:<br>Los dos pasajes le 17<br>cuestan setecientos dólares.<br>¿Quiere Vd. pagar con cheque o /con/ 18<br>tarjeta /de/ crédito? |
| MRS. DÍAZ: By check.<br>To whom do I make out (write) the check? | SRA. DÍAZ: Con cheque.<br>¿A quién escribo el cheque? |
| CLERK: Viajes al Sur, please. | DEPENDIENTE: Viajes al Sur, por favor. |
| MRS. DÍAZ: Is this right? | SRA. DÍAZ: ¿Está 19<br>en orden? |
| CLERK: Yes, it is. | DEPENDIENTE: Sí, lo está. |
| Do you want to reserve a seat now? | ¿Quiere Vd. reservar un asiento ahora? |
| MRS. DÍAZ: Can one?<br>Of course! | SRA. DÍAZ: ¿Se 20<br>puede?<br>¡Por supuesto! 21 |

CLERK: Do you want a seat in the front or back (part)?

MRS. DÍAZ: I don't know.
I don't smoke and I would like to be in the part where there is no smoking.

CLERK: Fine. I will give you a seat in the back (part).
Do you want to sit on the aisle or near a window?

MRS. DÍAZ: Near a window, please.

Is it a 747?

CLERK: Yes. On these flights we use only 747s.

Your seat number is 14A.

MRS. DÍAZ: Thank you. At what time is the flight?

CLERK: The flight to Bogotá leaves at seven thirty in the evening.

DEPENDIENTE: ¿Quiere Vd. un asiento en la parte /de/ adelante o /de/ atrás?

SRA. DÍAZ: No sé.
No fumo y me gustaría estar en la parte donde no se fuma.   22

DEPENDIENTE: Bueno. Le daré un asiento en la parte /de/ atrás.
¿Quiere Vd. sentar/se/ en el pasillo o cerca /de/ una ventana?

SRA. DÍAZ: Cerca /de/ una ventana, por favor.
¿Es un siete cuarenta y siete?

DEPENDIENTE: Sí. En estos vuelos usamos solamente aviones siete cuarenta y siete.
El número /de/ su    23
asiento es catorce A.

SRA. DÍAZ: Gracias.
¿A qué hora es    24
el vuelo?

DEPENDIENTE: El vuelo para Bogotá sale a /las/ siete    25
y media de la tarde.

| | |
|---|---|
| MRS. DÍAZ: /At/ what time are we going to arrive? | SRA. DÍAZ: ¿A qué hora vamos a llegar? |
| CLERK: The flight takes 6 hours. Therefore, you are going to arrive at one thirty the next morning. | DEPENDIENTE: El vuelo tarda seis horas. Así que van a llegar a /la/ una y media /de/ la próxima madrugada.   26 |
| MRS. DÍAZ: At what time do I have to be at the airport? | SRA. DÍAZ: ¿A qué hora <u>tengo que estar en el aeropuerto</u>?   27 |
| CLERK: You must be at the airport one hour before departure. Do you have a (north) American passport? | DEPENDIENTE: Vd. tiene que estar en el aeropuerto una hora antes /de la/ salida. ¿Tiene Vd. un pasaporte norte-americano? |
| MRS. DÍAZ: Yes, do I need a visa? | SRA. DÍAZ: Sí. ¿Necesito una visa? |
| CLERK: No. With an American passport you don't need /a/ visa for Colombia. | DEPENDIENTE: No. Con un pasaporte norteamericano <u>no necesita visa</u> para Colombia.   28 |
| MRS. DÍAZ: Do I need /a/ vaccination? | SRA. DÍAZ: <u>¿Necesito vacuna</u>?   28 |
| CLERK: Yes, you must have a vaccination certificate that shows that you have been vaccinated in the last two years. | DEPENDIENTE: Sí. <u>Debe tener un certificado /de/ vacunación que muestre que Vd. ha sido vacunada en los últimos dos años</u>.   29 |

| | | |
|---|---|---|
| MRS. DÍAZ: How much baggage can I take? | SRA. DÍAZ: ¿Cuánto equipaje puedo llevar? | |
| CLERK: You can take 44 lbs. gratis. | DEPENDIENTE: Vd. puede llevar cuarenta y cuatro libras gratis. | 30 |
| After that, you must pay. | Después /de/ esto, tiene que pagar. | |
| MRS. DÍAZ: Each (one), yes? | SRA. DÍAZ: Cada uno, ¿verdad? | 31 |
| CLERK: Yes, each (one). | DEPENDIENTE: Sí, cada uno. | |
| MRS. DÍAZ: If I want to return later, for how long is this ticket good (valid)? | SRA. DÍAZ: Si quiero volver más tarde, ¿por cuánto tiempo es válido este pasaje? | 32 |
| CLERK: Your ticket is good for a year. | DEPENDIENTE: Su pasaje es válido por un año. | 33 |
| MRS. DÍAZ: You have been very kind. Thank you very much. | SRA. DÍAZ: Vd. ha sido muy amable. Muchas gracias. | |
| CLERK: You are welcome, Mrs. Díaz. Good-bye. | DEPENDIENTE: De nada, señora Díaz. Adiós. | 34 |
| MRS. DÍAZ: Good-bye. | SRA. DÍAZ: Adiós. | |

NOTES

1. ¿En qué puedo servirla?: What can I do for you?
   Literally: In what can I serve you?
                         Dict(Idioms)

2. ¿Se pueden comprar boletos aquí?: Can one buy tickets here?
Use of reflexive construction in Spanish (se pueden comprar) - Passive voice in English (can be bought).
cf. Aquí se habla español: English is spoken here.   VIID3(Reflexive Construction)

3. ¿A dónde quiere Vd. ir?: Where do you want to go (to)?
While in English the preposition (to) may be left out, in Spanish a must always be expressed when direction is indicated.
cf. ¿Dónde está Vd?: Where are you?
XVIA1a(note (a))

4. El señor Díaz: Mr. Díaz.
The definite article (el) must be used before titles, when speaking about someone.
IIA2d(Use of Definite Article)
cf. ¿Cómo está Vd., Sr. Díaz?

5. Vamos /a/ visitar /a/ nuestros padres: We are going to visit our parents.
a nuestros padres: Use of personal a before a direct object referring to persons.
XVIA1m(Personal a)

6. Pasajes /de/ ida /y/ vuelta: Round trip tickets.   IA16(Compound Nouns)

7. Una reserva: a reservation.

8. /El/ próximo martes: Next Tuesday.
The definite article is used before the days of the week.   IIA2r(Use of Definite Article)

9. U otra línea: Or another line.
otro: another
o (or) changes to u before a word that begins in o.   XXIIIA(o)

10. No importa: /It/ doesn't matter.
It as a subject is never expressed in Spanish.
XIA3(it)
Dict(Idioms)

11. Este sería Lan Chile: This would be Lan Chile.
sería: conditional of ser.
XIVB1a(Conditional)

12. __Hacen escala__: They make a stop.
    Dict(Idioms)

13. __Dentro /de/__: within
    XVIB(Compound Prepositions)

14. __Los pasajes están confirmados__: The flights (passages) are confirmed.
    Use of __estar__ when speaking about the result of an action.
    XB3(estar)

15. __Eso es__: That's it.

16. __Vamos /a/ ver__: Let's see.
    Dict(Idioms)

17. __Los dos pasajes le cuestan 700 dólares__: The two tickets (will) cost you $700.
    Use of Present Tense in Spanish, Future in English.
    __costar__ is a stem changing verb (__o__ changes to __ue__)    IIIB1b(Stem changing verbs)

18. __¿Con cheque o /con/ tarjeta /de/ crédito?__: By (with) check or credit card?
    Prepositions are usually repeated in Spanish.
    La tarjeta /de/ crédito: the credit card.
    IA16(Compound Nouns)

19. __¿Está en orden?__: Is /it/ all right (in order)?

20. __¿Se puede?__: Can one?
    Use of reflexive construction in Spanish to express the impersonal __one__ in English.
    VIID3(Reflexives)

21. __¡Por supuesto!__: Of course!
    Dict(Idioms)

22. __Me gustaría estar en la parte donde no se fuma__: I would like to be in the part where there is no smoking (where one doesn't smoke).
    me gustaría: I would like. Use of Conditional in English and Spanish. XIV(Conditional)
    Use of __estar__ for location. XB2(estar)
    Use of reflexive construction in Spanish where English uses the impersonal __one__.
    VIID3(Reflexive in Spanish)

23.  El número de su asiento es catorce A:  Your
     seat number (the number of your seat) is 14A.
                    IA16 & Dict(Compound Nouns)
24.  ¿A qué hora?:  At what time?
                    XVF(time)
25.  A /las/ siete /y/ media de la tarde:  At 7:30
     in the afternoon.   XVE2(time)
26.  A /la/ una y media /de/ la próxima madrugada:
     At one thirty the next morning.
     La madrugada:  daybreak, very early in the
     morning.       XVF(time)
27.  Tengo /que/ estar en el aeropuerto:  I have to
     be at (in) the airport.
     Tener que:  to have to.  Tener is an
     irregular verb.    IVA1g(Present Tense)
     Use of estar for location.  XB2(estar)
28.  No necesita visa:  You do not need /a (any)/
     visa.
     ¿Necesito vacuna?:  Do I need /a/ vaccination?
     In questions and negative statements, the
     English a(any) is generally not translated.
                    IIB5d and XXA1(Omission of
                              a and any)
29.  Debe tener un certificado /de/ vacunación que
     muestre que Vd. ha sido vacunada en los últimos
     dos años:  You must have a vaccination
     certificate which shows that you have been
     vaccinated in the last two years.
     Un certificado de vacunación:  a vaccination
     certificate.   IA16 & Dict(Compound Nouns)
     Muestre is the subjunctive of mostrar.
                    XXVA1c(Subjunctive Forms)
     The subjunctive is used here because this is a
     requirement which must be fulfilled (debe
     tener...)      XXVD1a and f(Use of Subjunctive)
30.  44 libras:  44 pounds.
     la libra:  the pound    IA14(gender)
     cf. el libro:  the book.

31. <u>Cada uno</u>:  Each one.
32. <u>¿Por cuánto tiempo?</u>:  For how long?
                Dict(Idioms)
33. <u>Su pasaje es válido por un año</u>:  Your ticket is good (valid) for a year.
                XVIA7a(Use of <u>por</u>)
34. <u>De nada</u>:  You are welcome.
                Dict(Idioms)


TRANSLATE


1.  What can I do for you?
2.  Where do you want to go (to)?
3.  The plane stops in Miami.
4.  Can one buy tickets here?
5.  I want to be in the part where there is no smoking.
6.  You do not need any visa.
7.  The ticket is good (valid) for a year.
8.  I want a round trip ticket.
9.  You will leave next Wednesday.
10. Your seat number is 16B.

AIRLINES                              LÍNEAS AÉREAS

A. At the airport                     A. En el aeropuerto

Put all your baggage on               Ponga todo su
the scale, please.                    equipaje en la
                                      balanza, por favor.

You have twenty                       Tiene veinte libras
pounds excess baggage.                /de/ exceso /de/
                                      equipaje.

Announcer:                            Anunciador:

All flights have been                 Todos /los/ vuelos
cancelled because of                  han sido cancelados
the bad weather.                      a causa del mal                1
                                      tiempo.

Passengers for flight                 Pasajeros para /el/
number four fifteen                   vuelo número cuatro-
to (with destination)                 cientos quince con
Bogotá, kindly board                  destino Bogotá,
the plane.                            tengan la bondad de            2
Gate (exit) number                    subir al avión.
six.                                  Salida número seis.

B. On the plane                       B. En el avión

Stewardess:                           Azafata:

Good morning, ladies                  Buenos días, señores           3
and gentlemen.                        pasajeros.
Welcome aboard.                       Bienvenidos a bordo.
This is flight                        Este es /el/ vuelo
number 415 to (with                   número cuatrocientos
destination) Bogotá.                  quince con destino
                                      a Bogotá.

The plane will leave                  El avión saldrá
in a few minutes.                     en unos minutos.               4

Please, fasten                        Por favor,
your seat (safety)                    abróchen/se/ los               5
belts.                                cinturones /de/
                                      seguridad.

| | |
|---|---|
| Don't smoke during the take-off. | No fumen durante el despegue. |
| The flight will take (last) six hours. We will fly at an altitude of 5000 feet. | El vuelo durará seis horas. Volaremos a una altitud de cinco mil pies. |
| We shall arrive in Bogotá at 5:30 a.m. | Llegaremos a Bogotá a /las/ cinco /y/ media /de la/ mañana.    6 |
| Dinner will be served (we will serve dinner) in a few minutes. | Serviremos /la/ cena en unos minutos. |
| You may purchase alcoholic drinks at one dollar each (one). Soft (carbonated) drinks are free (gratis). | Pueden comprar bebidas alcohólicas a un dólar cada una. Las bebidas gaseosas son gratis. |
| If you have /to/ vomit, use the paper container. | Si tienen /que/ vomitar, usen la bolsa /de/ papel. |
| We shall be landing in half /an/ hour. | Aterrizaremos en media hora.    7 |
| We are arriving at Bogotá. | Estamos llegando a    8 Bogotá. |
| Fasten your seat (safety) belts, please. | Abróchense los cinturones /de/ seguridad, por favor. |
| Obey the "No Smoking" sign. | Obedezcan el letrero /de/ "No Fumar". |

C. <u>Emergency</u>           C. <u>Emergencia</u>

| | |
|---|---|
| Please, stay calm. | Por favor, permanezcan en calma.    9 |
| Everything is (all the services are) under control. | Todos los servicios están bajo control. |

| | | |
|---|---|---|
| Put on your life (saving) jackets. It is only a precaution. | Pónganse los chalecos salvavidas. Es solo una precaución. | 10 |

## NOTES

1. <u>A causa del mal tiempo</u>: Because of the bad weather.

2. <u>Tengan la bondad de subir al avión</u>: Kindly (have the kindness to) board (climb into) the plane.
   Tenga(n) la bondad de: kindly, please, be so kind as to.   Dict(Idioms)
   subir a   un avión: to board (climb into) a plane.   Dict(Idioms)

3. <u>Señores pasajeros</u>: Ladies and gentlemen (passengers).
   Señores means either <u>gentlemen</u> or <u>ladies and gentlemen</u>.
   cf. los padres: the fathers, the parents.
                   IB7(Plural Nouns)

4. <u>En unos minutos</u>: In a few minutes.

5. <u>Abróchense los cinturones de seguridad</u>: Fasten your seat (safety) belts.
   Abróchense los cinturones: Fasten your belts.
   Use of reflexive construction and definite article in Spanish, possessive adjective in English.        VIID2(Reflexives)
   el cinturón de seguridad: the safety belt.
                   IA16(Compound Nouns)

6. <u>A las cinco y media de la mañana</u>:
   At 5:30 a.m. (in the morning).
   Use of definite article (las cinco) with time.
                   IIA2g(Definite Article)
   A las cinco <u>de</u> la mañana:  at 5 a.m.
   Use of the preposition <u>de</u> (to translate <u>in</u>) after an expression of definite time.   XVIA3c($\overline{de}$)

7. <u>En media hora</u>:  In /a/ half hour.
8. <u>Estamos llegando</u>:  We are (in the midst of) arriving.
   Use of <u>estar</u> with present participle of the main verb to form the progressive form (the same as in English).   XVII(Progr. Forms) & XB4(estar)
9. <u>Permanezcan en calma</u>:  Stay calm (in peace).
                               Dict(Idioms)
   In the verb <u>permanecer</u> <u>c</u> changes to <u>zc</u> before <u>o</u> and <u>a</u>.        VIA1(Commands)
10. <u>Póngan/se/ los chalecos salvavidas</u>:  Put on your life (saving) jackets.
    Ponerse algo:  to put on something.  <u>Poner</u> is an irregular verb.     VIA1(Commands)
    Use of reflexive verb in Spanish - possessive adjective in English (your).
                       VIID2(Reflexive Verbs)


                         TRANSLATE


1. All flights have been cancelled because of bad weather.
2. Please, board the plane at exit number nine.
3. Fasten your seat belts, please.
4. We are now arriving in New York.
5. How long does the flight take?
6. Your baggage is five pounds overweight.
7. Don't smoke during the take-off.
8. Put on your life jackets, please.

## VOCABULARY

NOTE: Since nearly all nouns ending in -o are masculine, and nearly all nouns ending in -a are feminine in Spanish, we have not indicated the gender for these nouns. However, for nouns with other endings and nouns ending in -o or -a that do not fit into this pattern, the gender has been indicated in parenthesis.

We have also indicated in parenthesis any stem or spelling changes that may occur in verbs. Irregular verbs have been underlined.

Where there are several possible endings for an adjective or pronoun, these are indicated in parenthesis.

VOCABULARY

ESPAÑOL - INGLÉS

A

A (Prep.): at, to, for, on, in(to), by
A BORDO: aboard
A CAUSA DE: because of
A LA DERECHA: on(to) the right
A LA IZQUIERDA: on(to) the left
A LA SEMANA: per week, a week
A LA VEZ: at the same time
A LAS...: at...(time)
A MÁS TARDAR: at the latest
A MENUDO: often
¿A QUÉ HORA?: at what time?
A TIEMPO: in (on) time
A VECES: sometimes
ABANDONAR: to abandon, leave
ABIERTO(A): open
ABOGADO(A): lawyer
ABRIGO: overcoat, coat
ABRIGO DE PIEL: fur coat
ABRIR: to open
ABRIR UNA CUENTA: to open an account
ABROCHAR(SE): to fasten
ABSTENERSE DE: to abstain from
ACCIDENTE (m): accident
ACCIDENTE DE TRÁFICO: traffic accident
ACCIÓN (DE BOLSA): share

ACERA: curb
ACERCARSE(QU) A: to go (come) near
ACERCARSE(QU) MÁS: to move closer
ACOMPAÑAR: to accompany
ACOSTAR(UE) to put to bed (sleep)
ACOSTARSE(UE): to lie down, to go to bed
ACTUAL: present
ACTUAR(Ú): to act
ADEMÁS: moreover, besides
ADICTO(A): addict
ADICTO(A) A LAS DROGAS (NARCÓTICOS): drug (narcotics) addict
ADIÓS: good-bye
ADJUNTO(A): attached, enclosed
ADMINISTRACIÓN (f): administration
ADMINISTRACIÓN (f) DE VETERANOS: Veterans' Administration
¿A DÓNDE?: where to?
ADOPCIÓN: adoption
HOGAR DE ADOPCIÓN: foster home
AEROPUERTO: airport
AGENCIA DE VIAJES: travel agency
AGENTE (mf): agent
AGENTE (mf) DE VIAJES: travel agent
AGUA: water
AGUA CALIENTE: hot water
AGUA FRÍA: cold water
AHÍ: there

AHORA: now
AHORA MISMO: right now
AHORRAR DINERO: to save money
AHORROS: savings
AIRE (m): air
AL (A + EL): to the
AL (plus infinitive): upon
AL AIRE: exposed (to the air)
AL AÑO: per annum (year)
AL MES: per month
AL NOMBRE DE: in the name of
AL TELÉFONO: on the phone
AL TRABAJO: at work
ALARGAR(GU): extend
ALARGAR(GU): to extend
ALCOHOL (m): alcohol
ALCOHÓLICO(A) (n & adj.): alcoholic
ALERGIA: allergy
ALGUIEN: anyone, someone, somebody
ALGÚN(A): some, any
ALGUNA VEZ: sometime, ever
ALGUNAS VECES: sometimes
ALGUNO(A)S: a few, some
ALIMENTO(S): food
ALMACÉN (m): department store
ALMUERZO: lunch
ALQUILER (m): rent
DE ALQUILER (m): for rent (hire)
ALQUILERES (m.pl.): rentals
ALTITUD (f): altitude
ALTO(A): high
ALLÁ: (over) there

ALLÍ: (over) there
AMABLE: kind
AMARILLO(A): yellow
AMBO(A)S: both
AMBULANCIA: ambulance
AMERICANO(A): American
AMÍGDALA: tonsil
AMIGO(A): friend
ANOCHE: last night
ANTE: in front of
ANTES (Adv.): before
ANTES DE (Prep.): before
AÑO: year
EL AÑO PASADO: last year
APARTAM(I)ENTO: apartment
APETITO: appetite
APODO: nickname
APOYARSE (CONTRA): to lean on
APRENDER: to learn
APRENDER UNA LECCIÓN: to do (learn, study) a lesson
APROXIMADAMENTE: approximately, about
AQUEL(LA) (dem. adj.): that (over there)
AQUÍ: here
AQUÍ ESTÁ: here it is
AQUÍ (LO) TIENE: here it is
ARREGLAR: to settle, fix
ARREGLARSE: to work out
ARRESTAR: to arrest
ARRESTO: arrest
ARRESTO POR NARCÓTICOS: drug arrest
ARRIMARSE A LA ACERA: to pull over to the curb
ARROZ (m): rice
ARRUINAR: to ruin
ARRUINARSE: to get ruined
ASCENSOR (m): elevator

ASCENSORISTA (mf):
  elevator operator
ASÍ: so, like this
ASÍ QUE: therefore
ASIENTO: seat
ASIENTO JUNTO A LA
  VENTANA: window seat
ASIENTO JUNTO AL
  PASILLO: aisle seat
ASIGNAR: to assign
ASISTIR A LA ESCUELA:
  to attend school
ASISTIR A UNA CITA:
  to keep an appointment
ASUNTO: matter
ATACAR(QU): to attack
ATENCIÓN (f): attention
ATERRIZAR(C): to land
ATRACO: hold-up
ATRASADO: late,
  delayed, retarded
ATRASADO(A) MENTAL:
  mentally retarded
AUSENTE: absent
AUTO(MÓVIL) (m): car
AUTORIZACIÓN (f):
  authorization
AUXILIO: assistance
AUXILIO PÚBLICO
  (SOCIAL): Social
  Welfare, Social
  Service
AVENIDA: avenue
AVIÓN (m): aero(plane),
  (air)plane, airliner,
  plane
AVISAR: to notify
AYER: yesterday
AYUDA (f): aid, help,
  assistance
AYUDA ECONÓMICA:
  financial aid
AYUDA PÚBLICA: Welfare
AYUDAR: to help
AZAFATA: stewardess

AZAFATO: steward
AZOTEA: flat roof
AZUL: blue

B

BAJO(A) (adj.): low
BAJO (prep.): under
BAJO ARRESTO: under arrest
BAJO TRATAMIENTO MÉDICO:
  under medical treatment
BALANZA: scale
BALÓN (m): balloon
BANCO: bank
BANCO DE AHORROS: savings
  bank
BAÑERA: bathtub
BAR (m): bar
BARBA: beard
BASTANTE: enough
BASURA: rubbish
BEBÉ (m): baby
BEBER: to drink
BEBIDA: beverage, drink
BEBIDA ALCOHÓLICA:
  alcoholic beverage
  (drink)
BEBIDA GASEOSA:
  carbonated drink
BENEFICIARIO: beneficiary
BENEFICIO: benefit
BENEFICIOS DEL SEGURO
      CONTRA DESEMPLEO:
  Unemployment Insurance
  Benefits
BENEFICIOS DEL SEGURO
  SOCIAL: Social Security
  Benefits
BIEN: well, fine, all
  right
BIENVENIDO(A): welcome
BILLETERA(O): wallet
BLANCO(A): white
BODEGA: grocery store
  (Latin America)

BOGOTÁ: Bogotá
BOLETO (Latin America): ticket
BOLSA (BOLSA): stock market, stock exchange, bag, container
BOLSA DE PAPEL: paper bag
BOMBERO: fireman
BONDAD (f): kindness
TENGA LA BONDAD DE: kindly
BONO: bond
BONO DEL GOBIERNO: government bond
BORRACHO(A): drunk
BORRAR: to erase
BUEN(O,A): good
BUENAS NOCHES: good night, good evening
BUENAS TARDES: good afternoon
BUENO (ON PHONE): hello
BUENOS DÍAS: good morning
BUSCAR(QU): to look for

C

CABEZA: head
CABLE (m): cable, wire
CADA: each, every
CADA UNO: each one, every one
CAJA: box
CAJA DE SEGURIDAD: safe deposit box
CAJERO(A): (bank) teller
CALEFACCIÓN (f): heat(ing)
CALENDARIO: calendar
CALENDARIO ADJUNTO: calendar insert
CALIENTE: hot

CALMA: calm
CALMARSE: to calm down
CALLE (f): street
CAMA: bed
CAMARERO: waiter
CAMARERA: waitress
CAMBIAR: to (ex)change, cash
CAMBIO: (ex)change
CAMINAR: to walk
CAMINAR EN LÍNEA RECTA: to walk a straight line
CAMISA: shirt
CANCELAR LA LICENCIA: to suspend the license
CÁNCER (m): cancer
CAPATAZ (m): foreman
CAPAZ: able
CÁRCEL (f): jail
CARIE (f): cavity
CARTERA (DE BOLSILLO): wallet
CASA: house, home
CASA PRIVADA (PARTICULAR): private house
CASADO(A): married
CASERA: landlady
CASERO: landlord
CASI: nearly, almost
CASO: case
CATORCE: fourteen
CAUSA: cause
A CAUSA DE: because
CELDA: cell
CELDA DE DETENCIÓN: detention cell
CENA: dinner, supper
CENTAVO: cent
CERCA DE: near, around, about
CEREAL (m): cereal
CEREAL (m) CALIENTE: hot cereal
CEREAL (m) FRÍO: cold cereal

CERO: zero
CERRADO(A): closed
CERRADO(A) CON LLAVE: locked
CERRADURA: lock
CERRADURA DE SEGURIDAD: safety lock
CERRAR(IE): to close
CERRAR CON LLAVE: to lock
CERTIFICADO: certificate
CERTIFICADO DE NACIMIENTO: birth certificate
CERTIFICADO DE VACUNA-(CIÓN): vaccination certificate
CICATRIZ (f): scar
CIEGO(A): blind
CIEN: (one) hundred (before nouns)
CIENTO: (one) hundred
CINCO: five
CINCUENTA: fifty
CINE (m): movies
CINTURÓN (m): belt
CINTURÓN (m) DE SEGURIDAD: safety belt
CITA: appointment
CIUDAD (f): city
CIUDADANO(A): citizen
CLARAMENTE: clearly
CLASE (f): class, kind
CLUB (m): club
COBRAR: to collect
COCINA: kitchen
COLA: line (of people cars, etc.)
COLGAR(UE,GU): to hang (up)
COLOCAR(QU): to place
COLOR (m): color
COMER: to eat
COMISARÍA DE POLICÍA: Police Headquarters
COMO: as, like, about
CÓMO: how

¿CÓMO?: How?
¿CÓMO ESTÁ USTED?: How are you?
¿CÓMO SE SIENTE?: How do you feel?
¿CÓMO SE LLAMA?: What is your name?
¿CÓMO SE LLAMA USTED?: What is your name? (formal)
¿CÓMO TE LLAMAS (TÚ)?: What is your name? (familiar)
COMPARECER(ZC): to appear (before authority)
COMPARTIR: to share
COMPENSACIÓN (f): compensation
COMPENSACIÓN (f) OBRERA: Workmen's Compensation
COMPENSACIÓN (f) DEL SEGURO OBRERO: Workmen's Compensation
COMPLETO(A): complete, whole
COMPRA: purchase
IR DE COMPRAS: to go shopping
COMPRAR: to buy, purchase
COMPRENDER: to understand
COMUNICAR(QU): to communicate, to notify
COMUNIDAD (f): community
CON: with
CON CALMA: calmly
CON DESTINO A: to
CONDUCIR(ZC): to drive
CONDUCTOR(A): driver
CONFIRMAR: to confirm
CONMIGO: with me
CONSEGUIR(I,G): to get, obtain
CONSEJERO(A): counselor

CONSIDERAR: to consider
CONSULTA (CONSULTORIO) DEL MÉDICO: doctor's office
CONTESTACIÓN (f): answer
CONTIGO: with you (fam. sing.)
CONTRA: against
CONTRATO DE ARRENDAMIENTO: lease
CONTROL (m): control
CORAZÓN (m): heart
CORPORACIÓN: corporation
CORRECTO(A): correct
CORREDOR (m): hall(way)
CORREO: mail
CORTAR: to cut
CORTAR LA LUZ: to cut off the light
CORTE (f): Court
CORTO(A): short
COSA: thing
COSTAR: to cost
CRÉDITO: credit
CREER(Y): to think
CREER(Y) QUE SI: to think so
CREER(Y) QUE NO: to think not
¿CUÁL?: Which?, What?
EL (LO, LA) CUAL: which
CUALQUIERA: any
CUANDO (Rel. pron.): when
¿CUANDO?(Interr.): When?
¿CUÁNTO(A)?: How much?
¿CUÁNTOS(AS)?: How many?
¿CUÁNTOS AÑOS TIENE VD?: How old are you?
¿CUÁNTO TIEMPO HACE?: How long is it?
CUARENTA: forty
CUARTO: fourth, quarter, room

CUARTO DE BAÑO: bathroom
CUATRO: four
CUBA: Cuba
CUCHILLO: knife
CUENTA: account, bill
CUENTA DE BANCO: bank account
CUENTA CORRIENTE: checking account
CUENTA DE AHORROS: savings account
CUENTA DE ELECTRICIDAD: electric bill
CUENTA DE GAS: gas bill
CUENTA DE TELÉFONO: telephone bill
CUERPO DE BOMBEROS: Fire Department
TENER CUIDADO: to watch out
CUIDAR: to take care of
CULPABLE: guilty
CUMPLIR...AÑOS: to be... years old
CUPÓN (m): coupon
CUPONES PARA ALIMENTOS: food stamps
CURAR: to cure
CURAR UNA CARIE : to fill a tooth

CH

CHALECO SALVAVIDAS: live (saving) jacket
CHAQUETA: jacket
CHEQUE (m): check
CHUPARSE EL DEDO: to suck one's thumb

D

DADO QUE: since (causal)
DAR: to give

DAR PARTE DE: to report
DE: of, from
DE ESTA MANERA: in this way
DE LA MAÑANA: in the morning, a.m. (after specific time)
DE LA TARDE: in the afternoon, p.m. (after specific time)
DE MANERA QUE: so that
DE NADA: you are welcome
DE OTRO MODO: otherwise
DEBER: to owe, should
DECENTE: decent
DECIR: to say, to tell
DECLARACIÓN (f): declaration, statement
DECLARARSE INOCENTE: to plead not guilty
DEDO: finger
DEDO GORDO: thumb
DEDUCIR(ZC): to deduct
DEJAR: to leave, let
DEJAR SALIR EL AIRE: to let out air
DEJAR UN EMPLEO: to leave a job
LO DEMÁS: the rest
DEMASIADO(A): too (much)
DENTISTA (mf): dentist
DENTRO DE (Prep.): within
DENUNCIAR: to denounce, report
DEPARTAMENTO: department
DEPARTAMENTO DE INCENDIOS: Fire Department
DEPARTAMENTO DE VIVIENDAS: Housing Authority
DEPARTAMENTO DE SALUBRIDAD (f) (SANIDAD (f)) PÚBLICA: Health Department
DEPARTAMENTO DE SERVICIO SOCIAL: Welfare Department
DEPENDER: to depend
DEPENDIENTE (mf): clerk
DEPOSITAR: to deposit
DERECHO: right, straight ahead
DESAYUNO: breakfast
DESCRIBIR: to describe
DESCRIPCIÓN (f): description
DESDE: since, from
¿DESDE CUÁNDO?: since when?
DESDE QUE: since (time)
DESEAR: to want
DESEMPLEADO(A): unemployed
DESEMPLEO: unemployment
DESGRACIADAMENTE: unfortunately
DESPACIO: slow(ly)
DESPEDIR(I): to fire (dismiss) from a job, to let go
DESPEGUE (m): take-off (plane)
DESPERTAR(SE)(IE): to wake up
DESPUÉS (Adv.): after(wards)
DESPUÉS DE (Prep.): after
DESPUÉS DE ESO: thereafter
DESPUÉS (DE) QUE (Conj.): after
DESTINO: destination
DETECTIVE (mf): detective
DEUDA: debt
DEVOLVER(UE): to return (something)

DÍA (m): day
DÍA (m) DE FIESTA:
  holiday
DIECIOCHO: eighteen
DIECISÉIS: sixteen
DIECISIETE: seventeen
DIEZ: ten
DIFERENCIA: difference
DIFERENTE: different
DIFÍCIL: difficult
DIFICULTAD (f):
  difficulty
DIFICULTAD (f) PARA
  (EN) HABLAR: speech
  difficulty (problem)
DIFTERIA: diphtheria
DÍGAME: hello (on the
  phone)
DINERO: money
DIRECCIÓN (f): direction,
  address
DIRECTO(A): direct
DISCUTIR: to discuss
DISPÉNSEME: excuse me
DISPONER (DE): to
  dispose (of)
DISPONIBLE: available
DISPONIBLE PARA
  TRABAJAR: available
  for work
DISPUTA: dispute
DIVORCIADO(A): divorced
DOBLARSE: to bend
  (over)
DOCE: twelve
DOCTOR(A): doctor,
  physician
DÓLAR (m): dollar
DOLER(UE): to hurt,
  ache
DOLOR (m): pain
DOLOR (m) DE GARGANTA:
  sore throat
DONDE (rel. pron.):
  where

¿DÓNDE? (interrogative):
  Where?
¿A DÓNDE?: Where to?
¿DE DÓNDE?: From where?
DORMIR(UE,U): to sleep
DORMITORIO: dormitory,
  bedroom
DOS: two
DOSCIENTO(A)S: two
  hundred
DROGA: drug
DUCHA: shower
DUEÑO: landlord
DUEÑA: landlady
DURANTE: during
DURAR: to last, to take
  time
DURO(A): hard

E

E: and (before i or hi)
ECONÓMICO(A): financial
ECHAR: to throw (out)
EDAD (f): age
EDIFICIO: building
EDUCACIÓN (f): education
EJEMPLO: example
POR EJEMPLO: for
  example, for instance
EJÉRCITO: army
EL: the
ÉL: he,it,him (aft. prep.)
EL MÍO: mine
ÉL MISMO: himself
ELECTRICIDAD (f):
  electricity
ELÉCTRICO(A): electric
ELLA: she, it, her
ELLO(A)S: they,them
EMERGENCIA: emergency
EMPASTE (m): filling
  (of tooth)
EMPEZAR(IE,C): to
  begin, start

EMPLEO: employment, job
EMPUJAR: to push
EN: in, on
EN CASO DE (QUE): in case
EN DOS SEMANAS: in two weeks
EN EL FUTURO: in the future
EN EL NOMBRE DE...: in the name of...
EN PRIMER LUGAR: in the first place
EN UNA SEMANA: in a week
EN UNOS (POCOS) MINUTOS: in a few minutes
ENCONTRAR(UE): to find
ENFADARSE: to get angry
ENFERMEDAD (f): sickness, disease, illness, ailment
ENFERMEDAD DE CORAZÓN heart ailment (disease)
ENFERMEDAD MENTAL: mental illness
ENFERMERA(O): nurse
ENFERMO(A): sick
ENSEGUIDA: right away
ENSEÑAR: to teach
ENTERARSE DE: to find out about
ENTONCES: then
ENTRAR: to enter, come in
ENTRE: between
ENTRETANTO: in the meantime
ENTREVISTA: interview
ENVIAR(Í): to send
EPILÉPTICO(A): epileptic

EQUIPAJE (m): baggage
ES DECIR: that is to say
ESCALA: stop
HACER ESCALA: to make a stop
ESCALERA: stairs
ESCALERA DE INCENDIOS: fire escape
ESCAPAR(SE): to escape, run away
ESCRIBIR: to write
ESCUELA: school
ESCUELA PARA ATRASADOS MENTALES: School for Mentally Retarded
ESCUELA SECUNDARIA: secondary (high) school
ESE(A) (dem. adj.): that
ESO (dem. pron.): that
ESO ES: that's it
ESO ES TODO: that's all
ESPERA: wait
ESPERAR: to wait for, expect
ESPOSA: wife
ESPOSAS: handcuffs
ESPOSO: husband
ESQUINA: (outer) corner
ESTA (f) (dem. adj.): this
ÉSTA (f) (dem. pron.): this one
ESTA MAÑANA: this morning
ESTA TARDE (f): this afternoon (evening)
ESTÁ BIEN: all right, fine, okay
ESTACIÓN (f): station
ESTACIÓN (f) DE POLICÍA: police station
ESTADOS UNIDOS: United States
ESTAMPILLA: stamp
ESTAMPILLAS (CUPONES) PARA ALIMENTOS: food stamps
ESTAR: to be

ESTAR AL AIRE: to be exposed
ESTAR BAJO ARRESTO: to be under arrest
ESTAR BAJO CONTROL: to be under control
ESTAR BAJO TRATAMIENTO MÉDICO: to be under (medical) treatment
ESTAR BIEN: to be all right (fine, well)
ESTAR CASADO(A): to be married
ESTAR ENFERMO(A): to be sick
ESTAR EN ORDEN: to be in order
ESTAR FUERA: to be out(side)
ESTAR LISTO(A): to be ready
ESTAR MAL(O,A): to be sick
ESTAR SEGURO: to be sure
ESTAR SIN TRABAJO: to be out of work (unemployed)
ESTATAL: state (of the state)
ESTE(A) (dem. adj.): this
ESTE: east
ÉSTE(A) (dem. pron.): this one
ESTO(A)S: these (dem.adj.)
ESTÓMAGO: stomach
ESTUDIAR: to study
EXACTAMENTE: exactly
EXCEPTO: except
EXCESO: excess
EXCESO DE EQUIPAJE: excess baggage
EXCUSA: excuse
EXTERIOR: outside

EXTERIOR (m): exterior
EXTRA: extra

F

FÁBRICA: factory
FÁBRICA DE PLASTICOS: plastics factory
FÁBRICA DE VESTIDOS: dress factory
FÁCIL: easy
FALSO(A): false
FALTAR: to be missing (lacking)
FAMILIA: family
FAMILIAR: member of the family, relative
POR FAVOR: please
FECHA: date
FECHA DE HOY: today's date
FEDERAL: federal
FIEBRE (f): fever
FIEBRE (f) ESCARLATINA: scarlet fever
FIESTA: holiday
FILA: line (of people, cars, etc.)
FIRMA: firm (commercial company), signature
FIRMADO(A): signed
FIRMAR: to sign
FORMULAR: to formulate
FORMULAR UNA QUEJA: to file a complaint
FORMULARIO: form
FOTO(GRAFÍA): photo(graph)
FRENTE A: in front of
FRÍO(A): cold
FUEGO: fire
FUERA: outside, away
FUMAR: to smoke
FUNCIONAR: to work (machine)

## G

GANAR: to earn
GARGANTA: throat
GASEOSA: soda, carbonated drink, soft drink
GASTAR DINERO: to spend (lay out) money
GASTOS: expenses
GASTOS MÉDICOS: medical expenses
GENERALMENTE: generally
GENTE (fs): people
GOBIERNO: government
GOTERA: leak
GRABAR: to engrave
GRACIAS: thanks, thank you
GRACIAS A: thanks to
GRACIAS A DIOS: thank God
GRADO: degree (in school), class, degree (temperature)
GRANDE: big, large
GRATIS: gratis
GRAVEMENTE: seriously
GRITAR: to yell
GRITARSE: to yell at each other
GUSTAR: to be pleasing to, like
ME GUSTA: I like

## H

HABER: to have (auxiliary verb)
HÁBITO: habit
HÁBITO NERVIOSO: nervous habit
HABLAR: to speak
HABLAR EN VOZ ALTA: to speak up (loudly)
HABLAR MÁS ALTO: to speak louder
HACE CALOR: it is hot (warm)
HACE FRÍO: it is cold
HACE MUCHO TIEMPO: a long time ago
HACER: to do, to make
HACER COMPRAS: to make purchases
HACER DAÑO A: to hurt someone
HACER ESCALA: to make a stop (plane, train)
HACER PREGUNTAS: to ask questions
HACER UNA CITA: to make (give) an appointment
HACER UNA RESERVA(CIÓN): to make a reservation
HACIA: toward
HASTA (prep.): until
HASTA AHORA: up to now
HASTA (EL DÍA DE) HOY: until today
HASTA QUE (conj.): until
HAY: there is, there are, is there?, are there?
HELADO: ice cream
HERIDO(A): hurt, wounded, injured
HERIR(IE,I): to hurt
HERIRSE(IE,I): to be injured (hurt)
HERMANA: sister
HERMANO: brother
HERMANOS: brothers and sisters
HEROÍNA: heroine
HIJO: son, child

HIJOS: children (sons and daughters)
HOGAR (m): home
HOGAR (m) DE ADOPCIÓN (CRIANZA): foster home
¡HOLA!: hello!
HOMBRE (m): man
HORA: hour, time (of day)
HORAS EXTRA(ORDINARIAS) DE TRABAJO: overtime
HOSPITAL (m): hospital
HOSPITAL (m) DE (P)SIQUIATRÍA: psychiatric hospital
HOSPITALIZAR(C): to hospitalize
HOTEL (m): hotel
HOY: today
HOY MISMO: this very day
HUELLA: finger print
HUELLA DACTILAR (DIGITAL): finger print

I

IDENTIFICAR(QU): to identify
IMPORTE (m): amount
INCENDIO: fire
INCLUÍDO(A): included
INCLUIR(Y): to include
INFLAMABLE: (in)flammable
INFORMACIÓN (f): information
INFORMAR: to inform
INFORME (m): report
INGLÉS: English
INGRESO(S): income
INGRESO NETO: net income

INICIAR: to initiate
INMUNIZAR: to immunize
INSCRIBIR(SE): to register
INSPECCIÓN (f): inspection
INSTRUCCIONES (f): instructions
INTERESES (mpl): interests
INTOXICADO(A): intoxicated, drunk
INVALIDEZ (f): disability
INVÁLIDO(A): disabled
INVIERNO: winter
INYECCIÓN (f): injection
IR: to go
IR A: to be going to
IR DE COMPRAS: to go shopping
IRSE: to leave
IZQUIERDO(A): left

J

JOVEN (mf): young, young man, young woman, youngster
JOYAS (f.pl.): jewels, jewelry
JUGAR(UE,GU): to play (a game)
JUGO: juice
JUGO DE NARANJA: orange juice
JUICIO: trial
JURAR: to swear

L

LA (fem. def. art.): the; (dir. obj. pron.): her, it, you
LA MAYOR PARTE DE: most of
PUNTA: tip

LADRÓN(A): thief
¡QUÉ LÁSTIMA!: What a pity!
LAVAR(SE): to wash (oneself)
LE (dir. obj. pron.): him, you; (ind. obj. pron.): to (him,her,you)
LECCIÓN (f): lesson
LECHE (f): milk
LEER(Y): to read
LENGUA: tongue, language
LES: to you (pl.)
LETRERO: sign
LETRERO DE NO FUMAR: no smoking sign
LEVANTARSE: to get up, to stand up
LEVANTARSE DE LA CAMA: to get out of bed
LEY (f): law
LEY (f) ESTATAL: state law
LEY (f) FEDERAL: federal law
LIBRA: pound
LIBRETA DE AHORROS: bankbook
LIBRO: book
LIBRO DE CHEQUES: checkbook
LIBRO DE BENEFICIOS DE DESEMPLEO: unemployment booklet
LICENCIA: license
LICENCIA DE CONDUCIR: driver's license
LICOR (m): liquor
LÍMITE (m): limit
LIMPIO(A): clean
LÍNEA: line
LÍNEA AEREA: airline
LÍNEA RECTA: straight line
LÍQUIDO: liquid

LÍQUIDO INFLAMABLE: inflammable liquid
LO (neuter def. art.): the; (dir. obj. pron.): him, it, you
LO MÁS POSIBLE: as much as possible
LO QUE: what, that
LO SIENTO: I am sorry (about this)
LOS (m.pl. def. art.): the; (masc. dir. obj. pron.): them
LOS (LAS) DOS: both (of them)
LOS ESTADOS UNIDOS: The United States
LUCHAR: to fight
LUNES (m): Monday
LUZ (f): light
LUZ (f) DE TRÁFICO: traffic light
LUZ (f) ELÉCTRICA: electric light

LL

LLAMAR: to call
LLAMAR POR TELÉFONO: to call on the phone
LLAMARSE: to be called
LLAVE (f): key
LLEGAR: to arrive
LLENAR: to fill out
LLEVAR: to take (somewhere), to take away
LLEVAR ROPA: to wear clothes
LLEVARSE ALGO: to take something away (out)
LLEVARSE BIEN: to get along (well) with

M

MADRE (f): mother
MADRUGADA: early morning
MAESTRO(A) (DE ESCUELA): (school) teacher
MAL, MALO, MALA (adj.): bad; (adv.): badly
MAL TIEMPO: bad weather
MANDAR: to send
MANDAR POR CORREO: to (send by) mail
MANEJAR: to drive (Latin America)
MANO (f): hand
MANTENER: to keep, support
MAÑANA: tomorrow, morning
MARCAR(QU): to mark
MARIDO: husband
MARIGUANA (MARIJUANA): marihuana
MARRÓN: brown
MARTES (m): Tuesday
MARZO: March
MÁS: more
MAS DE: more than (after numeral)
MÁS QUE: more than
MATAR: to kill
MATRICULAR: to register
MÁXIMO(A): maximum
MAYO: May
(EL, LA) MAYOR: (the) oldest
LA MAYORÍA DE LAS VECES: most of the times
ME: (to) me
MEDIA HORA: half an hour
MÉDICO (mf): doctor (M.D.), physician
MÉDICO (mf) DE CABECERA: family doctor
MÉDICO (mf) DE LA ESCUELA: school doctor
MEDIDOR (m): meter (apparatus)
MEDIDOR (m) DE ALCOHOL: drunkometer
MEDIO(A): half
MEJILLA: cheek
MEJOR: better
MENORES (TRIBUNAL DE): Juvenile Court
MENOS: less
MENSUAL: monthly
MENTAL: mental
MERCANCÍA: merchandise
MES (m): month
METAL (m): metal
MI(S): my
MÍ (obj. of prep.): me
MIEMBRO: member
MIENTRAS (QUE): in the meantime
MIENTRAS TANTO: in the meantime
MIÉRCOLES (m): Wednesday
MIL (m): (one) thousand
MIL NOVECIENTOS: nineteen hundred
MINUTO: minute
MÍO(A): (of) mine; (poss. pron.): El(la,los,las) mío(a,os,as)
MIRAR: to look at
MISMO(A)(S): self, same
MITAD (f): half
LA MITAD (f) DE: half of
MONEDA: coin
MONTAR EN EL COCHE: to get into the car
MORDER(UE): to bite
MORDERSE(UE) LAS UÑAS: to bite one's nails

MORIR(UE,U):to die
MOSTRAR(UE): to show
MOVER(SE)(UE): to move
MUCHAS GRACIAS: thank you, thanks a lot, thank you very much
MUCHAS VECES: many times, often
MUCHO(A): much
MUCHO(A)S: many
MUDARSE: to change (clothing, residence)
MUEBLES (m.pl.): furniture
MUJER: woman, wife
MULTA: fine, ticket
MULTA DE TRÁFICO: traffic ticket

N

NACER(ZC): to be born
NACIMIENTO: birth
NADA: nothing, not anything
NADIE: no-one, nobody
NARANJA: orange
NARCÓTICO: drug
NARIZ (f): nose
NECESITAR: to need
NEGRO(A): black
NERVIOSO(A): nervous
NETO: net
NEUMONÍA: pneumonia
NI...NI: neither...or
NINGÚN(O,A): not any
NINGUNO(A): no-one, none
NIÑO(A): child
NIÑOS: children
NO: no, not
NO FUMAR: no smoking
NO IMPORTA: it doesn't matter
NO MÁS: no more

NO PODER: to be unable to
NOMBRAR UN ABOGADO: to appoint a lawyer
NOMBRE (m): name
NORTEAMERICANO(A): North American
NOS (obj. pron.): (to) us
NOSOTRO(A)S (subj. pron.): we
NOTA: note
NOTIFICAR(QU): to notify
NOVECIENTO(A)S: nine hundred
NOVENTA: ninety
NUESTRO(A)(S): our
NUEVA YORK: New York
NUEVE: nine
NUEVO(A): new
NÚMERO: number
NÚMERO DE ASIENTO: seat number
NÚMERO DE TELÉFONO: telephone number
NÚMERO DEL SEGURO SOCIAL: Social Security Number
NUNCA: never

O

O: or
OBEDECER(ZC): to obey
OBRERO(A): workman, worker
O(B)SCURO(A): dark
OBSTRUÍDO(A): obstructed
OBTENER: obtain, to get, receive
OCASIÓN (f): occasion
OCTAVO(A): eighth
OCUPACIÓN (f): occupation
OCURRIR: to occur, happen
OCHENTA: eighty
OCHO: eight
OCHOCIENTO(A)S: eight hundred

OESTE: west
OFERTA: offer
OFERTA DE TRABAJO:
  job offer
OFICIAL (mf): officer
OFICIAL DE NARCÓTICOS:
  narcotics officer
OFICINA: office
OÍR: to hear
OJO: eye
ONCE: eleven
ORDEN (mf): order
ORDINARIO(A): ordinary
ORGANIZACIÓN:
  organization
ORINAR(SE): to urinate
ORINARSE EN LA CAMA:
  to wet the bed
OTRO(A)S: other(s)
OTRA VEZ: again
OTRAS VECES: at
  other times

P

PADECER(ZC) DE: to
  suffer (from)
PADRE (m): father
PADRES (mpl): parents
PAGA: pay(ment)
PAGAR(GU): to pay (for)
PAGAR(GU) LOS GASTOS:
  to pay the expenses
PAGO: pay(ment)
PAGOS DEL SEGURO CONTRA
  EL DESEMPLEO:
  Unemployment Insurance
  Benefits
PALABRA: word
PANTALÓN (m): pants
PANTALONES (mpl): pants
PANTALONES (mpl) DE
  VAQUERO: (blue)
  jeans, dungarees
PAÑUELO: handkerchief

PAPEL (m): paper
PAPERAS: mumps
PAQUETE (m): package
PARAR(SE): to stop
PARAR EN: to stop at
PARCIAL: partial
PARECER(ZC): to seem
PARQUE (m): park
PARROQUIA: parish
PARTE (f) DE ADELANTE:
  front (part)
PARTE (f) DE ATRÁS:
  rear (part)
PASADO(A): past
EL MES PASADO: last month
PASAJE (m): ticket
PASAJE (m) DE IDA: one
  way ticket
PASAJE (m) DE IDA Y
  VUELTA: round trip
  ticket
PASAJE (m) DE PRIMERA
  CLASE: first class
  ticket
PASAJE (m) DE VUELTA:
  return ticket
PASAJE (m) TURISTA:
  tourist class ticket
PASAJERO(A): passenger
PASAPORTE (m): passport
PASAR: to pass, enter,
  happen
PASAR TIEMPO: to spend
  time
¿QUÉ PASA?: What is going
  on?; What is the matter?
PASILLO: aisle, hallway
PATRÓN(O): employer,
  boss, landlord
PEDIR(I): to ask for,
  request
PELEAR: to fight
PELO: hair
PEQUEÑO(A): small
PERDER(IE): to lose

PERDIDO(A): lost, missing
PERÍODO: period
PERÍODO DE ESPERA: waiting period
PERÍODO DE INVALIDEZ: period of disability
PERMANECER(ZC): to stay
PERMANECER(ZC) EN CALMA: to stay calm
PERMANECER(ZC) SOBRE UNA PIERNA: to stand on one leg
PERO: but
PERSONA: person
PERSONA PERDIDA: missing person
PERTENECER(ZC) A: to belong to
PERTENECIENTE A: pertaining to
PESAR: to weigh
PIE (m): foot
DE PIE: standing (up)
PIES (mpl): feet
PIEL (f): fur
PIERNA: leg
PIEZA: piece (of machinery, etc.)
PISO: floor, apartment
PLÁSTICO(A): plastic
POLICÍA (m): policeman, patrolman, police officer (f) police (force)
POLLO: chicken
PONER: to put
PONER ATENCIÓN: to pay attention
PONER UNA MULTA: to give a ticket
PONERSE ALGO: to apply something to oneself.

PONERSE DE PIE: to stand up
PONERSE EN CONTACTO CON: to get in touch with
PONERSE EN FILA: to get on line
PONERSE ROPA: to put on clothes
POPULAR: popular
POR: by, for, per
POR AQUÍ: this way
(TANTO) POR CIENTO: percent
POR CORREO: by mail
POR CORREO AÉREO: by airmail
¿POR CUÁNTO TIEMPO?: for how long?
POR DÍA: per diem (day)
POR EJEMPLO: for example (instance)
POR ESO: for that
POR FAVOR: please
POR LA MAÑANA: in the morning
POR LO COMÚN: usually
¿POR QUÉ? (interr.): why?
POR SEMANA: per (a) week
POR SUPUESTO: of course
POR TELÉFONO: by telephone
PORQUE: because
POSEER(Y): to possess, own
POSIBLE: possible
PRECAUCIÓN (f): precaution
PRECINTO: precinct
PRECINTO DE POLICÍA: police precinct
PREFER(IE,I): to prefer
PREGUNTA: question
PREGUNTAR: to ask (a question)

PREOCUPARSE: to worry about
PRESENTAR: to present
PRESIÓN (f): pressure
PRESIÓN (f) (ARTERIAL) ALTA: high blood pressure
PRESIÓN (f) ARTERIAL: blood pressure
PRESIÓN (f) (ARTERIAL) BAJA: (low) blood pressure
PRIMER(O,A): first
PRIMERA CLASE: first class
LA PRIMERA VEZ: the first time
PRIVADO(A): private
PROBLEMA (m): problem
PRODUCIR(ZC): to produce
PROGRAMA (m): program
PROGRAMA (m) (CONTRA USO)DE NARCÓTICOS: narcotics program
DE PROMEDIO: on the average
PROMETER: to promise
PROPINA: tip
PROPIO(A): own
PROVEER(Y): to provide
PRÓXIMO(A): next
PROYECTO: project
PRUEBA: test
PRUEBA DE ALCOHOL: drunkometer test
PSIQUIATRA (mf): psychiatrist
PSIQUIATRÍA: psychiatry
PÚBLICO(A): public
PUEDE SER: may be
PUERTA: door
PUERTORRIQUEÑO(A): Puerto Rican

PUES: then
PULGADA: inch
PUNTA DE LA NARIZ: tip of the nose
PUÑO: handle (knife)

Q

QUE (rel. pron.): that, which, who, whom
¿QUÉ?: What?
¿QUÉ CLASE DE?: What kind of?
¿QUÉ EDAD TIENE EL BEBÉ?: How old is the baby?
¿QUÉ HORA ES?: What time is it?
¡QUÉ LÁSTIMA!: What a pity!
¿QUÉ TE (LE) DUELE?: What hurts you?
¿QUÉ PASA?: What is the matter?
¿QUÉ PASÓ?: What happened?
¿QUÉ TIENE UD?: What is the matter (wrong, the trouble) with you?
QUEJA: complaint
QUEMADO(A): burnt (out)
QUEMAR: to burn
QUEMARSE: to get burned (burnt)
QUERER: to want
¿QUIÉN? (interr.): Who?
¿A QUIÉN?: (to) whom?
¿QUIÉNES? (pl. interr.): Who?
QUINCE: fifteen
QUINIENTO(A)S: five hundred
QUITAR: to take away (off)
QUITARSE ROPA (SOMBRERO, ZAPATOS, ETC.): to take (slip) off clothes (hat, shoes, etc.)

## R

RADIO (mf): radio, radium
RÁPIDAMENTE: rapidly
RATO: little while
RAZÓN (f): reason, right
REALMENTE: really
RECIBIR: to receive, get
RECIBO: receipt
RECIENTE(MENTE): recent(ly)
RECLAMACIÓN (f): claim
RECLAMAR BENEFICIOS: to claim benefits
REGISTRAR: to register, to search someone
REGISTRO DEL AUTOMÓVIL (COCHE, CARRO)(DE LA MÁQUINA): automobile,(car) registration
REGRESAR: to go (come) back, to return
REGRESAR A CASA: to go (return) home
REGULAR: regular, fair
REHUSAR: to refuse
REPARTIR MERCANCÍAS: to deliver merchandise
REPORTE (m): report
RESBALAR(SE): to slip
RESERVA(CIÓN): reservation
RESPONSABILIDAD (f): responsibility
RESTO: rest
RESULTADO: result
RESULTAR HERIDO(A): to be (become) hurt (injured)
RETRETE (m): toilet
REUMATISMO: rheumatism
ROBO: robbery, theft, burglary
ROJO(A): red
ROPA (fs): clothes, clothing

## S

SABER: to know
SACAR(QU): to pull out, take out
SACAR(QU) LA LENGUA: to stick out one's tongue
SALA: living (sitting) room
SALA DE CLASE: classroom
SALIDA: departure, exit, gate (airport)
SALIR: to leave
SALVAVIDAS (m): life preserver
SARAMPIÓN (m): measles
SARGENTO: sergeant
SE: (to) himself, (to) herself, (to) itself, (to) yourself, (to) themselves, (to) yourselves
SECRETARIO(A): secretary
SECRETARIO(A) DE LA ESCUELA: school secretary
SECUNDARIO(A): secondary
SEGUIR(I,G): to continue
SEGUIR(I,G) DERECHO: to continue straight ahead
SEGUNDO(A): second
SEGURIDAD (f): safety
SEGURO (n): security, insurance
SEGURO(A) (adj.): sure

SEGURO CONTRA (DE) DESEMPLEO: unemployment insurance
SEGURO DE ENFERMEDAD: health insurance
SEGURO DE HOSPITAL: hospital insurance
SEGURO SOCIAL: social security
SEIS: six
SELLO: stamp
SELLOS PARA ALIMENTOS: food stamps
SEMANA: week
LA SEMANA QUE VIENE: next week
SEMANALMENTE: weekly
SEMESTRE (m): semester
SENTARSE(IE): to sit down
SENTIR(IE,I): to be sorry
SENTIRSE(IE,I) BIEN (MAL): to feel well (bad)
SEÑAL (f): sign, mark
SEÑAL (f) DE TRÁFICO: traffic light
SEÑAL (f) DE ALTO (PARADA): stop, stop sign
SEÑAL (f) DE TRÁNSITO (TRÁFICO): traffic light
SEÑAS (DEL DOMICILIO): address
SEÑOR (SR.) (m): Sir, Mr.
SEÑORA (SRA.) (f): Mrs., Madam
SEÑORITA (SRTA.) (f): Miss
SEPARADO(A): separate(d)
SEPARARSE: to move apart

¡SEPÁRENSE!: Break it up!
SE(P)TIEMBRE: September
SER: to be
SER DE...PIES DE ALTO(A): to be...feet tall
SER HOSPITALIZADO(A): to be hospitalized
SERVICIO: service
SERVIR(I): to serve
SESENTA: sixty
SETECIENTO(A)S: seven hundred
SETENTA: seventy
SEXTO(A): sixth
SI: if
SI NO: if not
SÍ: yes
SIEMPRE: always
SIETE: seven
SIGUIENTE: next
SILENCIO: silence
SILLA: chair
SIN (prep.): without
SIN EMBARGO: however
SIQUIATRA (mf): psychiatrist
SIQUIATRÍA: psychiatry
SITIO: place, spot
SITUACIÓN (f): situation
SOBRE: on, upon
SOBRE (m): envelope
SOBRE (m) DE PAGO(A): pay envelope
SOCIAL: social
SOCIEDAD (f): society, club, organization
SOLAMENTE: only
SOLDADO: soldier
SOLDADOR: welder
SOLER(UE): to be accustomed to, to be in the habit of, to do (have) usually
SOLICITAR: to apply for, to claim

SOLICITAR BENEFICIOS:
  to apply for benefits
SOLICITUD:  application
SOLO:  alone
SÓLO:  only
SOLTERA:  single
  (unmarried) woman
SOLTERO:  single
  (unmarried) man
SOMBRERO:  hat
SOMETER A UNA PRUEBA:
  to oblige to take
  a test
SOPLAR:  to blow (up),
  inflate
SOSPECHOSO(A):
  suspicious
SOSTENER:  to hold,
  support
SÓTANO:  basement
SU(S) (poss. adj.):
  his, her, its,
  their, your, one's
SUBIR AL AVIÓN:  to
  board the plane
SUCIO(A):  dirty
SUEGRA:  mother-in-law
SUELDO:  salary, wages
SUELO:  floor (of the
  room)
SUERTE (f):  luck
SUFRIR (DE):  to
  suffer (from)
EL(LA,LOS,LAS)
  SUYO(A,OS,AS) (poss.
  pron): his, hers,
  yours, theirs,
  one's

T

TAL:  such (a)
TAL VEZ:  maybe
TALÓN(ARIO) DE PAGO:
  pay stub

TAMBIÉN:  also, too
TAMPOCO:  neither
TAN:  so
TAN...COMO...:  as...as
TAN PRONTO COMO...:  as
  soon as
TAN PRONTO COMO SEA
  POSIBLE:  as soon as
  possible
TANTO(A):  so (as) much
TAPARSE LA BOCA:  to
  cover one's mouth
TARDAR:  to take (time)
TARDE:  late
TARDE (f):  afternoon,
  evening
TARJETA:  card
TARJETA DE ASISTENCIA
  MÉDICA (MEDICAID):
  Medicaid card
TARJETA DE CRÉDITO:
  credit card
TARJETA DE DESEMPLEO:
  unemployment card
TARJETA DE RECLAMACIÓN:
  claim card
TATUAJE (m):  tatoo
TAXI (m):  taxi(cab)
TE:  (to) you, (to)
  yourself (fam.)
TECHO:  ceiling
TEJADO:  roof
TELÉFONO:  (tele)phone
(AL) TELÉFONO:  on the
  (tele)phone
TELE(VISIÓN):  television
TELEVISOR (m):  television
  set
TEMER:  to be afraid of
TEMOR (m):  fear
TEMPERATURA: temperature
TEMPRANO:  early
TENER:  to have
TENER...AÑOS:  to be...
  years old

TENER CUIDADO: to
  watch out
TENER DOLOR EN...:
  to have a pain
  in...
TENER DOLOR DE ESTÓMAGO:
  to have a stomach ache
TENER EL DERECHO DE:
  to have the right to
TENER HERIDO(A) EL (LA)
  ...: to be hurt
  (wounded) in...
TENER MIEDO DE...:
  to be afraid of...
TENER QUE: to have to
TENER QUE VER CON...:
  to have to do with...
TENER RAZÓN: to be
  right
NO TENER RAZÓN: to
  be wrong
TENER SUERTE: to be
  lucky
TENGA (n) LA BONDAD
  DE: kindly, please
TERCERO(A): third
TERCIO: a third
TERMINAR: to finish
TESTIGO (mf): witness
TI: you (fam.) (obj.
  of prep.)
TÍA: aunt
TÍO: uncle
TIEMPO: time, weather
TIEMPO PARCIAL: part
  time
TIENDA: store, shop
TIENDA DE LICORES:
  liquor store
TIPO: type
TIRAR: to throw
  (away)
TODO(A)(S): all, every
TODAVÍA: still
TODO EL DÍA: all day
  long
TODO EL MUNDO: everybody,
  everyone
TOMAR: to take, eat,
  drink
TOMAR LAS HUELLAS
  DIGITALES: to
  finger print
TORCER(UE,Z): to turn
TOSER: to cough
TOTAL: total
TRABAJADOR(A): worker
TRABAJADOR(A) SOCIAL:
  social worker
TRABAJAR: to work
TRABAJAR A DESTAJO: to
  do piecework
TRABAJAR DURO: to work
  hard
TRABAJO: work, job
TRABAJO A DESTAJO:
  piecework
TRAER: to bring
TRÁFICO: traffic
TRATAMIENTO: treatment
TRATAMIENTO MÉDICO:
  medical treatment
TRATAR: to treat
TRATAR DE: to try to
TRECE: thirteen
TREINTA: thirty
TRES: three
TRESCIENTO(A)S: three
  hundred
TRIBUNAL DE MENORES:
  Juvenile Court
TU(S): your (fam.)
TÚ: you (fam. sing.)
TUBERCULOSIS (f):
  tuberculosis
TURISTA (mf): tourist

U

U: or (before o or ho)
UD. (abbrev. of usted):
  you (form. sing.)

UDS. (abbrev. of
  ustedes): you
  (form. pl.)
ÚLTIMO(A): last
UN(O,A): a, one
UN MOMENTO: (just)
  a moment
UN POCO: a little
UN POCO MÁS: a
  little more
ÚNICO(A): only
UNIDAD DE PROBLEMAS
  FAMILIARES: Family
  Crisis Unit
UNIVERSIDAD (f):
  university
UN(O,A): a, one
UNO(A)S: some, a few,
  about
UÑA: nail
USAR: to use
USO: use
USO DE NARCÓTICOS:
  narcotics usage
USTED (UD., VD.):
  you (sing. formal)
USTEDES (UDS., VDS.):
  you (pl. formal)
USUALMENTE: usually

V

VACACIONES (f. pl.):
  vacation
DE VACACIONES: on
  vacation
VACUNA(CION) (f):
  vaccination
VACUNAR: to vaccinate
VALER LA PENA: to be
  worthwhile
VÁLIDO(A): valid
VALOR (m): worth
VALORES (mpl): assets
VAMOS A VER: let's
  see

VARIAR(Í): to vary
VARIO(A)S: several
VARIAS VECES: several
  times
VARICELA: chicken pox
VECES: times (in a series)
VECINDAD (f)
  (VECINDARIO (m)):
  neighborhood
VECINO(A): neighbor
VEINTE: twenty
VEINTICINCO: twenty five
VENDEDOR (m): salesman
VENDEDORA: saleslady
VENDER: to sell
VENIR: to come
VENIR POR: to come for
  (someone or something)
VENTANA: window
VENTANA DE LA ESCALERA DE
  INCENDIOS: fire escape
  window
VER: to see
VERANO: summer
VERDAD (f): truth
¿VERDAD?: aren't you?,
  do you?, is that so?,
  yes?, etc.
VESTÍBULO: hall
VESTIDO: dress
VESTIR(I): to dress
VESTIRSE(I): to get
  dressed
VETERANO(A) DEL EJÉRCITO:
  (army) veteran
VEZ (f): time (in a
  series)
A LA VEZ: at the same
  time
VIAJE (m): travel
VIEJO(A): old; (n) old
  man (woman)
VIERNES: Friday
VIGILANTE (mf) ESCOLAR:
  truant officer

VIRUELA(S): small pox
VIRUS (m): virus
VISA(DO): visa
VISITAR: to visit,
  to see (someone)
VIUDA: widow
VIUDO: widower
VIVIENDA: housing
VIVIR: to live
VOLAR(UE): to fly
VOLVER(UE): to come
  back, return
VOMITAR: to vomit
VUELO: flight
VUELO DE REGRESO:
  return flight
VUELO DIRECTO:
  direct flight

Y

Y: and
YA: already
YA QUE: since (causal)
YO: I

Z

ZURDO(A): left-handed

ENGLISH - SPANISH

A

A: un(o,a)
A FEW: (alg)uno(a)s
A LITTLE: un poco
A LITTLE MORE: un poco más
A LITTLE WHILE: un rato
A LONG TIME AGO: hace mucho tiempo
A THIRD: un tercio
A (PER) WEEK: por semana
TO ABANDON: abandonar
ABLE: capaz
ABOARD: a bordo
ABOUT: aproximadamente, cerca de, como, uno(a)s
ABSENT: ausente
TO ABSTAIN FROM: abstenerse de
ACCIDENT: accidente (m)
TO ACCOMPANY: acompañar
ACCOUNT: cuenta
BANK ACCOUNT: cuenta de banco
CHECKING ACCOUNT: cuenta corriente
SAVINGS ACCOUNT: cuenta de ahorros
TO ACHE: doler(ue)
TO ACT (AS, FOR): actuar
ADDICT: adicto(a)

ADDRESS: dirección (f), señas del domicilio
ADOPTION: adopción (f)
AEROPLANE: avión (m)
AFTER (adv.): después; (prep.): después de; (conj.): después de que
AFTERNOON: tarde (f)
AGAIN: otra vez
AGAINST: contra
AGE: edad (f)
AGENT: agente (mf)
AID: ayuda
AILMENT: enfermedad (f)
AIR: aire (m).
AIRLINE: línea aérea
AIRLINER }
AIRPLANE  : avión (m)
AIRPORT: aeropuerto
AISLE: pasillo
ALCOHOL: alcohol (m)
ALCOHOLIC (adj. & noun): alcohólico(a)
ALL: todo(a)(s)
ALL DAY LONG: todo el día
ALL RIGHT: (está) bien, pues
ALLERGY: alergia
ALMOST: casi
ALREADY: ya
ALSO: también
ALTITUDE: altitud (f)
ALWAYS: siempre

AMBULANCE: ambulancia
AMERICAN: americano(a)
AMOUNT: importe (m)
AND: y;(before i or hi): e
ANSWER: contestación (f)
ANY: cualquiera
ANYONE: alguien
TO APPROACH: acercarse (qu) a
APARTMENT: apartam(i)ento, piso
TO APPEAR (BEFORE AN AUTHORITY): comparecer(zc)
APPETITE: apetito
APPLICATION: solicitud (f)
TO APPLY FOR: solicitar
TO APPLY FOR BENEFITS: solicitar beneficios
TO APPLY SOMETHING TO ONESELF: aplicarse (qu) (ponerse) algo
TO APPOINT A LAWYER: nombrar un abogado
APPOINTMENT: cita, entrevista
TO KEEP AN APPOINTMENT: asistir a una cita
APPROXIMATELY: aproximadamente
ARE THERE?: ¿hay?
ARMY: ejército
AROUND: cerca de
ARREST: arresto
DRUG ARREST: arresto por narcóticos
TO ARREST: arrestar
TO ARRIVE: llegar(gu)
AS: como
AS...AS: tan...como
AS MUCH AS: tanto(a)

AS MUCH AS POSSIBLE: lo más posible
AS SOON AS: tan pronto como
AS SOON AS POSSIBLE: tan pronto como sea posible
TO ASK A QUESTION: hacer una pregunta, preguntar
TO ASK FOR: pedir(i)
ASSETS: valores (mpl)
TO ASSIGN: asignar
ASSISTANCE: auxilio, ayuda
AT: a
AT...O'CLOCK: a la(s)...
AT OTHER TIMES: otras veces
AT THE LATEST: a más tardar
AT THE SAME TIME: a la vez
AT WHAT TIME?: ¿A qué hora?
AT WORK: al trabajo
ATTACHED: adjunto(a)
TO ATTACK: atacar(qu)
TO ATTEND SCHOOL: asistir a la escuela
ATTENTION: atención (f)
AUNT: tía
AUTHORIZATION: autorización (f)
AUTOMOBILE (CAR) REGISTRATION: registro del automóvil (coche, carro)
AVAILABLE: disponible
AVAILABLE FOR WORK: disponible para trabajar
AVENUE: avenida
AWAY: fuera

B

BABY: bebé (m), nene(a).
BACHELOR: soltero
BAD: mal(o,a)
BADLY: mal
BAG: bolsa
PAPER BAG: bolsa de papel
BAGGAGE: equipaje (m)
BALLOON: balón (m)
BANK: banco
SAVINGS BANK: banco de ahorros
BANK BOOK: libro (libreta) de banco (cheques)
BANK TELLER: cajero(a)
BAR: bar (m)
BASEMENT: sótano
BATHROOM: cuarto de baño
BATHTUB: bañera
TO BE: ser, estar
TO BE ACCUSTOMED TO: soler(ue)
TO BE AFRAID OF: tener miedo de, temer
TO BE ALL RIGHT: estar bien
TO BE BORN: nacer(zc)
TO BE CALLED: llamarse
TO BE CAREFUL: tener cuidado
TO BE EXPOSED: estar al aire
TO EXTEND: alargar(gu)
TO BE...FEET TALL: ser de...pies de alto
TO BE FINGERPRINTED: tomar las huellas digitales a alguien.
TO BE GOING TO: ir a
TO BE HOSPITALIZED: ser hospitalizado(a)

TO BE HURT;(INJURED): ser (resultar) herido (a); herirse(ie,i) tener herido(a) el(la)...
TO BE IN ORDER: estar en orden
TO BE IN THE HABIT OF: soler(ue)
TO BE LUCKY: tener suerte
TO BE MARRIED: estar (ser) casado(a)
TO BE MISSING: faltar
TO BE OUT: estar fuera
TO BE OUT OF WORK: estar sin trabajo
TO BE READY: estar listo(a)
TO BE RIGHT: tener razón
TO BE SICK: estar enfermo(a), (mal(o,a))
TO BE SORRY: sentir (ie,i)
TO BE SURE: estar seguro(a)
TO BE UNABLE TO: no poder
TO BE UNDER ARREST: estar bajo arresto
TO BE UNDER CONTROL: estar bajo control
TO BE UNDER MEDICAL TREATMENT: estar bajo tratamiento médico
TO BE WELL: estar bien
TO BE WORTHWHILE: valer la pena
TO BE WOUNDED: estar (resultar) herido(a)
TO BE WRONG: no tener razón
TO BE...YEARS OLD: tener (cumplir)...años
BEARD: barba
BECAUSE: porque
BECAUSE OF: a causa de
BED: cama

BEDROOM: dormitorio
BEFORE (adv): antes
  (prep): antes de;
  (conj): antes(de) que
TO BEGIN: empezar(ie,c)
TO BELONG TO:
  pertenecer(zc) a
BELT: cinturón (m)
TO BEND (OVER):
  doblarse
BENEFICIARY:
  beneficiario
BENEFIT: beneficio
BESIDES: además
BETTER: mejor
BETWEEN: entre
BEVERAGE: bebida
ALCOHOLIC BEVERAGE:
  bebida alcohólica
BIG: grande
BILL: cuenta
ELECTRIC BILL:
  cuenta de electricidad
TELEPHONE BILL:
  cuenta de teléfono
BIRTH: nacimiento
BIRTH CERTIFICATE:
  certificado de
  nacimiento
TO BITE: morder(ue)
TO BITE ONE'S NAILS:
  morderse(ue) las
  uñas
BLACK: negro(a)
BLIND: ciego(a)
BLOOD PRESSURE:
  presión (f)
  (arterial)
TO BLOW (UP): soplar
BLUE: azul
TO BOARD THE PLANE:
  subir al avión
BOND: bono

GOVERNMENT BOND: bono
  del gobierno
BOOK: libro
BOTH: lo(a)s dos, ambo(a)s
BOX: caja
BREAK IT UP!: ¡sepárense!
BREAKFAST: desayuno
TO BRING: traer
BROTHER: hermano
BROTHERS AND SISTERS:
  hermanos
BROWN: marrón
BUILDING: edificio
BURGLARY: robo
TO BURN: quemar
BURNED (BURNT):
  quemado(a)
BUT: pero
TO BUY: comprar
BY: por
BY AIRMAIL: por correo
  aéreo
BY HIM (HER) SELF: solo
BY MAIL: por correo
BY PHONE: por teléfono

C

CALENDAR: calendario
CALENDAR INSERT:
  calendario adjunto
TO CALL: llamar
TO CALL ON THE PHONE:
  llamar por teléfono
CALM: calma
TO CALM DOWN: calmarse
CANCER: cáncer (m)
CAR: automóvil (m),
  coche (m), máquina,
  (Cuba): carro
CARBONATED WATER:
  (agua) gaseosa
CARD: tarjeta
CASE: caso

CAUSE: causa
CAVITY: caries (f)
CEILING: techo
CELL: celda
DETENTION CELL: celda de detención
CENT: centavo
CEREAL: cereal (m)
COLD CEREAL: cereal (m) frío
HOT CEREAL: cereal (m) caliente
CERTIFICATE: certificado
VACCINATION CERTIFICATE: certificado de vacuna(ción)
CHAIR: silla
CHANGE: cambio
TO CHANGE: cambiar
TO CHANGE CLOTHING (RESIDENCE): mudarse
TO CASH: cambiar
CHECK: cheque (m)
CHEEK: mejilla
CHICKEN: pollo
CHICKEN POX: varicela
CHILD: niño(a), hijo(a)
CHILDREN: hijos, niños
CITIZEN: ciudadano(a)
CITY: ciudad (f)
CLAIM: reclamación (f)
CLAIM CARD: tarjeta de reclamación
TO CLAIM BENEFITS: solicitar (reclamar) beneficios
CLASS: clase (f)
CLASSROOM: sala de clase
CLEAN: limpio(a)
CLEARLY: claramente
CLERK: dependiente (mf)
TO CLOSE: cerrar(ie)
CLOSED: cerrado(a)
CLOTHES, CLOTHING: ropa (fs)

CLUB: club (m), sociedad (f)
COAT: abrigo
COIN: moneda
COLD: frío(a)
IT IS COLD: hace frío
TO COLLECT: cobrar
COLOR: color (m)
TO COME: venir
TO COME BACK: regresar, volver(ue)
TO COME FOR: venir por
TO COME IN: entrar
COMMUNITY: comunidad (f)
COMPENSATION: compensación (f)
COMPLAINT: queja
TO CONFIRM: confirmar
TO CONSIDER: considerar
CONTAINER: bolsa
TO CONTINUE: seguir(i,g)
TO CONTINUE STRAIGHT AHEAD: seguir(i,g) derecho
CONTROL: control (m)
CORNER (OUTER): esquina
CORPORATION: corporación (f)
CORRECT: correcto(a)
TO COST: costar(ue)
TO COUGH: toser
COUNSELOR: consejero(a)
COUPON: cupón (m)
COURT: Corte (f)
TO COVER ONE'S MOUTH: taparse la boca
CREDIT: crédito
CREDIT CARD: tarjeta de crédito
CURB: acera
TO CURE: curar
TO CUT: cortar
TO CUT OFF THE LIGHT: cortar la luz

D

DARK: o(b)scuro(a)
DATE: fecha
TODAY'S DATE: fecha de hoy
DAY: día (m)
DEBT: deuda
DECENT: decente
DECLARATION: declaración (f)
TO DEDUCT: deducir(zc)
DEGREE (TEMPERATURE): grado
DELAYED: atrasado(a)
TO DELIVER MERCHANDISE: repartir mercancías
DELIVERY OF MERCHANDISE: entrega de mercancías
DENTIST: dentista (mf)
DEPARTMENT: departamento
DEPARTMENT STORE: almacén (m)
DEPARTURE: salida
TO DEPEND: depender
TO DEPOSIT: depositar
TO DESCRIBE: describir
DESCRIPTION: descripción (f)
DESTINATION: destino
DETECTIVE: detective (mf)
TO DIE: morir(ue)
DIFFERENCE: diferencia
DIFFERENT: diferente
DIFFICULT: difícil
DIFFICULTY: dificultad (f)
DINNER: cena
DIPHTERIA: difteria
DIRECT: directo(a)
DIRECT FLIGHT: vuelo directo
DIRECTION: dirección (f)
DIRTY: sucio(a)

DISABILITY: invalidez (f)
DISABLED: inválido(a)
TO DISCUSS: discutir
DISEASE: enfermedad (f)
TO DISMISS (FROM A JOB): despedir(i)
TO DISPOSE OF: disponer de
DISPUTE: disputa
DIVORCED: divorciado(a)
TO DO: hacer
TO DO A LESSON: aprender una lección
TO DO PIECEWORK: trabajar a destajo
TO DO USUALLY: soler(ue)
DOCTOR: doctor(a), médico
DOCTOR'S OFFICE: consulta (consultorio) del médico
DOLLAR: dólar (m)
DOOR: puerta
DRESS: vestido
TO DRESS: vestir(se)(i)
DRESS FACTORY: fábrica de vestidos
DRINK: bebida
CARBONATED (SOFT) DRINK: (bebida) gaseosa
TO DRINK: beber, tomar
TO DRIVE: conducir(zc), (Lat. Amer.): manejar
DRIVER: conductor(a)
DRUG: droga, narcótico
DRUG ADDICT: adicto(a) a las drogas (narcóticos)
DRUNK: intoxicado(a), borracho(a)
DRUNKOMETER: medidor (m) de alcohol
DRUNKOMETER TEST: prueba de alcohol
DURING: durante

E

EACH: cada
EACH ONE: cada uno(a)
EARLY: temprano
EARLY MORNING: madrugada
TO EARN: ganar
EAST: este
EASY: fácil
TO EAT: comer, tomar
EDUCATION: educación (f)
EIGHT: ocho
EIGHT HUNDRED:
 ochociento(a)s
EIGHTEEN: dieciocho
EIGHTH: octavo(a)
EIGHTY: ochenta
ELECTRIC: eléctrico(a)
ELECTRIC LIGHT: luz (f)
 eléctrica
ELECTRICITY:
 electricidad (f)
ELEVATOR: ascensor (m)
ELEVATOR OPERATOR:
 ascensorista (mf)
ELEVEN: once
EMERGENCY: emergencia
EMPLOYER: patrono(a)
EMPLOYMENT: empleo
ENGLISH: inglés
TO ENGRAVE: grabar
ENOUGH: bastante
TO ENTER: entrar
ENVELOPE: sobre (m)
EPILEPTIC:
 epiléptico(a)
TO ERASE: borrar
TO ESCAPE: escapar(se)
EVENING: tarde (f)
THIS EVENING: esta tarde
EVER: alguna vez
EVERY: cada, todo(a)s
EVERYBODY, EVERYONE:
 todo el mundo,
 cada uno

EXACTLY: exactamente
EXAMPLE: ejemplo
EXCEPT: excepto
EXCESS: exceso
EXCESS BAGGAGE: exceso de
 equipaje
TO EXCHANGE: cambiar
EXCHANGE: cambio
EXCUSE: excusa
EXCUSE ME: dispénseme
EXIT: salida
TO EXPECT: esperar
EXPENSE: gasto
EXPOSED: al aire
TO EXTEND: alargar(gu)
EXTERIOR: exterior
EXTRA: extra
EYE: ojo

F

FACTORY: fábrica
FAIR: regular
FALSE: falso(a)
FAMILY: familia
FAMILY CRISIS UNIT:
 unidad (f) de problemas
 familiares
FAMILY DOCTOR: médico
 de cabecera
TO FASTEN THE SEAT BELT:
 abrocharse el cinturón
 de seguridad
FATHER: padre (m)
FEAR: temor (m)
FEDERAL: federal
FEDERAL LAW: ley (f)
 federal
TO FEEL BAD (WELL):
 sentirse(ie,i) mal
 (bien)
FEET: pies (mpl)
FEVER: fiebre (f)
FIFTEEN: quince
FIFTY: cincuenta

TO FIGHT: luchar, pelear
TO FILE A COMPLAINT:
  formular una queja
TO FILL OUT: llenar
FILLING OF TOOTH:
  empaste (m)
FINANCIAL AID: ayuda
  económica
TO FIND: encontrar(ue)
TO FIND OUT ABOUT:
  enterarse de
FINE: está bien;(n): multa
FINGER: dedo
FINGER PRINT: huella
  dactilar (digital)
TO FINISH: terminar
FIRE: fuego, incendio
FIRE DEPARTMENT:
  departamento de
  incendios, cuerpo
  de bomberos
FIRE ESCAPE: escalera
  de incendios
FIRE ESCAPE WINDOW:
  ventana de la escalera
  de incendios
FIREMAN: bombero
FIRM (n): firma
FIRST: primero(a)
FIRST CLASS TICKET:
  pasaje (boleto) de
  primera clase
THE FIRST TIME: la
  primera vez
FIVE: cinco
FIVE HUNDRED:
  quiniento(a)s
TO FIX: arreglar
FLAMMABLE: inflamable
FLIGHT: vuelo
DIRECT FLIGHT: vuelo
  directo
FLOOR (OF BUILDING):
  piso, (of room):
  piso, suelo

TO FLY: volar(ue)
TO FOLLOW: seguir(i,g)
FOOD: alimentos
FOOD STAMPS: estampillas
  (cupones, sellos) para
  alimentos
FOOT: pie (m)
FOR: por, para
FOR EXAMPLE: por ejemplo
FOR HIRE: de alquiler
FOR HOW LONG?: ¿Por
  cuánto tiempo?
FOR EXAMPLE (INSTANCE):
  por ejemplo
FOR RENT: de alquiler
FOR THAT: por eso
FOREMAN: capataz (m)
FORM: formulario
TO FORMULATE: formular
FORTY: cuarenta
FOSTER HOME: hogar (m)
  de adopción (crianza)
FOUR: cuatro
FOURTEEN: catorce
FOURTH: cuarto
FRIDAY: viernes (m)
FRIEND: amigo(a)
FROM: de, desde
FRONT PART: parte (f) de
  adelante
FUR COAT: abrigo de piel
FURNITURE: muebles (mpl)

G

GATE (AIRPORT): salida
GENERALLY: generalmente
TO GET: obtener, recibir,
  conseguir(i,g),
TO GET ALONG WELL WITH:
  llevarse bien con
TO GET ANGRY: enfadarse
TO GET DRESSED:
  vestirse(i)

TO GET IN TOUCH WITH:
  ponerse en contacto
  con
TO GET INTO THE CAR:
  montar en el coche
TO GET ON LINE: ponerse
  en fila, hacer cola
TO GET OUT OF BED:
  levantarse de la cama
TO GET RUINED:
  arruinarse
TO GET UP: levantarse
TO GIVE: dar
TO GIVE A TICKET (FINE)
  TO: poner una multa a
TO GIVE AN APPOINTMENT:
  hacer una cita
TO GO: ir
TO GO NEAR: acercarse
  (qu) a
TO GO ON VACATION: ir
  de vacaciones
TO GO SHOPPING: ir de
  compras
TO GO TO BED:
  acostarse(ue)
GOOD: bueno(a)
GOOD AFTERNOON: buenas
  tardes
GOOD BYE: adiós
GOOD MORNING: buenos
  días
GOOD NIGHT: buenas
  noches
GROCERY STORE   (Lat.
  Amer.): bodega
GOVERNMENT BOND: bono
  del gobierno
GRADE (IN SCHOOL): grado
GRATIS: gratis
GUILTY: culpable

H

HABIT: hábito

NERVOUS HABIT: hábito
  nervioso
HAIR: pelo
HALF: medio(a), mitad (f)
HALF AN HOUR: media hora
HALF OF: la mitad de
HALL(WAY): vestíbulo,
  corredor (m), pasillo
HAND: mano (f)
HANDCUFFS: esposas
HANDKERCHIEF: pañuelo
HANDLE (OF KNIFE):
  puño, mango
TO HANG (UP): colgar(ue,
  gu)
TO HAPPEN: ocurrir,
  pasar
HARD: duro(a)
HAT: sombrero
TO HAVE: tener, (auxil.):
  haber
TO HAVE A RIGHT TO: tener
  derecho a
TO HAVE A STOMACH ACHE:
  tener dolor de estómago
TO HAVE PAIN IN: tener
  dolor en
TO HAVE TO: tener que
TO HAVE TO DO WITH: tener
  que ver con
TO HAVE...USUALLY:
  soler(ue) tener
HE: él
HEAD: cabeza
HEALTH INSURANCE: seguro
  de enfermedad
TO HEAR: oír
HEART: corazón (m)
HEART AILMENT (DISEASE):
  enfermedad (f) de
  corazón
HEAT(ING): calefacción (f)
HELLO: ¡hola! (on the
  phone): bueno, dígame
HELP: ayuda

TO HELP: ayudar
HER: (poss. adj.): su(s),
  (dir. obj. pron.): la,
  (obj. of prep.): ella
HERE: aquí
HERE IT IS: aquí está,
  aquí (la) tiene
HEROINE: heroína
HERS: (poss. pron.): el
  (la, los, las)
  suyo(a,os,as)
(TO) HERSELF: se
HIGH: alto(a)
HIGH BLOOD PRESSURE:
  presión (arterial)
  alta
HIM: (dir. obj. pron.):
  le, lo,(obj. of
  prep.): él
TO HIM: le
(TO) HIMSELF: se, él
  mismo
HIS: (poss. adj.):
  su(s), (poss. pron.):
  el (la, los, las)
  suyo(a,os,as)
TO HOLD: sostener
HOLD-UP: atraco
HOLIDAY: día (f) de
  fiesta
HOME: casa, hogar (m)
HOSPITAL: hospital (m)
HOSPITAL INSURANCE:
  seguro de hospital
(TO) HOSPITALIZE:
  hospitalizar(c)
HOT: caliente
IT IS HOT: hace calor
HOTEL: hotel (m)
HOUR: hora
HOUSE: casa
PRIVATE HOUSE: casa
  privada (particular)
HOUSING: vivienda

HOUSING AUTHORITY:
  Departamamento de
  Vivienda
HOW?: ¿Cómo?
HOW ARE YOU?: ¿Cómo está
  Vd?
HOW DO YOU FEEL?: ¿Cómo
  se siente Vd?
HOW LONG IS IT THAT...?:
  ¿Cuánto tiempo hace
  que...?
HOW MANY?: ¿Cuánto(a)s?
HOW MUCH?: ¿Cuánto(a)?
HOW OLD ARE YOU?:
  ¿Cuántos años tienes
  (tiene Vd.)? ¿Qué edad
  tienes (tiene Vd.)?
HOWEVER: sin embargo
HUNDRED: ciento,
  (before noun): cien
TO HURT (ACHE): doler(ue)
TO HURT SOMEONE:
  herir(ie,i), hacer daño
  a
HURT: herido(a)
HUSBAND: esposo, marido

I

I: yo
ICE CREAM: helado
TO IDENTIFY:
  identificar(qu)
IF: si
IF NOT: si no
ILLNESS: enfermedad (f)
TO IMMUNIZE: inmunizar(c)
IN: en, a
IN A FEW MINUTES: en unos
  (pocos) minutos
IN A WEEK: en una semana
IN CASE: en caso (de) que
IN FRONT OF: ante,
  frente a

IN THE AFTERNOON: por la tarde, (after spec. time): de la tarde
IN THE FIRST PLACE: en primer lugar
IN THE FUTURE: en el futuro
IN THE MEANTIME: entretanto, mientras (que)(tanto)
IN THE MORNING: por la mañana, (after spec. time): de la mañana
IN THE NAME OF: a (en el) nombre de
IN THIS WAY: de esta manera
IN TWO WEEKS: en dos semanas
INCH: pulgada
INCLUDED: incluído(a)
INCOME: ingreso(s)
INFLAMMABLE: inflamable
INFLAMMABLE LIQUID: líquido inflamable
TO INFLATE: soplar, inflar
TO INFORM: informar
TO INITIATE: iniciar
INJECTION: inyección (f)
INJURED: herido(a)
INSPECTION: inspección (f)
INSTRUCTIONS: instrucciones (fpl)
INTERESTS: intereses (mpl)
INTERVIEW: entrevista
INTOXICATED: intoxicado(a), borracho(a)
ISN'T THAT SO?: ¿(no es) verdad?
IS THERE?: ¿hay?
IT: (subj. pron): él, ella (dir. obj.):lo, la

IT DOESN'T MATTER: no importa
ITS: (poss. adj.): su(s), (poss. pron.): el(la, los, las) suyo(a,os,as)
(TO) ITSELF: se

J

JACKET: chaqueta
JAIL: cárcel (f)
JEANS: pantalones (mpl) de vaquero
JEWELRY, JEWELS: joyas
JOB: empleo, trabajo
JOB OFFER: oferta de trabajo
JUICE: jugo
JUST A MOMENT: un momento
JUVENILE COURT: Tribunal de Menores

K

TO KEEP: mantener
KEY: llave (f)
TO KILL: matar
KIND (adj.): amable (n): clase
KINDLY: tenga(n) la bondad de
KINDNESS: bondad (f)
KITCHEN: cocina
KNIFE: cuchillo
TO KNOW: saber

L

TO LAND: aterrizar(c)
LANDLORD: casero, dueño
LANGUAGE: lengua
LARGE: grande
LAST: último(a)
LAST NIGHT: anoche

LAST MONTH: el mes pasado
LAST YEAR: el año pasado
TO LAST: durar
LATE: tarde
LAW: ley (f)
LAWYER: abogado(a)
TO LAY OUT MONEY: gastar dinero
LEAK: gotera
TO LEAN AGAINST: apoyarse contra
TO LEARN: aprender
TO LEARN A LESSON: aprender una lección
LEASE: contrato de arrendamiento
TO LEAVE: salir, irse (abandon): abandonar, (to leave a job): dejar un empleo, (to leave behind): dejar
LEFT: izquierdo(a)
LEFT-HANDED: zurdo(a)
LEG: pierna
LESS: menos
LESSON: lección (f)
TO LET: dejar, permitir, (rent): alquilar, arrendar(ie)
TO LET OUT THE AIR: dejar salir el aire
LET'S SEE: vamos a ver
LICENSE: licencia
TO LIE DOWN: acostarse(ue)
LIFE PRESERVER: salvavidas (m)
LIFE SAVING JACKET: chaleco salvavidas
LIGHT: luz (f)
LIKE: como

TO LIKE: gustar (I like: me gusta)
LIKE THIS: así
LIMIT: límite (m)
LINE: línea, (of people, cars, etc.): fila, cola
STRAIGHT LINE: línea recta
LIQUID: líquido
LIQUOR: licor (m)
LIQUOR STORE: tienda de licores
TO LIVE: vivir
LIVING ROOM: sala
LOCK: cerradura
SAFETY LOCK: cerradura de seguridad
TO LOCK: cerrar(ie) con llave
TO LOOK AT: mirar
TO LOOK FOR: buscar(qu)
TO LOSE: perder(ie)
LOST: perdido(a)
LOW: bajo(a)
LOW BLOOD PRESSURE: presión (arterial)baja
LUCK: suerte (f)
TO BE LUCKY: tener suerte
LUNCH: almuerzo

M

MADAM: señora (Sra.)
MAIL: correo
TO (SEND BY) MAIL: mandar por correo
TO MAKE A RESERVATION: hacer una reserva(ción)
TO MAKE A STOP: hacer escala
TO MAKE AN APPOINTMENT: hacer una cita
TO MAKE PURCHASES: hacer compras

MAN: hombre (m)
MANY: mucho(a)s
MANY TIMES: muchas veces
MARCH: marzo
MARIHUANA: mariguana, marijuana
MARK: señal (f)
TO MARK: marcar(qu)
MARRIED: casado(a)
MATTER: asunto
MAXIMUM: máximo(a)
MAY: mayo
MAYBE: puede ser, tal vez
(TO) ME: me, (obj. of prep.): mí
MEASLES: sarampión (m)
MEDICAL: médico(a)
MEDICAL EXPENSES: gastos médicos
MEDICAL TREATMENT: tratamiento médico
MEDICAID CARD: tarjeta de Asistencia Médica (Medicaid)
MEMBER: miembro
MEMBER OF FAMILY: familiar (m)
MENTAL ILLNESS: enfermedad (f) mental
MERCHANDISE: mercancía(s)
METAL: metal (m)
METER (apparatus): medidor (m)
MILK: leche (f)
(OF) MINE: el(la, los, las) mío(a,os,as)
MINUTE: minuto
MISS: señorita (Srta.)
MISSING: perdido(a)
MISSING PERSON: persona perdida
MONDAY: lunes (m)

MONEY: dinero
MONTH: mes (m)
LAST MONTH: el mes pasado
MONTHLY: mensual
MORE: más
MORE THAN: más que, (after numeral): más de
MOREOVER: además
MORNING: mañana
THIS MORNING: esta mañana
MOST OF: la mayor parte de
MOST OF THE TIMES: la mayoría de las veces
MOTHER: madre (f)
MOTHER-IN-LAW: suegra
TO MOVE: mover(se)(ue)
TO MOVE APART: separarse
TO MOVE CLOSER: acercarse(qu) más
MOVIES: cine (m)
MR.: señor (Sr.)
MRS.: señora (Sra.)
MUCH: mucho(a)
MUMPS: papera(s)
MY: mi(s)

N

NAIL: uña
NAME: nombre (m)
LAST NAME: apellido
NARCOTICS: narcóticos
NARCOTICS ADDICT: adicto(a) a las drogas (narcóticos)
NARCOTICS OFFICE: oficina de narcóticos
NARCOTICS PROGRAM: programa(contra uso)de narcóticos
NEAR: cerca de
NEARLY: casi
TO NEED: necesitar
NEIGHBOR: vecino(a)
NEIBHBORHOOD: vecindario
NEITHER: tampoco

NEITHER...NOR: ni...ni
NERVOUS: nervioso(a)
NEVER: nunca
NEW YORK: Nueva York
NEXT: próximo(a), siguiente
NEXT WEEK: la semana que viene
NICKNAME: apodo
NINE: nueve
NINE HUNDRED: noveciento(a)s
NINETEEN HUNDRED: mil novecientos
NINETY: noventa
NO: no
NO MORE: no más
NO-ONE; NOBODY: nadie, ningún(o)
NO SMOKING: no fumar
NO SMOKING SIGN: letrero de no fumar
NORTH AMERICAN: norteamericano(a)
NOSE: nariz (f)
NOT: no
NOT ANYTHING: nada
NOTE: nota
NOTHING: nada
TO NOTIFY: notificar(qu)
TO NOTIFY: comunicar(qu), avisar, hacer saber
NOW: ahora
NUMBER: número
NURSE: enfermero(a)

O

O.K.: está bien
TO OBEY: obedecer(zc) a
TO OBLIGE TO TAKE A TEST: someter a una prueba
OBSTRUCTED: obstruído(a)
TO OBTAIN: obtener, conseguir(i,g)
OCCASION: ocasión (f)
OCCUPATION: ocupación (f)
TO OCCUR: ocurrir
OF: de
OF COURSE: por supuesto
OFFER: oferta
OFFICE: oficina
OFFICER: oficial (mf)
OFTEN: muchas veces, a menudo
OLD: viejo(a)
OLD MAN: viejo
OLD WOMAN: vieja
THE OLDEST: el(la) mayor
ON: en, sobre
ON THE AVERAGE: de promedio
ON THE LEFT: a la izquierda
ON THE PHONE: al teléfono, en el teléfono
ON THE RIGHT: a la derecha
ON TIME: a tiempo
ON VACATION: de vacaciones
ONE: uno(a)
ONE'S: su(s), el(la, los, las) suyo(a,os,as)
ONLY (adj.): único(a), (adv.): sólo, solamente
TO OPEN: abrir
OPEN: abierto(a)
TO OPEN AN ACCOUNT: abrir una cuenta
OR: o, (before o or ho): u
ORANGE: naranja
ORANGE JUICE: jugo de naranja
ORDER: orden (m)
ORDINARY: ordinario(a)

ORGANIZATION:
  organización (f),
  sociedad (f)
OTHER(S): otro(a)(s)
OTHERWISE: de otro
  modo
OUR: nuestro(a)(s)
OUT: fuera
OVERCOAT: abrigo
OVERTIME: horas extra-
  (ordinarias) de
  trabajo
TO OWE: deber
OWN (adj.): propio(a)
TO OWN: poseer(y)

P

PACKAGE: paquete (m)
PAIN: dolor (m)
PANTS: pantalón(es)(mpl)
PAPER: papel (m)
PARENTS: padres (mpl)
PARISH: parroquia
PARK: parque (m)
PART TIME: tiempo
  parcial
PARTIAL: parcial
PASSENGER: pasajero(a)
PATROLMAN: policía (m)
PAY: pago(a)
PAY ENVELOPE: sobre
  (m) de pago(a)
PAY STUB: talón(ario)
  de pago
TO PAY(FOR): pagar(gu)
TO PAY ATTENTION:
  poner atención
TO PAY EXPENSES:
  pagar(gu) los gastos
PAYMENT: pago(a)
PEOPLE: gente (fs)
PER: por
PER ANNUM: por (al)
  año

PER DAY(DIEM): por (al)
  día
PER MONTH: por (al) mes
PER WEEK: por (a la)
  semana
PERCENT:(tanto)por ciento
PERIOD: período
PERIOD OF DISABILITY:
  período de invalidez
PERSON: persona
PERTAINING TO:
  perteneciente a
PHOTO(GRAPH): foto-
  (grafía)
PHYSICIAN: médico (mf)
TO PICK UP (SOMETHING):
  recoger(j)
PIECE (OF MACHINERY):
  pieza
PLACE: sitio
TO PLACE: colocar(qu)
PLASTICS FACTORY: fábrica
  de plásticos
TO PLAY: jugar(ue, gu)
TO PLEAD NOT GUILTY:
  declararse inocente
PLEASE: por favor, tenga
  la bondad de
PNEUMONIA: neumonía
POLICE FORCE: policía
POLICE HEADQUARTERS:
  Comisaría de Policía
POLICEMAN: policía (m)
POLICE OFFICER: policía (mf)
POLICE PRECINCT: precinto
  de policía
POLICE STATION: estación(f)
  de policía
POPULAR: popular
TO POSSESS: poseer(y)
POSSIBLE: posible
POUND: libra
PRECAUTION: precaución (f)
TO PREFER: preferir(ie,i)
PRESENT: actual

TO PRESENT: presentar
PRESSURE: presión (f)
PRIVATE: privado(a)
PROBLEM: problema (m)
TO PRODUCE: producir(zc)
PROGRAM: programa (m)
PROJECT: proyecto
TO PROMISE: prometer
TO PROVIDE: proveer(y)
PSYCHIATRIC HOSPITAL: hospital (m) de (p)siquiatría
PSYCHIATRIST: (p)siquiatra (mf)
PSYCHIATRY: (p)siquiatría
PUBLIC: público(a)
PUBLIC ASSISTANCE: ayuda pública
PUERTO RICAN: puertorriqueño(a)
TO PULL OVER TO THE CURB: arrimarse a la acera
PURCHASE: compra
TO PURCHASE: comprar
TO PUSH: empujar
TO PULL OUT: sacar(qu)
TO PUT: poner
TO PUT ON CLOTHES: ponerse (la) ropa
TO PUT TO BED (SLEEP): acostar(ue)

Q

QUESTION: pregunta

R

RADIO: radio(mf)
RADIUM: radio
RAPIDLY: rápidamente
TO READ: leer(y)
REALLY: realmente

REAR PART: parte (f) de atrás
REASON: razón (f)
RECEIPT: recibo
TO RECEIVE: recibir, obtener
RECENTLY: reciente(mente)
RED: rojo(a)
TO REFUSE: rehusar
TO REGISTER: registrar(se), matricular(se), inscribir(se)
REGULAR: regular
RELATIVE: familiar (m)
RENT: alquiler (m)
RENTALS: alquileres (mpl)
REPORT: reporte (m), informe (m)
TO REPORT: dar parte de, (denounce): denunciar
TO REQUEST: pedir(i)
RESERVATION: reserva(ción) (f)
RESPONSIBILITY: responsibilidad (f)
REST: resto
THE REST: lo demás
RESULT: resultado
TO RETURN: regresar, volver(ue)
TO RETURN HOME: regresar a casa
TO RETURN SOMETHING: devolver(ue)
RETURN TICKET: pasaje (m) (boleto) de vuelta
RHEUMATISM: reumatismo
RICE: arroz (m)
RIGHT: derecho
RIGHT AWAY: enseguida
RIGHT NOW: ahora mismo
ROBBER: ladrón(a)
ROBBERY: robo
ROOF: tejado, (flat roof): azotea

ROOM: cuarto
ROUND TRIP TICKET: pasaje (boleto) de ida y vuelta
RUBBISH: basura
TO RUIN: arruinar
TO RUN AWAY: escaparse

S

SAFE DEPOSIT BOX: caja de seguridad
SALARY: sueldo, salario, paga(o)
TO SAVE MONEY: ahorrar dinero
SAVINGS: ahorros
TO SAY: decir
SCALE: balanza
SCAR: cicatriz (f)
SCARLET FEVER: (fiebre) escarlatina
SCHOOL: escuela
SECONDARY SCHOOL: escuela secundaria
SCHOOL DOCTOR: médico de la escuela
SCHOOL FOR MENTALLY RETARDED: escuela para atrasados mentales
SCHOOL SECRETARY: secretario(a) de la escuela
TO SEARCH (SOMEONE): registrar a
SEAT: asiento
AISLE SEAT: asiento junto al pasillo
WINDOW SEAT: asiento junto a la ventana
SEAT NUMBER: número de asiento
SECOND: segundo(a)
SECONDARY: secundario(a)
SECRETARY: secretario(a)

SECURITY: seguridad (f), seguro
TO SEE: ver; (visit): visitar
TO SEEM: parecer(zc)
SELF: mismo(a)
TO SELL: vender
SEMESTER: semestre (m)
TO SEND: enviar(í), mandar
TO SEND BY MAIL: mandar por correo
SEPARATE(D): separado(a)
SEPTEMBER: se(p)tiembre (m)
SERGEANT: sargento
SERIOUSLY: gravemente
TO SERVE: servir(i)
SERVICE: servicio
TO SETTLE: arreglar
SEVEN: siete
SEVEN HUNDRED: seteciento(a)s
SEVENTEEN: diecisiete
SEVENTY: setenta
SEVERAL: vario(a)s
SEVERAL TIMES: varias veces
SHARE (OF STOCK): acción (de bolsa)
TO SHARE: compartir
SHE: ella
SHIRT: camisa
SHOP: tienda
SHORT: corto(a)
TO SHOW: mostrar(ue)
SHOWER: ducha
SICK: enfermo(a)
SICKNESS: enfermedad (f)
SIGN: letrero, señal (f)
TO SIGN: firmar
SIGNATURE: firma
SIGNED: firmado(a)
SILENCE: silencio

SINCE: (prep. of time):
  desde; (conj. of
  time): desde que;
  (causal conj.): dado
  (puesto) que, ya que
SINCE WHEN?: ¿Desde
  cuándo?
SINGLE: soltero(a)
SINGLE MAN: soltero
SINGLE WOMAN: soltera
SIR: señor (Sr.)
SISTER: hermana
TO SIT DOWN: sentarse
  (ie)
SITTING ROOM: sala
SITUATION: situación (f)
SIX: seis
SIXTEEN: dieciseis
SIXTH: sexto(a)
SIXTY: sesenta
TO SLEEP: dormir(ue)
TO SLIP: resbalar(se)
TO SLIP OFF CLOTHES
  (SHOES): quitarse
  ropa (zapatos)
SLOW(LY) despacio
SMALL: pequeño(a)
SMALLPOX: viruela(s)
TO SMOKE: fumar
SO: así; (adv.): tan
SO THAT: de manera que
SOCIAL SECURITY:
  seguro social
SOCIAL SECURITY BENEFITS:
  beneficios del
  seguro social
SOCIAL SECURITY NUMBER:
  número del seguro
  social
SOCIAL SERVICE (WELFARE):
  Auxilio Público
  (Social)
SOCIAL WORKER:
  trabajador(a) social
SOCIETY: sociedad (f)

SODA(WATER): soda,
  gaseosa
SOLDIER: soldado
SOME: alguno(a)(s)
SOMETIME: alguna vez
SOMEBODY, SOMEONE:
  alguien
SOMETIMES: a(algunas)
  veces
SON: hijo
SONS AND DAUGHTERS:
  hijos
SORE THROAT: dolor (m)
  de garganta
I AM SORRY: lo siento
TO SPEAK: hablar
TO SPEAK LOUDER: hablar
  más alto
TO SPEAK UP (LOUDLY):
  hablar en voz alta
SPEECH DIFFICULTY:
  dificultad (f) para
  hablar
TO SPEND MONEY: gastar
  dinero
TO SPEND TIME: pasar
  tiempo
SPOT: sitio
STAIRS: escalera(s)
STAMP: sello, estampilla
TO STAND ON ONE LEG:
  permanecer(zc) sobre
  una pierna
TO STAND UP: levantarse,
  ponerse de pie
STANDING (UP): de pie
TO START: empezar(ie,c)
STATE: estado; (adj.):
  estatal
STATE LAW: ley (f)
  estatal
STATEMENT: declaración (f)
STATION: estación (f)
TO STAY: permanecer(zc)

TO STAY CALM: permanecer
  (zc) en calma
STEWARDESS: azafata
TO STICK OUT ONE'S
  TONGUE: sacar(qu)
  la lengua
STILL: todavía
STOCK MARKET: bolsa
  (de valores)
STOMACH: estómago
STOP: escala
STOP SIGN: señal de
  stop (parada, alto)
TO MAKE A STOP: hacer
  escala (trip)
TO STOP: parar(se)
STORE: tienda
STRAIGHT AHEAD: (todo)
  derecho
STREET: calle (f)
TO STUDY: estudiar
TO STUDY A LESSON:
  estudiar (aprender)
  una lección
SUCH (A): tal
TO SUCK ONE'S THUMB:
  chuparse el dedo
TO SUFFER FROM: sufrir
  (padecer/zc/) de
SUMMER: verano
SUPPER: cena
TO SUPPORT: mantener
SURE: seguro(a)
TO SUSPEND THE LICENSE:
  cancelar la licencia
SUSPICIOUS: sospechoso(a)
TO SWEAR (TO): jurar

T

TO TAKE: tomar
TO TAKE AWAY (OFF):
  quitar
TAKE-OFF (OF AIRPLANE):
  despegue (m)
TO TAKE CARE OF: cuidar
TO TAKE OFF CLOTHES (HAT,
  SHOES): quitarse ropa
  (sombrero, zapatos)
TO TAKE OUT: sacar(qu)
TO TAKE SOMETHING OUT
  (AWAY): llevarse algo
TO TAKE (TIME): durar,
  tardar
TATOO: tatuaje (m)
TAXI (CAB): taxi (m)
TO TEACH: enseñar
TEACHER: maestro(a)
TELEPHONE: teléfono
TELEPHONE NUMBER: número
  de teléfono
TELEVISION: televisión (f)
TELEVISION SET:
  televisor (m)
TEMPERATURE: temperatura
TEN: diez
TEST (EXAM): prueba,
  análisis; (in school):
  examen (m)
THANK GOD: gracias a Dios
THANK YOU: gracias
THANKS TO: gracias a
THANK YOU VERY MUCH:
  muchas gracias
THAT (demon. adj.): ese(a);
  (over there): aquel(la);
  (rel. pron.): que
THAT'S ALL: eso es todo
THAT'S IT: eso es
THAT IS TO SAY: es decir
THE: el(la, los, las),
  (neuter): lo
THEFT: robo
THEIR: su(s)
THEIRS (poss. pron.):
  el(la, los, las)
  suyo(a, os, as)
THEM (dir. obj. pron.):
  los, las

TO THEM: les,(obj. of prep.): ello(a)s
THEMSELVES: se
THEN: después, entonces, pues
THERE: ahí, allí, (over there): allá
THERE ARE (IS): hay
THEREAFTER: después de eso
THEREFORE: así que
THEY: ello(a)s
THIEF: ladrón(a)
THING: cosa
TO THINK: creer(y)
TO THINK NOT: creer(y) que no
TO THINK SO: creer(y) que sí
THIRD: tercero(a)
THIRTEEN: trece
THIRTY: treinta
THIS: este(a) , esto
THIS MORNING: esta mañana
THIS ONE: éste(a)
THIS VERY DAY: hoy mismo
THIS WAY: por aquí
(ONE) THOUSAND: mil
THREE: tres
THREE HUNDRED: tresciento(a)s
THROAT: garganta
TO THROW AWAY: tirar
TO THROW OUT: echar
THUMB: dedo gordo
TICKET: pasaje(m), (Lat. Amer.): boleto; (fine): multa
TIME: tiempo,(of day): hora, (in a series): vez
TIMES: veces (fpl)
TIP: punta; propina (fee)

TIP OF THE NOSE: punta de la nariz
TO: a, hacia
TO THE: al, a la, a los, a las
TO THE RIGHT: a la derecha
TODAY: hoy
TOILET: retrete (m)
TOMORROW: mañana
TONGUE: lengua
TONSIL: amígdala
TOO: también
TOO MUCH: demasiado
TOTAL: total
TOURIST: turista (mf)
TOURIST CLASS TICKET: pasaje (m) turista
TOWARD: hacia
TRAFFIC: tráfico, tránsito
TRAFFIC ACCIDENT: accidente (m) de tráfico
TRAFFIC LIGHT: luz (f) (señal/f/) de tráfico (tránsito)
TRAFFIC TICKET: multa de tráfico
TRAVEL: viaje (m)
TRAVEL AGENCY: agencia de viajes
TRAVEL AGENT: agente (mf) de viajes
TO TREAT: tratar
TREATMENT: tratamiento
TRIAL: juicio
TRUANT OFFICER: vigilante (mf) escolar
TRUTH: verdad (f)
TO TRY TO: tratar de
TUBERCULOSIS: tuberculosis (f)
TUESDAY: martes (m)
TO TURN: torcer(ue,z)

TWELVE: doce
TWENTY: veinte
TWENTY FIVE:
  veinticinco
TWO: dos
TWO HUNDRED:
  dosciento(a)s
TYPE: tipo

U

UNCLE: tío
UNDER: (prep.): bajo,
  debajo de
UNDER ARREST: bajo
  arresto
UNDER MEDICAL
  TREATMENT: bajo
  tratamiento médico
TO UNDERSTAND:
  comprender
UNEMPLOYED: desempleado
  (a)
UNEMPLOYMENT: desempleo
UNEMPLOYMENT BOOKLET:
  libro de beneficios
  de desempleo
UNEMPLOYMENT CARD:
  tarjeta de desempleo
UNEMPLOYMENT INSURANCE:
  seguro contra
  desempleo
UNEMPLOYMENT INSURANCE
  BENEFITS: beneficios
  (pagos) del seguro
  contra desempleo
UNFORTUNATELY,
  desgraciadamente
THE UNITED STATES:
  Los Estados Unidos
UNIVERSITY:
  universidad (f)
UNTIL: (prep.): hasta,
  (conj.): hasta que
UNTIL TODAY: hasta
  (el día de) hoy

UP TO NOW: hasta ahora
UPON: al (plus
  infinitive)
TO URINATE: orinar(se)
(TO) US: nos, (obj. of
  prep.): nosotro(a)s
USE: uso
TO USE: usar
USUALLY: usualmente, por
  lo común

V

VACATION: vacaciones
  (fpl)
TO VACCINATE: vacunar
VACCINATION: vacuna(ción)
VALID: válido(a)
VALUE: valor (m)
TO VARY: variar(í)
VETERAN: veterano(a) del
  ejército
VETERANS' ADMINISTRATION:
  Administración (f) de
  Veteranos
VIRUS: virus (m)
VISA: visa(do)
TO VISIT: visitar
TO VOMIT: vomitar

W

WAGES: sueldo, pago
TO WAIT: esperar
WAIT: espera
WAITER: camarero
WAITING PERIOD: período
  de espera
WAITRESS: camarera
TO WAKE UP:
  despertar(se)(ie)
TO WALK: caminar
TO WALK A STRAIGHT LINE:
  caminar en línea recta
WALLET: billetero(a),
  cartera (de bolsillo)

TO WANT: desear, querer
TO WASH (ONESELF):
    lavar(se)
TO WATCH OUT: tener
    cuidado
WATER: agua
COLD WATER: agua fría
HOT WATER: agua caliente
WE: nosotro(a)s
TO WEAR CLOTHES:
    llevar ropa
WEATHER: tiempo
BAD WEATHER: mal tiempo
GOOD WEATHER: buen
    tiempo
WEDNESDAY: miércoles (m)
WEEK: semana
WEEKLY: semanalmente
TO WEIGH: pesar
WELCOME: bienvenido(a)
WELDER: soldador(a)
WELFARE: Ayuda Pública
    (Social)
WELFARE DEPARTMENT:
    Departamento de
    Auxilio (Ayuda) Social
WELL: bien
TO BE WELL: estar bien
WEST: oeste
TO WET THE BED: mojar
    (orinarse) en la cama
WHAT?: ¿Qué?; ¿Cuál?
WHAT A PITY!: ¡Qué
    lástima!
WHAT HAPPENED?: ¿Qué
    pasó?
WHAT HURTS YOU?: ¿Qué
    le (te) duele?
WHAT IS THE MATTER
    (TROUBLE)?: ¿Qué
    pasa? ¿Qué tiene
    Vd. (tienes)?

WHAT IS YOUR NAME?:
    ¿Cómo se (te) llama(s)?
WHAT KIND OF?: ¿Qué
    clase de?
WHAT TIME IS IT?: ¿Qué
    hora es?
WHEN?: ¿Cuándo?
WHERE?: ¿Dónde?
FROM WHERE?: ¿De dónde?
WHERE TO?: ¿A dónde?
WHICH: ¿Cuál?, ¿Qué?;
    (rel. pron.): que,
    el(la, lo), cual
WHITE: blanco(a)
WHO?: ¿Quién(es)?
    (rel. pron.): que,
    quien(es)
WHOLE: completo(a)
WHOM?: ¿A quién(es)?
WHY?: ¿Por qué?
WIDOW: viuda
WIDOWER: viudo
WIFE: esposa, mujer (f)
WINDOW: ventana
WINTER: invierno
WIRE: cable (m)
WITH: con
WITH ME: conmigo
WITH YOU (fam. sing.):
    contigo
WITHIN (prep.): dentro
    de
WITHOUT (prep.): sin
WITNESS: testigo (m.f.)
WORD: palabra
WORK: trabajo
TO WORK: trabajar;
    (machine): funcionar
TO WORK HARD: trabajar
    duro (mucho)
TO WORK OUT: arreglarse
WORKER: trabajador(a)
WORKMAN: trabajador,
    obrero

WORKMEN'S COMPENSATION:
  Compensación Obrera
  (del seguro obrero)
TO WORRY: preocuparse
WORTH: valor (m)
WOUNDED: herido(a)
TO WRITE: escribir

Y

YEAR: año
LAST YEAR: el año pasado
TO YELL: gritar
TO YELL AT EACH OTHER:
  gritarse
YELLOW: amarillo(a)
YES: sí
YESTERDAY: ayer
YOU (subj. pron.)
  (fam. sing.): tú;
  (form. sing.): usted;
  (form. & fam. pl.):
  ustedes; (dir. obj.
  pron.)(fam. sing.):
  te; (form. sing.):
  le, la, lo; (fam.
  & form. pl.):lo(a)s;(obj.
  of prep)(fam. sing.):
  ti; (form. sing.):
  usted; (fam. & form.
  pl.): ustedes
TO YOU (ind. obj.
  pron.) (fam. sing.):
  te; (form. sing.):
  le; (fam. & form.
  pl.): les
YOU ARE WELCOME: de
  nada
YOUNG: joven
YOUNG LADY: señorita
  (Srta.)
YOUNG MAN (WOMAN):
  joven (mf)
YOUNGSTER: joven (mf)
YOUR (fam. sing.): tu;
  (form. sing. & pl.): su

YOURSELF (fam. sing.):
  te; (form. sing.): se
YOURS (poss. pron.):
  el(la, los, las)
  suyo(a, os, as)
YOURSELVES (form. sing.
  & pl.): se; (fam. pl.
  in Spain): os

Z

ZERO: cero